Don't Alienate the Kids!

Other Books by Bill Eddy

*It's All Your Fault! 12 Tips for Managing People Who Blame Others for
Everything (2008)*
HCI Press

New Ways for Families in Separation and Divorce:
    Professional Guidebook (2009)
    Parent Workbook (2009)
    Collaborative Parent Workbook (2009)
HCI Press

High Conflict People in Legal Disputes (2006, 2008)
HCI Press

Managing High Conflict People In Court (2008)
HCI Press

Splitting: Protecting Yourself While Divorcing a Borderline or Narcissist (2004)
Eggshells Press

The Splitting CD: An Interview with Bill Eddy (2006)
Eggshells Press

Working with High Conflict Personalities (2004, 2006)
*(A Six-Hour Internet Course for Mental Health
Professionals at www.continuingEdCourses.net)*

Don't Alienate the Kids!

Raising Resilient Children While Avoiding High-Conflict Divorce

Bill Eddy

P R E S S

High Conflict Institute, LLC
Scottsdale, Arizona

Published by: HCI Press, A Division of High Conflict Institute, LLC
7701 E. Indian School Rd., Ste. F, Scottsdale, AZ 85251, (602) 606-7628, (888) 768-9874
www.hcipress.com

This publication is designed to provide accurate and authoritative information about the subject matters covered. It is sold with the understanding that the publisher is not rendering legal, mental health, medical or other professional services in this book, either directly or indirectly. If expert assistance, legal services or counseling is needed, the services of a competent professional should be sought.

Names and identifying information of private individuals have been changed to preserve anonymity. Most of the examples contained herein are based on real families, but details have been changed to protect confidentiality, and many examples include a composite of several individuals.

Eddy, Bill, 1948-
Don't alienate the kids : raising resilient children while avoiding high-conflict divorce / Bill Eddy
ISBN 978-1-936268-03-0

First Edition: 2010

First Printing: April 2010
Second Printing: May 2010

Printed in the United States of America

Edited by: Megan Hunter
Designed by: Elle Phillips Design

Publisher:
Published by HCI Press
www.hcipress.com

P R E S S Printed in the United States of America

For my father,
C. Roland Eddy

A scientist and teacher,
whose joy of learning and sense of humor
have always been contagious.

TABLE OF CONTENTS

A NOTE OF CAUTION
TO THE READER

This book addresses issues of High Conflict People and their high-conflict personalities. Knowledge is power. The information I provide is intended to help you be more successful in your interactions with people as an individual or as a professional.

However, this personality information can also be misused and can inadvertently make your life more difficult. Therefore, I caution you not to openly label people in your life, nor to use this information as a weapon in personal relationships. Before you go further, I ask that you make a commitment to use this information with caution, compassion, and respect.

My explanations and tips address general patterns of behavior and may not apply to your specific situation. You are advised to seek the advice of a therapist, an attorney, or other conflict resolution professional in handling any dispute.

The author and the publisher are not responsible for any decisions or actions you take as a result of reading this book.

Bill Eddy

FOREWORD

When I met lawyer, therapist and mediator Bill Eddy several years ago, I discovered we were comrades at heart. I had co-authored *Stop Walking on Eggshells* and the Stop Walking on Eggshells workbook about borderline personality disorder, and he had written *High Conflict People in Legal Disputes* for legal professionals. It was so validating to meet someone else with the same mission: develop innovative ways to help people understand personality disorders and develop skills for dealing with these high conflict personalities. Knowing how desperately divorcing people needed Bill's information, I published (through my company Eggshells Press) *Splitting: Protecting Yourself While Divorcing a Borderline or Narcissist* (an expanded version will be available through New Harbinger Publications in 2011). *Splitting* was so successful we followed it up with a CD companion to Splitting; we also collaborated on several teleseminars about relationships with borderlines and narcissists.

Now Bill has written another exceptional book, *Don't Alienate the Kids!* He addresses the concerns of parents and professionals dealing with a difficult or "high-conflict" parent in divorce. For parents, this book gives a foundation for assisting a child during the divorce process – or at any time – without getting emotionally "hooked" by a high-conflict parent, whether or not they have a personality disorder. His information and tips can help any parent at any time.

Frequently, professionals involved with divorce decisions improperly become embroiled in the conflict between the parents, which can sway their judgment about what's best for the children. Bill offers professionals guidelines on how to make these decisions with compassion and understanding. His new approach may, at first, be surprising. Once professionals understand that high conflict individuals require a different mindset, they realize the wisdom of Bill's approach.

As a former therapist and mediator with an interest in high conflict personalities, Bill is probably the most qualified expert in the world to write about this topic. He knows how bad it can get on the front lines of modern divorce in family court, and how families can become endlessly split over their children. He writes about these issues with expertise and sensitivity, with tips for everyone, from parents, family members and friends, to counselors, lawyers and judges.

This book takes a giant step in its effort to calm the conflict over child alienation. His "1000 Little Bricks" approach gives hope and really spells out what parents and professionals can do to help the kids build a Foundation of Resilience, even during a divorce, for everyone's benefit in the future. The ideas in this book may change how people get divorced for years to come.

Randi Kreger

Co-Author of *Stop Walking on Eggshells: Taking Your Life Back When Someone You Care About Has Borderline Personality Disorder*

Author of *The Essential Family Guide to Borderline Personality Disorder: New Tools and Techniques to Stop Walking on Eggshells*

Author of *The Stop Walking on Eggshells Workbook: Practical Strategies for Living With Someone Who Has Borderline Personality Disorder*

INTRODUCTION

I wrote this book out of frustration – and hope. It's intended for parents, professionals, and anyone concerned about the next generation. It's about two growing problems that overlap:

1. More and more children and parents are suffering from "high-conflict" divorces – unnecessarily. (When I speak of "divorce" throughout this book, I include the separation of unmarried parents, who face the same problems.)

2. Recent research suggests that "high-conflict" personalities are increasing in our society, and one of the contributing factors may be the life-long dysfunctional lessons children learn from high-conflict divorces.

Therefore, the information in this book is designed to assist parents and professionals in helping children learn skills for resilience for a lifetime – even during a divorce.

Frustration

For the past 17 years I have been a family law attorney – a Certified Family Law Specialist. I have represented clients in family court in many high-conflict divorces. Over time, in many of these cases, the children have become "alienated" from a parent. I use that term broadly to mean that the child resisted or totally refused all contact with that parent.

In some of these cases, I represented the "rejected parent" who the child didn't want to see. In other cases, I represented the "favored parent," who seemed to win the child's loyalty and total agreement. However, in both types of cases, the children were stressed and unhappy, and learned dysfunctional ways of handing close relationships – ways which may negatively affect them for the rest of their lives.

I was frustrated in both types of cases. I had many restless nights, trying to figure out how to protect my clients and their children. The opposing parent would hate me. The opposing lawyer would criticize me. And the judge would frown and disregard much of what I had to say.

Out of about 400 cases I had as an attorney representing one party, approximately 40 included an issue of child alienation. Out of all the issues I handled in family court (child support, property division, custody and visitation, even child sexual abuse), I found child alienation to be the most frustrating – because it seemed to be based on nothing. There was no credible evidence, but lots of opinions. No one could figure out these cases, so there was a lot of blaming. Anger grew as everyone's frustration grew – for parents, lawyers, counselors, and judges. This anger was contagious, and the children absorbed it as well.

I always intended to focus my law practice on divorce mediation. After 15 years of representing clients in family court, as well as handling about 1000 mediation cases, I finally stopped taking court cases. Some of my last court cases were alienation cases.

In one case, my client was the rejected father. His case had gone on for about 6 years, in and out of court, until his daughter totally stopped spending any time with him. At my last court hearing, the judge said there was nothing he could do.

In the other case, my client was the mother, who became the rejected parent. The father had been ordered into domestic violence treatment near the start of the case. Even though he had about one-third of the parenting time, he returned to court repeatedly seeking primary custody of their son. Even after the judge sanctioned the father once for a totally unnecessary hearing, he kept bringing the mother back to court. For ten years, the mother was the primary custodial parent. Then, after relentless pressure by his father, the son "ran away" to his father's and stayed there. She gave up, exhausted.

Neither of these children had rejected either parent prior to their parents going to court.

The Wall of Alienation

Somehow, the adversarial structure of court focused on determining who was the "all-good parent" and who was the "all-bad parent." The allegations went back and forth:

"The father must be abusing the child. That's why she doesn't want to see him and cries before his visits."

Or: "Her mother must be alienating her. That's why she refuses to see me."

Or: "The father must be alienating the child. That's why he refuses to see the mother."

Or: "The mother must have done something to make the child estranged from her."

The court process was all about who put the wall up between a parent and the child.

"It's all his fault. He has only himself to blame. I've done nothing wrong."

Or: "It's all her fault. I have been a loving parent while she just spews vituperative venom against me." (Yes, these statements are drawn from real court documents.)

The whole battle over picking the "all-good parent" and the "all-bad parent" was a long, drawn out tug-of-war until one parent lost. Most of the time it was the rejected parent. But sometimes, the rejected parent won a change of primary custody and the previously favored parent left the city, the state or the country. (Yes, I saw each of these happen.) Or attempted to commit suicide, as occurred in more than one case.

It has become an ugly contest.

It's not a gender issue...
It's not about who has custody...

What Alienation is Not

From all of these experiences, I learned a lot about what alienation is not:

- It's not a gender issue: I have represented fathers and mothers who were the "rejected" parent.

- It's not about who has custody: While most rejected parents have been the "non-custodial" parent with less parenting time, I have represented several custodial parents who became the rejected parent.

- It's not just a defense against child sexual abuse allegations: Child alienation is an issue in over 20% of contested custody cases at court, yet child sexual abuse is alleged in only about 2-5% of contested custody cases.

- It's not just a defense against domestic violence allegations: From my experience, perpetrators of domestic violence engage in more alienating behaviors than victims of domestic violence.

- It's not just a defense against child abuse allegations: I have seen cases where one parent had abusive behaviors and the other parent had alienating behaviors. I also know of cases where a parent with abusive behaviors also engaged in alienating behaviors, and the other parent had neither abusive nor alienating behaviors. I learned that abuse and alienation are independent sets of behavior.

- It's not a common symptom of child abuse or domestic violence: Most abused children are not alienated. Most love their parents, but want the abuse to stop. Many fear their abusive parents and are very careful not to upset them. Most would never say they hated the parent or would risk running away – behaviors I have seen much more common in alienation cases.

- It's not caused by one disparaging remark or incident: From my experience, alienation is a gradual process which may begin before separation, but mostly grows during the divorce process.

So, if alienation is not about the above common theories, then what is it?

Learning About Child Abuse

I was a social worker for many years before becoming a lawyer. My first job out of college was as a social worker in New York City. In 1981, I got my Masters in Social Work degree, and I counseled children and adults for much of that decade. Many of them had been abused.

In the 1980's, child abuse, especially child sexual abuse, was starting to be taken more seriously. Some of my clients were teenagers who had been sexually abused and some of my adult clients had been sexually abused as children. Some cases were extremely shocking. Others seemed mild, but the long-term effects were still quite damaging.

Learning About Family Systems

In 1980, as I was in training as a family therapist, I learned that families are like a system – like the solar system – in which everyone has a pull on everyone else. Each family's "system" of relating is influenced and maintained by everyone in the family – but in different ways. Usually, everyone in the family system is blind to their own role in reinforcing problems and blind to their potential role in solving problems.

My job as a family therapist was to help enough members of the family system to shift their behavior, to change the whole family for the better – especially for the benefit of the children. That was the only way that family problems could really be improved. No one person could really change, unless most in the family changed. Children's behavior was often the result of unresolved issues between the parents. This was rarely obvious on the surface.

I learned that other family members (grandparents, aunts and uncles, etc.) were hidden parts of the family system as well, and could have a powerful influence over the problems on the surface. And, of course, therapists, teachers and others involved with a family also became part of the family system. Everyone reinforced the problems (in hidden ways), so they needed to reinforce the solutions.

During the 1980's, I was also volunteering as a mediator with community mediation programs that resolved conflicts between neighbors, landlords and tenants, and businesses and consumers. They had similar dynamics, with everyone contributing to the problem and/or the solution.

I really liked mediation and decided to pursue it as a career, but there were no paying jobs available. I noticed that lawyers were getting paid to do mediation, so I decided to go to law school. When I graduated and passed the bar in 1992, I set up my own Law and Mediation office. I also decided to practice family law in court for a couple years, while establishing my mediation practice. I ended up taking court cases for 15 years.

Learning About Divorce Disputes

My social work background was really helpful in my law practice, as many cases involved substance abuse, child abuse and/or domestic violence. However, I never heard of Parental Alienation Syndrome until I was practicing as a lawyer in the 1990's.

The battle over abuse versus alienation was a surprise to me. ("The father's an abuser." "No, the mother's an alienator"). Because of my background, I could see there was a lot that parents and professionals in the family court system misunderstood about children and abuse. Because of my training in family systems, I knew that families weren't as simple as "the abuser" versus "the alienator."

However, as I began practicing family law, it became clearer to me that parents are not usually equal when there is abuse in a family – more often only one parent is an offender (child abuse, domestic violence, substance abuse, etc.) and the other is not. Some divorcing parents had high-conflict personalities (which I will explain in Chapter One), while others did not. From my experience and my surveys of family law professionals, I believe that half to two-thirds of high-conflict families have only one parent with a high-conflict personality who is driving the dispute, while the other parent is mostly acting reasonably and just trying to protect the children from the high-conflict parent.

However, because families operate as a system, everyone adapts and reinforces problems in hidden little ways. Even reasonable people would over-react and reinforce problems. I realized that the problem of a child rejecting a parent wasn't all one parent's fault or all the other's. And it wasn't always fathers who were rejected, and it wasn't always mothers who were favored. I represented both about equally.

However, I realized that my clients who were the rejected parent were in a real bind. When they were understandably angry toward the other parent or the child, they made things worse. While they usually weren't the cause of the alienation, they reinforced the alienation without realizing it.

When they did nothing and cooperated with the child's rejection ("if you really want me to stop seeing you, I'll stop"), nothing ever got better. When they supported their child going to individual counseling, the alienation continued. When they went to "reunification" counseling with their child, the alienation continued. As the rejected parent, they were blamed for all of these failures. Yet everyone in the family system seemed to reinforce these problems.

Even my clients who were the favored parents didn't really win. They were also very frustrated, defensive and at times depressed. I remember one judge railing at me about my client, the mother, after the child said she didn't want to see her father:

"Mr. Eddy, I know what your client is doing. She's telling the child negative things about her father to alienate the child."

I responded: "Your honor, my client is trying to be very careful not to say anything to the child against her father. Since she was criticized for discussing the case with the child four years ago, she has been very careful not to say anything negative."

And I believe she was being very careful. But the alienation didn't change, and the judge gave up. While my client was favored by the child, everyone else (the father, the father's attorney, and the judge) blamed her for being a despicable person (along with her lawyer - me).

Professionals in the Family System

I started realizing that the problem was bigger than just the parents. Lawyers sometimes contributed to the problem. They often made extreme and emotional arguments in court that devastated one or the other parent. As a lawyer, I learned early on (after temporarily losing a custody battle), that I couldn't just say that my client was doing a good job. I had to attack the other parent as doing a horrible job. I learned that's what worked in the adversarial process of custody battles.

Judges sometimes contributed with their anger at the parents and made extreme orders in an effort to gain control – such as supervised visitation or no contact – while an investigation labored on for weeks or months, to see if allegations were really true. They criticized one or both parents. They tried having long hearings. They tried having short hearings. They tried ordering counseling, ordering lawyers for the children (Guardians ad litem), ordering psychological evaluations. They made threats. They fulfilled threats. But children remained alienated or became even more alienated.

Even counselors seemed to contribute to the problem at times. Each parent's counselor would report that his or her client was really great and had no problems to work on. For example:

The mother's therapist: "The father just doesn't understand how hurtful he has been to the child. The mother is merely trying to protect the child from his negative behavior and poor judgment. She is doing a good job."

The father's therapist: "The father has a lot of insight into himself and frankly I can see no behavior on his part that is causing the child to resist seeing him."

Then, of course, individual child therapists are often ordered for the child in these alienation cases. Everyone hopes or expects that the individual child therapist will be able to turn the child's attitude around, then the child and the rejected parent will reconcile. Sometimes, these individual child therapists work valiantly to be supportive of both parent's relationships with the child. But sometimes they succumb to agreeing with the child's rejection of one parent. They agree that the child is realistically estranged from that parent, and that this is a reasonable position for the child to take. For example:

"The boy is so angry with his mother that I wouldn't even recommend a joint session with the mother yet. The boy needs to stop being so angry at what she has done first. She should work on herself to be more accepting of his negative feedback about her new relationship." She worked on herself, but the boy never stopped being angry with her, so nothing ever changed and the boy stopped seeing her.

"The daughter despises her father. He is an embarrassment to her. She doesn't want him coming to her school. She feels he does not respect her. If he respected her, he would stay away until she feels more comfortable with him."

In some cases, the judge would wait until the child's therapist said the child was ready to spend more time with his or her other parent. Of course, this never happened.

In one such case, I wrote a letter to the child's therapist, who was not used to treating children in family court cases. He had immediately taken sides against my client, at the request of the child. In my letter, I quoted research and tried to be friendly and understanding of his lack of knowledge about how to handle such cases. He wrote back a letter angry with me and stating that I totally misunderstood his intentions in the case. This correspondence made it into a court hearing, and the judge made a finding that I had been too "adversarial" in writing my letter to the therapist. Even I was part of the problem!

1000 Little Bricks

Out of all of these experiences, plus a lot of reading, attending seminars and having sometimes heated discussions, I came to the conclusion that no one parent or single professional can solve this problem – because I realized that the wall between a child and one parent is not built by just one parent or just one event or disparaging remark.

I now believe that the wall of alienation is built with at least 1000 little bricks, which have come from a "perfect storm" of three Cultures of Blame:

1. The family's Culture of Blame when a high-conflict parent is involved

2. The family court Culture of Blame when one or more professionals get emotionally "hooked"

3. Our society's rapidly escalating Culture of Blame, which contributes to alienation and also affects children's personality development

These three Cultures of Blame repeatedly teach children three bad behaviors, which they absorb:

All-or-nothing thinking

Unmanaged emotions

Extreme behaviors

I think of these three bad behaviors as little bricks which add up over the weeks, months and years, to create and reinforce alienation in close relationships for many children in divorce. When children are exposed to enough of these bad behaviors (bricks), their unconscious solution to the family conflict is to absorb an all-or-nothing view of each parent – one "all-good" and one "all-bad." They express their feelings with great intensity and often have uncontrollable outbursts against their rejected parent.

Extreme behaviors become normal, as parents yell at each other in front of the children at parenting exchanges. Lawyers argue for extreme measures (no contact or total custody reversals). Counselors say that it is reasonable that a child has rejected a parent (realistic estrangement), so just accept it. And judges make extreme orders (no contact, total custody reversals) or just give up.

Hope

Despite all of this, I have hope! I believe we have the knowledge and potential to turn the corner and change these Cultures of Blame into Cultures of Learning Skills. We just need enough reasonable people to learn the skills – and teach them to the kids. These three big skills are:

Flexible Thinking

Managed Emotions

Moderate Behaviors

These are the skills for handling a rapidly changing world and an unknown future. They are the key skills for close relationships, decision-making and leadership. Children who learn these skills will have unlimited potential, because they will be able to handle problems without becoming overwhelmed or distracted by blaming others. The children who learn these skills will be the problem-solvers of the future.

So how do we do this? First, *we all* need to really understand that the problem isn't about bad parents, but about bad behaviors – *many people's* bad behaviors. Then, *all of us* need to be involved in working on the solution. No one person – parent or professional – can prevent or repair alienation. It has to be a change in these cultures (family, court, society) surrounding the child.

What really give me hope are three new developments:

1. Abusive cultures can change. For example, a recent comprehensive study by the U. S. federal government showed that child abuse reduced between 1993 and 2006 at a rate of 23% for physical abuse, 33% for emotional abuse and 44% for sexual abuse. Unfortunately, the economic downtown since 2008 has increased child abuse once again – but we now know that we have the ability to make a large scale change for the benefit of children when enough people work at it.

2. Brain research has new discoveries about how children learn. In this book, I will explain some very new discoveries which can be used to help parents help their children develop skills for resilience, rather than alienation.

3. Cognitive-behavioral therapy methods are having success in changing people's behavior. Even some people with personality disorders can change, by learning small skills in small steps with lots of structure and encouragement. Some no longer have a disorder. (Personality disorders are rigid patterns of distressful thinking, unmanaged emotions and behavior problems dating from childhood. Examples in Chapter 1.) By recognizing that many people going through the legal system have these disorders, courts can require efforts to learn skills, rather than focusing on shame and blame. By recognizing these disorders, courts can become more effective at understanding who can change and who can't, which is essential in the protection of children.

For these reasons, I have hope. But as I will explain in this book, it is urgent that we work together to help children learn these skills now. The future of our society may depend on it.

If You Are a Reasonable Parent

If you are a reasonable parent going through a separation or divorce, or are considering separating, this book is designed to help you avoid experiencing a high-conflict divorce. Even if neither of you is a high-conflict parent, the actions you take and the ways you deal with your children can unintentionally teach them high-conflict behaviors which can become part of their personality development for a lifetime.

If you are a reasonable parent who is separating from or divorcing a parent with a high-conflict personality, you need to be careful not to fall into some very common traps. When someone is violent, makes false statements, or otherwise engages in extreme behavior, it's easy to over-react or under-respond. Instead, you often need to do the opposite of what you *feel* like doing.

In this book, I will explain ways of dealing with a high-conflict parent while teaching your child resilience at the same time. Remember, actions often speak louder than words.

If You Are a Divorce Professional

If you are an experienced divorce professional, you know how bitter high-conflict divorces can be. You also know how they can seriously impact the children. However, you also may have strong feelings about the two big theories of alienation: Child Abuse versus Parental Alienation Syndrome. I want to encourage you to have an open mind in regard to the recent personality research and brain research discussed in this book, which sheds new light on how we can handle alienation cases more successfully in the future.

If you are a new divorce professional, this book should help you avoid making some common mistakes – whether you are a lawyer, judge, therapist, mediator, collaborative professional, or other related professional. If you are a graduate student considering a career working with families of separation and divorce, you will have a clear advantage by being up to date on the science and legal issues presented here.

If you are an advocate for victims of child abuse or domestic violence, or an advocate fighting for victims of parental alienation, I encourage you to take a fresh look at what I explain in this book. You have made contributions in the past and can make more in the future. However, it is important that you are well-informed about alternate theories and can demonstrate that you have considered them in helping any particular parent or child. The most calm and knowledgeable advocates are the ones who are most credible in family courts and with parents – especially on the controversial subject of child alienation.

This Book

Part I of this book explains how to avoid the dynamics of high-conflict divorce and child alienation, including a discussion of the Parental Alienation Syndrome, child abuse and the proposed theory of "1000 Little Bricks."

Part II focuses on what we can all do – as parents, family and friends, counselors, lawyers and family court judges. Since I am a counselor and a lawyer, and I give seminars to judges, I am in a unique position to talk about how everyone can – and must – practice the same skills to build a foundation of resilience for children of separation and divorce. Rather than fighting with each other over the problem, we can immediately become part of the solution. I end with my view of the most constructive role for family courts in the future.

This book focuses on helping your child or children build resilience during a divorce. If you are looking for a book for yourself on navigating a complete divorce with a high-conflict other parent, including strategies for court, you should see my related book: *SPLITTING: Protecting Yourself While Divorcing a Borderline or Narcissist.*

I have written this book in a conversational tone, because that's how I am and I want it to be easy to read for parents and non-professionals. However, I also wrote it for professionals, so some of the information may seem technical and not of interest to everyone. Feel free to read what interests you and skip over what does not.

To make the chapters easier to read, I put all of the references for facts, figures and other's ideas in the back of the book. Much has been thought and written by others, and they deserve the majority of the credit for the information presented in this book.

Examples

Throughout this book I give lots of examples of alienating behavior, alienated children, and ways to teach skills of resilience. Most of these examples are based on real families, but details have been changed to protect confidentiality, and many individuals are a composite of several parents and children with similar problems.

ACKNOWLEDGEMENTS

First of all, I thank the many parents who have been my clients in high-conflict divorces and on all sides of the issue of child alienation. You have allowed me to learn from your painful experiences, and you have taught me to keep going in efforts to protect your children from harm.

I especially want to thank my wife, Alice, who is a therapist and whose encouragement, wisdom and good nature keep me going. I write knowing that she will be my first critic, so it better be good and it better be practical. I thank her for our low-conflict marriage.

I thank Megan Hunter, my business partner with High Conflict Institute, for pushing me to develop these theories, write books, develop programs and give seminars to professionals interested in managing high conflict disputes. Her insight and confidence has moved these concepts from a hobby to serious work that seems to be meeting an important need.

I thank Michelle Jensen, our Program Coordinator for High Conflict Institute, who is just starting a career combining social work and law. Her new energy and insights are helping us assist divorcing families with our New Ways for Families program. I also thank Mark Baumann, family lawyer, for his insights and great editing suggestions.

I want to acknowledge my mother, Margaret, my role model who influenced my life in the direction of social service and compassion for others, well before her untimely death when I was 23. I want to acknowledge my stepmother, Helen, a role model of creativity throughout my adult life, who has kept painting and volunteering even up to age 98.

Most of all for this book, I want to thank my father, Roland, for raising me to be interested in the science of human behavior. Even though he was a chemist, his curiosity about why people act the way they do motivated me to try to find the answers. His book about the brain, *Oceans of the Mind* (2003), helped inspire me to learn more. He especially taught me to have flexible thinking – that science is not exact, and that we must always have an open mind to new information. At the age of 95, he continues to inspire me with his writing, teaching, learning and sense of humor, and I thank him for it.

An Open Mind

I hope everyone will read this book with an open mind. The subject of child alienation has been a highly controversial issue for 25 years or more, and it's easy to fight about it. But it seems to be growing as a problem in divorce, and it seems to be growing as a problem for the future of our society. It's time to really understand what it is, how to reduce its impact, and how to prevent it from occurring in the first place.

The "1000 Little Bricks" theory is new and certainly not perfect. It is based on our new awareness that children's brains absorb almost everything that goes on in their environment – their family's culture, the family court culture, and society's larger culture. Cultures are contagious!

Therefore, I am addressing the information in this book broadly – to parents, professionals and anyone concerned about the future of our society. Hopefully, this book will help us to be more self-aware, so that we don't alienate the kids, but teach the kids skills of resilience instead – through our *contagious reasonable behavior* as well as our words.

PART 1:

Building a Wall
(What to Avoid)

*Suppose when parents separate or divorce, they are given a pile of 1000 little bricks. They can use these bricks to build a wall against the other parent, or they can use these bricks to build a foundation of resilience for their child. When they build a wall, the bricks they use are **all-or-nothing thinking, unmanaged emotions** and **extreme behaviors**. When they build a foundation of resilience, the bricks they use become **flexible thinking, managed emotions** and **moderate behaviors**. There are many people today who will help parents build a wall or a foundation. The problem is that we're all blind and we don't know which one we're building. We have to become informed and self-aware.*

High-Conflict Divorce

The couple had a vicious fight that resulted in the mother getting custody of their young daughter. They had continuing battles, as the child grew older until she ultimately reached the age of majority. The father, however, never got over his anger. When the daughter announced that she was going to get married, the father offered to not only pay for the wedding, but also to throw in an extra $10,000 to the daughter if she did not invite the mother. The daughter took the offer. (Borof, 2003, p. 3)

This example is typical of the fallout from a "high-conflict" divorce. Many sources agree that up to one-third of divorces these days are high-conflict. This means that one or both parties are stuck in fighting over something – usually the children – for years. There are repeated court hearings about extreme behaviors: substance abuse, child abuse, domestic violence, lying, hiding money, false allegations of abuse and parental alienation. There is lots of blame, without positive change. Families are caught in a spin cycle of high-conflict behavior.

In high-conflict divorce, emotions are high and often increase over time. For some parents, simmering anger turns into yelling rages at parenting exchanges, anger at family members, anger at professionals, and yelling or running out of court hearings. There's angry emails, angry voicemails, taping phone conversations, videotaping "bad" behavior – even going on YouTube and the news to prove how bad the other parent is. Of course, these actions make things worse, not better.

These emotions are also contagious, as family members, professionals, news reporters, and even children get swept up in emotionally taking sides – bitterly questioning the intelligence, sanity, morality, ethics and competence of the other parent and professionals involved in the case.

Of course, you've known about high-conflict divorce for years. You probably thought it was just an unavoidable fact of modern life. But if you're considering a separation or divorce, you probably think you are going to avoid this. I want to help you do that, but you need to have your eyes wide open to the many little ways that you can accidently create a high-conflict divorce.

Over the past decade, sources from the Wall Street Journal to family court judges say that high-conflict divorces have increased. Well-known family law researcher, Janet Johnston, and colleagues (2009) said:

> About one fourth to one third of divorcing couples report high degrees of hostility and discord over the daily care of their children many years after separation... For about one tenth of all divorcing couples, the unremitting animosity will shadow the entire growing-up years of the children... [O]ver a span of two decades, more than five million children will be affected by ongoing parental conflict; for two million children, this condition may well be permanent. (p. 4)

The long-term effects of high-conflict divorce are becoming obvious when the children become adults. Suddenly, this isn't just a problem we can ignore any more while other families go through it. The children of high-conflict divorce are having problems that will eventually affect everyone. Something must be done, and it must be done soon.

High-Conflict Parents

High-conflict divorces are driven by one or two "high-conflict" parents. Over time, these often turn into cases with an alienated child – a child who intensely rejects one parent. The case at the beginning of this chapter is a perfect example of a parent using the three "bad" bricks or "wall" bricks of a high-conflict parent:

All-or-Nothing Thinking

Unmanaged Emotions

Extreme Behavior

The father wanted the mother to be totally excluded from the wedding. He wasn't willing to just avoid her at the wedding or briefly say hello. His solution was all-or-nothing: She will not participate – at all!

His anger was still so unmanaged that he couldn't get over it years after the divorce. It drove his decision to exclude his ex-wife from the wedding. And his behavior was extreme. He offered his daughter $10,000 to keep the mother away.

Of course, we don't know how the mother behaved over all of these years. Perhaps her actions were equally bad or worse after their separation or divorce. On the other hand, she may have been a reasonable parent just trying to protect her daughter from her ex-husband's anger and high-conflict behavior.

From my experience over thirty years with divorcing families, and from my surveys of divorce professionals, I would say that half to two-thirds of high-conflict divorces include one high-conflict parent with the above characteristics and one reasonable parent, who has been walking on eggshells for years.

Why Do People Act This Way?

Why would someone act so extremely? If someone is a high-conflict person (HCP), then he or she may have a personality disorder. If so, this means that they are stuck – that these characteristics are part of who they are.

I believe that about half of HCPs have a personality disorder and about half have some of these traits, but not a full personality disorder. This means that they are still difficult, but may respond more easily to approaches designed for people with personality disorders.

It helps to understand some of these traits, but it is important not to tell someone you think they have a personality disorder. They may become very defensive and angry with you, as defensiveness is a common characteristic of those with personality disorders and those just with traits.

Personality disorders appear to be growing in our society. Over the last few years, the National Institutes of Health (NIH) sponsored a study which concluded that about 20% of the general population of the United States meets the criteria for a personality disorder. They broke down their results into age groups and gender. I will give the percentage results below, but it is important to know that there is a lot of overlap, as some people may have more than one such disorder.

The five personality patterns that most commonly appear in high-conflict divorces are the following, in my opinion. You can see why they constantly get into conflicts with those closest to them:

Borderline HCPs: They have extreme mood swings - friendly and loving one minute and angry and blaming the next. They are preoccupied with fears of abandonment. When they feel abandoned (even if they aren't), they can become enraged, vindictive, and sometimes violent. They can be highly manipulative – mostly to avoid abandonment or to punish someone who they feel abandoned them. Sometimes, they make false statements and spread rumors. They often "split" people into all-good or all-bad in their eyes.

The NIH study said that 5.9% of the general population meets the criteria for borderline personality disorder. The gender results were 53% female and 47% male. But remember, many people may have some traits of this disorder some of the time, but not have the full disorder.

Narcissistic HCPs: They can be very arrogant and preoccupied with themselves. They try hard to be seen as superior and very important. They seek constant admiration and praise, and get angry when they don't get it. They can be highly manipulative, and very disdainful and demeaning to those around them. When they feel insulted or disrespected (even if they aren't), they can become enraged, vindictive and sometimes violent. They may make false statements and spread rumors to regain a sense of control when they feel powerless and inferior. They also engage in "splitting" those around them into superior and inferior people.

The NIH study said that 6.2% of the general population meets the criteria for narcissistic personality disorder. The gender results were 62% male and

38% female. Almost 40% of those with narcissistic personality disorder meet the criteria for borderline personality disorder as well.

Paranoid HCPs: They are very fearful and suspect that other people want to manipulate them or hurt them. They often imagine that others are conspiring against them. They are mistrustful and expect that people close to them will betray them sooner or later. They will sometimes attack others first (verbally or physically), in order to prevent being attacked themselves by surprise (even though no one was planning to attack them).

The NIH study said that 4.4% of the general population meets the criteria for this disorder. The gender results were 57% female and 43% male.

Antisocial HCPs: They can be the most dangerous and uncaring. They often enjoy other people's suffering, and like to dominate and be in control. They don't care about the rules of society. Instead, they just want what they want and they will do anything to get it. They are chronic liars and lack remorse. They can be highly manipulative and often persuade others that they (the antisocial HCPs) are victims, when in fact they are perpetrators of bad behavior. They view people as powerful or as suckers, who deserve what they get. Violent revenge or causing other people suffering is often seen as justified in their eyes.

The NIH study said that 3.6% of the general population meets the criteria for this disorder. The gender results were 74% male and 26% female. Approximately 20% of those with borderline personality disorder and narcissistic personality disorder also have antisocial personality disorder.

Histrionic HCPs: They are generally over-dramatic and very intense. They constantly are talking about being a victim of this or that, and can go on and on about dramatic details which may or may not be true. They are attention seekers and once they have your attention they don't like to let go. They look to others to solve their problems. They are prone to lots of exaggeration – of facts and of emotion.

The NIH study said that 1.8% of the general population meets the criteria for this disorder. The gender results were 51% male and 49% female.

Throughout this book, I will avoid the term "personality disorder" in describing these patterns, as I believe that half of HCPs don't have these disorders but just some traits of these disorders. What is important is to understand their possible patterns of behavior so you can deal with them, not deciding if they have a disorder – which you can't do without extensive training.

It's also important not to think of these characteristics as defining a whole person. People with personality disorders or traits can be high functioning in society – such as in their work – while they are very difficult in close relationships. They can have the full range of intelligence, from very low to very high. So when someone is referred to as "a borderline" or "a narcissist," it's like calling someone a diabetic or a painter or a Californian – it's just one aspect of the person.

"Splitting" People

For decades, mental health professionals have recognized that many people with these personality traits "split" people into "all-good" and "all-bad." In their eyes, the "all-good" people can do nothing wrong - they have no negative qualities. And they believe that the "all-bad" people can do nothing right - they can't think of a single positive quality about them. They don't just think this way – they feel it intensely, as though they were at war with the bad people.

The following is an excellent description of this splitting process by psychiatrist, Jerold J. Kreisman (1989). It is most commonly identified with borderlines, but I have seen this with all HCPs in high-conflict disputes:

> The world of a borderline, like that of a child, is split into heroes and villains. A child emotionally, the borderline cannot tolerate human inconsistencies and ambiguities; he cannot reconcile another's good and bad qualities into a constant coherent understanding of another person. At any particular moment, one is either "good" or "evil"; there is no in-between; no gray area….Lovers and mates, mothers and fathers, siblings, friends, and psychotherapists may be idolized one day, totally devalued and dismissed the next.

> When the idealized person finally disappoints (as we all do, sooner or later) the borderline must drastically restructure his one-dimensional conceptualization. Either the idol is banished to the dungeon, or the borderline banishes himself in order to preserve the all-good image of the other person.

> This type of behavior, called "splitting," is the primary defense mechanism employed by the borderline. Technically defined, splitting is the rigid separation of positive and negative thoughts and feelings about oneself and others, that is, the

inability to synthesize these feelings. Normal persons are ambivalent and can experience two contradictory feeling states at one time; borderlines characteristically shift back and forth, entirely unaware of one feeling state while in another.

Splitting creates an escape hatch from anxiety: The borderline typically experiences a close friend or relation (call him "Joe") as two separate people at different times. One day, she can admire "Good Joe" without reservation, perceiving him as completely good; his negative qualities do not exist; they have been purged and attributed to "Bad Joe." Other days, she can guiltlessly and totally despise "Bad Joe" and rage at his badness without self-reproach – for now his positive traits do not exist; he fully deserves the rage. (pp. 10-11)

Splitting commonly has three components to it: all-or-nothing thinking, unmanaged emotions, and extreme behaviors. Some of the developers of cognitive therapy, Aaron Beck and colleagues, have described (1990) how these three components are connected together:

Borderline individuals can experience the full range of cognitive distortions, but one particular distortion that Beck refers to as "dichotomous thinking" is particularly common and is particularly problematic. Dichotomous thinking is the tendency to evaluate experiences in terms of mutually exclusive categories (e.g. good or bad, success or failure, trustworthy or deceitful) rather than seeing experiences as falling along [a continuum]. The effect of this "black-or-white" thinking is to force extreme interpretations on events that would normally fall in the intermediate range of a continuum, since there are no intermediate categories. According to the cognitive view, **extreme evaluations of situations** lead to **extreme emotional responses** and **extreme actions**. (p. 187) [bold added]

Ralph and Yolanda

You can see how the idea of splitting can drive high-conflict divorces. In many of these cases, one parent sees the other as "all-bad." This leads to extreme behavior. Take Ralph, for example. I was the family lawyer for his wife, Yolanda.

Ralph was a bully to his wife Yolanda throughout their short marriage. They had two children, both daughters, ages 3 and 5. He hit her from time to time, on her back and buttocks, so no one would see. He frequently called her disparaging names. She told me that he liked to call her stupid and a pig.

Based on what she told me about the abuse, I went to court and obtained a restraining order. Ralph had to stay 100 yards away from Yolanda and he could not contact her. He didn't have an attorney, which meant that he would be calling me directly.

I am always cautious about believing what my clients tell me. However, when Ralph called me up to demand that Yolanda should do this and that for him, he was very rude. At one point, he started referring to her as "that pig" or "stupid pig." "You tell that pig that she better do what I'm telling you."

I remember telling him: "Don't talk about my client that way, or I'll have to hang up."

"I'll call that stupid pig whatever I want!" he said.

"Then I'm hanging up," I replied, and calmly hung up the phone.

After that, he called her that name one more time with me, but then quickly said that he didn't want me to hang up and that he wouldn't call her that. We eventually negotiated most of a settlement out of court for their parenting plan and finances. He agreed to have a family member present when he had his parenting time with the children. He didn't really want to spend much time with them anyway. While they were sometimes afraid of him, they didn't resist seeing him with a family member present. They were still pretty young.

He seemed to be an HCP and to be "splitting." He was arrogant and never admitted to doing anything wrong. In his eyes she couldn't do anything right. He believed that she deserved everything that happened to her and he was constantly trying to manipulate situations to his extreme advantage. Because he saw her as "all-bad" or "all-stupid," he felt justified in hitting her. This is one of the dangerous aspects of splitting – it allows the person to hurt other people. It's okay in their own minds, because whatever they do is okay – and the other person "deserved" it.

He finally got his own lawyer to help finish the settlement out of court. It was much easier then, since I didn't have to deal with him directly. Of course, his attorney adopted some of this splitting and spoke of Yolanda as "the difficult client," even though the lawyer had never met her.

"I know your client is really difficult, but could you ask her if she could change the parenting time next week." Who said she was difficult? I never did. Yet his attorney spoke this way to me, as though this was an agreed-upon fact. In fact, I thought my client was not an HCP. She asked for my advice and generally followed it. She seemed flexible in thinking of solutions, which helped in reaching agreements.

Ralph's attorney seemed to have been emotionally influenced by Ralph – who was very intense. Splitting is contagious. Even professionals can catch it.

Mack and Mona

Mona was my client. She had a 4-year-old daughter, Annie. She and the father, Mack, had never been married. He had lived in another state most of her life, so he rarely saw Annie. Then, he moved back and wanted regular weekends and a weekday with Annie. She was very angry about that.

After one of the first weekends, Mona told me over the phone that Annie seemed unusually sad.

"I asked Annie what was wrong," Mona said. "She said nothing was wrong. But I insisted and she started to cry. That's when I knew that her father had

done something to her. I've always thought he was evil. You can't trust him for a minute." Then she really raised her voice: *"You've got to do something to protect her. I know he has abused her – sexually! She finally admitted it."*

Next thing, Child Protective Services was involved. But they said that they were closing their case, because family court was involved. Soon we're in court with her allegations of child sexual abuse. The judge ordered a psychological evaluation and limited time with the father, but not supervised. The judge said angrily to my client: "Nothing you have described sounds anything like child sexual abuse to me. But we will see what the psychologist has to say."

The psychologist eventually said there was no evidence of any child sexual abuse and Annie seemed happy when she saw her father. The psychologist had observed Annie with her father, and he seemed appropriate and Annie seemed to value their time together.

Mona was furious. She yelled at me over the phone: "I know he did something to her. I just know it! He's an evil man! I knew he would do something to her someday."

Mona viewed Mack as totally "evil." When you see someone as "all-bad," it's easy to jump to the conclusion that they could do the worst things in the world. And the worst thing you could do to someone's young child would be to sexually abuse her.

I believe that Mona was splitting in her mind. She saw herself as "all-good" and Mack was "all-bad." I had no doubt that she believed everything she told me. She intensely believed he had harmed her, even though no professionals did.

I didn't get emotionally hooked into her all-or-nothing view. Splitting isn't contagious, if you know about it and you learn to emotionally avoid it. For a year, I tried to help her take a more flexible approach. The psychologist recommended a shared parenting plan, with Mona having the majority of the time. After all, she had done most of the child-rearing during Annie's first four years. She made an effort to cooperate with the shared schedule, but she never got over her intense belief that he had harmed her.

Finally, she fired me and went back to court. I don't know how it turned out, but I had warned her that continued efforts to prove something without facts to support it can backfire at family court. I wouldn't be surprised if the court reduced her parenting time, since the state law says that the preferred parent for custody is the one who supports the other parent's relationship with the child.

Mona had all-or-nothing thinking about Mack. Seeing him as evil fed her upset emotions, which she couldn't manage for more than a year. These emotions drove her back to court, which was an extreme behavior because all logic and all professionals had told her that it would backfire. Yet she was unable to stop herself.

These are just two examples of splitting. In one case, the father appeared to be a high-conflict person (HCP) and his splitting led to violence against his wife, the "all-bad" person in his mind. In the other case, the mother appeared to be an HCP and her splitting led to false allegations of abuse, which she appeared to believe because the father was an "all-bad" person in her eyes.

This fits the description of the cognitive researchers above about splitting:

Extreme evaluations of situations (all-or-nothing thinking)

Leads to:
↓
Extreme emotional responses

Leads to:
↓
Extreme actions

It is very important to know that splitting is not a conscious process and that HCPs lack self-awareness of much of their behavior. Make sure that you do not confront an HCP and say "You're an HCP" or "You're splitting." HCPs can get angry at almost anything you say or do. Remember, you can easily become the "all-bad" person in their eyes, without a moment's notice. Everyone around them is at risk of being blamed for anything, possibly having rumors spread about them, or even being verbally or physically assaulted as the HCP's "target of blame."

Splitting is possible even if you have been a good friend or family member, even for many years. Remember, in both cases above, the "target" of the splitting was the other parent. These parents had been close and intimate at one point in time. As described above, someone can be the "all-good" person one day and become the "all-bad" person the next. Don't let this happen to you. This can be mostly avoided by practicing the skills described in this book.

Avoiding High-Conflict Divorce

The key to avoiding high-conflict divorce is to understand HCPs, to understand splitting, and to avoid joining in the splitting process. However, this isn't easy. Unfortunately, reasonable parents and professionals get repeatedly emotionally "hooked" into splitting in reaction to high-conflict behavior. This keeps high-conflict divorce cases going and feeds child alienation, as the chart shows on the next page.

The key to avoiding high-conflict
divorce is to understand HCPs, to understand splitting, and to avoid joining in the
splitting process. This isn't easy.

I really wrote this book for reasonable parents and reasonable divorce professionals. As the chart suggests, I have reached several surprising conclusions about how to avoid high-conflict divorce and its alienating effects on children:

1. **High-conflict divorces aren't driven by the issues.** They're driven by people with high-conflict personalities (HCPs). From my experience and surveys, half to two-thirds of high-conflict divorces are driven by one HCP. The other parent is a reasonable person who is just trying to cope and to protect the children. Some professionals are also HCPs, perhaps 10-20%.

2. **Reasonable parents and professionals respond to HCPs with high-conflict behaviors.** They get emotionally "hooked." They think they can get the HCP to change by getting angry with them, trying to control them, and trying to shame them into behaving better. However, these high-conflict responses inadvertently escalate the case and just make matters worse.

3. **Most HCPs won't change.** This is because they lack the ability to be self-aware of the effects of their high-conflict behavior, for reasons I will explain in this book. However, there has been some progress in helping some HCPs change by learning small skills in small steps with lots of structure and support.

4. **Reasonable parents and professionals can change.** If you learn how HCPs think, feel and act, and you learn to respond differently – often by doing the opposite of what you have done in the past – I believe that you can reduce the conflict, reduce your own stress and increase your child's resilience. In this book I have compiled the tips I believe will most effectively help you accomplish this.

BUILDING ALIENATION

HIGH CONFLICT PARENT	+	"HOOKED" OTHER PARENT	+	"HOOKED" FAMILY, FRIENDS, AND PROFESSIONALS	=	ALIENATED CHILD
All-or-Nothing Thinking		**All-or-Nothing Thinking**		**All-or-Nothing Thinking**		**All-or-Nothing Thinking**
Seeing other parent as "all-bad" with no redeeming value		Seeing other parent as "all-bad" with no redeeming value		Seeing one parent as "all-bad" with no redeeming value		Seeing rejected parent as "all-bad" with no redeeming value
Seeing himself or herself as "all-good" with nothing to change or improve		Seeing self as "all-good" with nothing to change or improve		Seeing other parent as "all-good" with nothing to change or improve		Seeing favored parent as "all-good" with nothing to change or improve
Demanding no contact with the children for the other parent		Advocating for no contact with the children and the "all-bad" parent		Advocating for no contact with the children and the "all-bad" parent		Demanding no contact with rejected parent
Demanding 50-50, with no flexibility		Or demanding 50-50, with no flexibility		Or demanding 50-50, with no flexibility		Demanding that family and professionals advocate for no contact with rejected parent
Having only one solution to each problem		Having only one solution to each problem		Having only one solution to each problem		Having only one solution to each problem
Unmanaged Emotions	+	**Unmanaged Emotions**	+	**Unmanaged Emotions**	=	**Unmanaged Emotions**
Yelling at other parent or making threats during exchanges of the children		Angry lectures at other parent, at children, slamming down phone, making threats		Angry lectures at bad parent, at children, slamming down phone, making threats		Yelling at rejected parent or making threats (run away) if rejected parent asserts self
Sudden outbursts of anger when discussing problems and solutions with other parent		Sudden outbursts of anger when discussing problems and solutions with other parent		Sudden outbursts of anger when discussing problems and solutions with professionals		Sudden outbursts of anger when discussing problems or solutions about rejected parent
Intense blaming of the other parent, to children, friends, family and professionals		Intense blaming of the other parent, to children, friends, family and professionals		Intense blaming of one parent/professional, to children, friends, family and professionals		Intense blaming of rejected parent, to children, friends, family and professionals
Intense or prolonged crying in front of the children about divorce and other parent		Intense or prolonged complaining to children, own family, friends, professionals		Intense or prolonged complaining to own family, friends and professionals about case		Intense or prolonged anxiety and/or anger about spending time with other parent
Trying to make children feel anxious or guilty while they are with other parent		Trying to make parents, children, and professionals feel anxious/guilty if disagree		Trying to make parents, children, and/or professionals feel anxious/guilty if disagree		Desperate to contact other parent when conflicts/problems arise with rejected parent
Extreme Behaviors	+	**Extreme Behaviors**	+	**Extreme Behaviors**	=	**Extreme Behaviors**
Not exchanging the child as scheduled, including hiding child, disappearing with child		Seeking radical changes of custody/access, including no contact with other parent		Seeking no contact orders with one parent		Refusing to spend time with rejected parent
Interfering with other parent's time, such as scheduling appointments or fun activities		Ending or accepting an end to all contact with child, including leaving the city, state		Seeking radical changes of custody/access		Seeking to cancel rejected parent's time, by scheduling activities or time with friends
Hiding money or withholding or threatening to withhold payments of financial obligations		Sharing information about parental alienation or about child abuse with children		Allowing interferences with one parent's time, making excuses for other parent		Hiding important school information, activities, big events from rejected parent
Threatening to eliminate the other parent from children's lives through the court		Hiding money or withholding or threatening to withhold payments of financial obligations		Hiding important negative information about a parent, plans to move, surprise attacks		Threatening to never see or speak to the rejected parent ever again in his or her life
Domestic violence: hitting, shoving, threatening to hurt other parent and/or child		Publically calling other parent "the alienator" or "the abuser" to groups, internet and press		Threatening to eliminate one parent from children's lives through the court		Hitting rejected parent, running away to favored parent, threatening suicide, actually committing suicide
				Publically labeling as "alienator" or "abuser"		

DON'T ALIENATE THE KIDS! © 2010 Bill Eddy www.HighConflictInstitute.com

Conclusion

The next five chapters explain the "wall" bricks of child alienation – all-or-nothing thinking, unmanaged emotions, and extreme behaviors – so that you can avoid them, even if the other parent is engaging in them on a regular basis.

Short Summary

Parents: If your spouse and/or co-parent is a high-conflict person (HCP), it helps to understand that this is an unconscious problem. It's not about you and most of their behavior is not on purpose (although some may be). Some HCPs can change, but you can't make them. Don't tell them "You're an HCP" or "You have a personality disorder." You need skills to deal with them, such as described in this book.

Family and Friends: If you have a loved one who is divorcing or separating from an HCP, avoid speaking in all-or-nothing terms about either person. It is easy to slip into "splitting," by seeing one as all-good and the other as all-bad, but you can resist this by recognizing it. Acknowledge that your loved one may be truly dealing with a difficult person (an HCP), and help him or her avoid getting "emotionally hooked."

Professionals: Recognize that high-conflict people often need different strategies for helping them and helping those around them. They can range from slightly manipulative to seriously dangerous. Avoid making assumptions, positive or negative. They can mislead you with their charm, fear and anger. However, they often can be managed with certain skills. You can be a role model for your client and make your own life easier.

Child Alienation

Katie, age 4, hides behind the couch and screams: "No, mommy! Don't make me go! Don't wanna see Daddy!" Daddy is knocking on the door to pick her up for his parenting time with her. Why didn't she want to go? Is Katie afraid of him because he has abused her? Or has her mother intentionally turned her against him?

Jonathan, age 14, yells at his mother over the phone: "No, I'm not going to spend any more time with you! You're stupid and your new boyfriend is a real jerk! I want nothing to do with either of you! I wish I had a real mother I could talk to! Dad isn't going to force me to see you, so just leave me alone – forever! Goodbye!" Why didn't he want to go? Is Jonathan realistically estranged from his mother because she's really stupid? Or because he was abused by her, or her boyfriend? Or has his father intentionally turned him against her?

Something is terribly wrong when a child resists or totally refuses contact with one of his or her parents after a separation or divorce. This is not a passing phase for many children, but lasts into their adult lives and can significantly interfere with their adult relationships.

Refusal to have a meaningful relationship with one of a child's parents appears to be a growing problem. Researchers indicate that in 11-15% of all divorces a child aligns with one parent and resists or totally rejects the other parent. In cases of custody litigation, when parents fight at court over who should have the majority of the time, 20-27% of cases have a child who strongly resists or totally rejects one parent. Why does this happen?

Two Theories

For the past 25 years, battles have raged unresolved in families and family courts around the world over two opposing theories about the cause of this resistance or refusal in divorce, each held by millions of parents and professionals, many of whom absolutely despise each other:

1. **Parental Alienation Syndrome (PAS):** This theory is that one parent has engaged in a pattern of "parental alienation," intentionally turning the child against the other parent for an advantage in court. The child favors that parent and joins in the negative campaign against the rejected parent. Those who believe in this theory say it is the *favored parent's fault* that there is a wall between the rejected parent and the child. Therefore, the child should have reduced contact or no contact with the favored parent, often referred to by supporters of this theory as "the alienator."

   This theory was developed in the 1980's by psychiatrist Richard Gardner. Gardner (2004) summed up his theory in an article that was published after his death: "The primary cause of the disorder is the programming parent who hopes to gain leverage in court by indoctrinating a campaign of denigration into the child against a good, loving parent." (p. 612)

2. **Child Abuse Presumption:** Others strongly believe that a resistant child must have been abused or otherwise mistreated by the rejected parent. In other words, the child resists contact because of the rejected parent's own actions and that it is realistic that the child has become

estranged from that parent. Some call this type of resistance "realistic estrangement." Since it is the ***rejected parent's fault*** that there is a wall between him or her and the child, they say the child should be allowed to limit or refuse contact with the rejected parent, often referred to as "the abuser."

This is the theory favored by many advocates against child abuse, especially child sexual abuse. It has been actively promoted, also since the 1980's. It wasn't until the 1980's that society truly accepted child sexual abuse as a real problem, rather than a child's fantasy. Children were allowed to testify and considered credible as witnesses. Therefore, when some men were prosecuted for child sexual abuse, they turned to Parental Alienation Syndrome as a defense against the child's own statements. If the court was convinced there was PAS, then the defendant would go free and custody would often be changed to the defendant to undo the alienation. This brought a strong objection from child abuse advocates, including Carol Bruch (2001).

> To the extent that PAS results in placing children with a parent, who is, in fact, abusive, the youngsters will be bereft of contact with the parent who might help them. Parent groups and investigative reporting describe, for example, numerous cases in which trial courts have transferred children's custody to known or likely abusers and custodial parents have been denied contact with the children they have been trying to protect.

Paul Fink, M.D., past president of the American Psychiatric Association agrees, stating, "I am very concerned about the influence Gardner and his pseudo-science is having on the courts . . . . Once the judge accepts PAS, it is easy to conclude that the abuse allegations are false, and the courts award custody to alleged or proven perpetrators . . . . Gardner . . . undermines the seriousness of sexual abuse allegations." (pp. 533-534)

You can see how these two worlds collided and why advocates of each theory were so frustrated by each other. However, over these two decades, Parental Alienation Syndrome has not been widely accepted as a "syndrome" by mental health professionals or family courts. A syndrome is a scientific term for an automatic "cause and effect" pattern of behavior – if you can prove the pattern of behavior exists, then the cause is automatically known and you don't need to prove that it was the cause.

Also, many courts may seem to have a child abuse "presumption" – that someone is guilty until proven innocent if anyone suspects abuse, just to be safe. A presumption is a legal term for something which is assumed to be true, unless evidence can overcome the presumption and prove it's not true. For example "You're innocent until proven guilty" is a presumption in the criminal justice system.

However, there is no child abuse presumption and many mental health professionals and family courts are becoming more skeptical of abuse allegations made during divorce proceedings – as just a manipulation to get an advantage in court. In only 2-5% of custody litigation cases are there allegations of child sexual abuse, so that courts see many more cases of a child resisting or refusing contact with a parent (20-27%) where child sexual abuse is not even an issue. Instead, poor parenting or insensitivity are raised as reasons that a child is "realistically estranged" from the rejected parent. The courts are becoming more skeptical of that.

Neither theory has been generally accepted. Nevertheless, both theories seem to have more advocates than ever. There is an appealing logic to each of these theories, but, from my experience and the writings of many others, both of these theories have serious weaknesses. Making extreme assumptions based on one or the other theory often makes the problem worse. Yet both of these theories are alerting us to real problems. Child abuse is real and child alienation is real. Both should be taken seriously.

In 25 years, I have not seen a satisfactory resolution of the conflict between these two theories in family courts around the world. However, I am hopeful now, because some of those on both sides of the "abuse versus alienation" debate are starting to come together and agree on a larger view.

For example, the Association of Family and Conciliation Courts is the largest international organization addressing the issues of custody and access in divorce. In 2010, they held a large conference to address the issue of alienation. Many researchers seem to agree on several points:

- Alienation is usually caused by several factors, rather than just one parent's "bad" behavior.

- The problem seems to be growing, or at least getting more attention in the news and in the courts of appeal in the United States and Canada.

- There is no one good label for this problem. However, many prefer to use the term "the alienated child" or "child alienation," rather than "parental alienation," because parental alienation assumes that it is all caused by one parent's bad behavior. I prefer to use the term "child alienation," because it describes the problem without making assumptions. Each case of refusal to see a parent may have a very different cause or combination of causes, from child sexual abuse to child alienation – or both! This term will be discussed more later in this chapter.

- In some cases there is child abuse or domestic violence by the parent who is rejected, and in other cases this rejection occurs without any abuse by the rejected parent. Sometimes an abusive parent also has an alienating influence on the child and the rejected parent is also the victim of the abuse.

- All agree that when allegations of abuse are reported by children, they should be taken seriously and investigated thoroughly. While recent reports indicate that child abuse rates have reduced, most agree that they are increasing again with the economic hard times and that child abuse is still a wide-spread problem that needs many more resources for investigations.

- In other words, many advocates for the child abuse theory or the parental alienation theory are getting away from all-or-nothing viewpoints and seriously considering several causes and trying many different solutions.

- Many researchers strongly believe that children need two parents, with some extreme exceptions, and there is growing research to support that now.

- Some cases have mild alienation from a parent, some have moderate, and some have very extreme alienation. Different approaches are needed for these different problems, and there is no one approach that fits all.

- Many agree that it is very hard – but not impossible – to recover a loving relationship between an alienated child and a parent. All agree it is best to try to address alienation as soon as possible, before a child is totally rejecting a parent. Most agree that counseling involving the whole family is best (except in cases of known serious abuse), with strong court instructions and consequences. However, there are still disagreements over how strong a role the courts should play.

With this new openness in mind, let me explain some common dynamics of child abuse and alienation cases over the years, with examples. In the next chapter, I will explain a new, third theory of alienation which I call "1000 Little Bricks" and which, I believe, fits the more recent thinking of many professionals trying to resolve this issue.

Child Abuse

Let's start with the case of James. He was a young teenager with a girlfriend his age. For some reason, his father also liked teenage girls. They lived in a secluded area and his father encouraged him to bring girls home from school to hang out at their house. So James brought home his young friends from school and they would hang out for hours with his "cool" dad and stepmom.

One day, while James and his girlfriend were hanging out at his house, his father asked him to go to the store to pick up some food. While he was gone, stepmom was not around and Dad sexually abused his own son's girlfriend.

The girlfriend was devastated and told her mother. They contacted the police, who did an investigation. James' father denied any sexual contact. But he didn't know that he had been recorded in a phone call he made afterward to the girl, admitting the sexual encounter and asking her to get together again. The girl and her mother moved to another state, and James' father went to jail.

When this incident happened, James immediately contacted his mother and moved back in with her. His parents had divorced many years earlier and he had lived with his mother most of his life until his father persuaded him to move to his house when he became a teenager. After this child abuse incident, James was furious with his father. He wanted nothing to do with his father. You could say that he was "realistically estranged" from his father.

But a strange thing happened. James' father only spent 3 months in jail (half of a six month sentence because it was his first offense and he showed "good behavior" in jail). After he got out, James initiated contact again with his father. They started meeting secretly, because there was a family court order preventing contact by his father with James, and James told his mother he wanted nothing to do with his father. He wasn't estranged for very long. In fact, he started picking up some of his father's manipulative and antisocial behaviors. If ever a father had betrayed a son, it was this one. Yet, James wasn't realistically estranged from his father at all.

Years of Abuse

One of my first clients when I was a child therapist was a teenage girl who had been sexually abused for five years by her step-father. Jane was one of the most resilient people I had ever met (child or adult). Her mother had an evening job, but finally discovered that her husband was sexually abusing her daughter in the evenings. The mother kicked him out of the house and went to the police. But surprisingly, Jane would sneak out to see him even while the police investigation was going on.

Her mother brought her in for therapy. I said that Jane would probably want a female therapist, but Jane wanted a man. She was furious with her mother. She had fallen in love with her step-father and was alienated from her mother. As I worked with her in therapy, she described how he had helped her build a lot of confidence in herself through music. Playing in the band, she had become a leader with her peers, although he didn't let her have boyfriends.

My job as a therapist was to be supportive and non-directive – to talk about whatever she wanted to discuss. After several months of counseling, she decided on her own that what he had done to her was really wrong. He had terrified her when he first started coming into her bedroom in the evenings and abusing her. She realized that she didn't want any other child to go through this. She eventually testified at his trial and helped put him in jail for several years.

You would think that she would have been alienated or "realistically estranged" from her stepfather. But even after putting him in jail, she still said she appreciated his contributions to her self-esteem through encouraging her music. This was true even after she completely reconciled with her mother.

Criminal Behavior

Many years ago I volunteered in a program to drive children to see their parents in state prison on Sundays. I would take a van full of excited, talkative youngsters for over an hour's drive to see the worst parents in the world: drug dealers, thieves, attempted murderers, and others. Their parents were spending many years in prison for their crimes. These weren't alleged criminals; these were convicted criminals. They were parents who no longer denied their crimes.

After an hour's visit, the children would get back in the van and ride in almost total silence on the ride back. The sadness of having to see their parents and then leave them again was devastating. One tearful child said, "My Dad said not to grow up like him. I really miss him." These kids loved their parents. And they learned from them: what NOT to do. They weren't alienated or "realistically estranged" either – even from the worst parents in the world!

These are just a few examples of child abuse, where you would expect a child to reject a parent. But they didn't. To my knowledge, there is no research showing that "realistic estrangement" is a common result of child abuse. It may seem logical, but what I have observed as a social worker is the opposite: When a child had a repeatedly-abusive parent, he or she adapted to that parent years ago. What I have seen is that children mostly love their parents, but hate the abuse.

In the cases where they are truly angry with their abusive parents, they are too afraid to upset that parent and will do anything to avoid further abuse. The abused children I saw did not feel safe to challenge an abusive parent by running away or expressing anger at them – at all!

Yet running away or expressing anger at an alleged abusive parent is often raised in cases where a child rejects a parent – as evidence of child abuse. Yet there is no such pattern associated with child abuse. Similarly, bed-wetting is not a certain sign of child sexual abuse – it is more often a sign of a high-conflict divorce. It should still be investigated until the problem is resolved, but there should be no assumptions. In other words, there's no Child Abuse "Presumption" that can be applied when a child rejects a parent.

In all my years as a social worker, I never worked with a child who directly confronted their abusive parent or ran away from their abusive parent. While I know there are cases of this, especially among older teenagers, I believe it is the exception rather than the rule. Also, the term "parental alienation syndrome" never came up in my work as a social worker in the 1980's, even though it was coined in the 1980's when I was counseling children and parents. Rejection of a parent was not an issue or an option for the abused clients I saw.

Parental Alienation Syndrome

Frank was one of my first family law clients. He and his ex-wife Christine had handled all of their own divorce paperwork when their daughter, Patti, was 2 years old. When she was four, Frank remarried and wanted to change their parenting agreement to give him more time with Patti. He met with me to discuss his options and he retained me to be his attorney. We developed a plan for him to approach his ex-wife with his request for more parenting time.

Suddenly one morning, I received a call from a lawyer for his ex-wife. He gave me notice of an emergency hearing that afternoon at court, because Frank had sexually abused their daughter during the past weekend's visitation. Child Protective Services had met with Patti and Christina and said his contact should be restricted. I rushed down to court with no idea what to expect. I had never before had my own client accused of child sexual abuse.

At the hearing, the mother said that little Patti had been growing more and more fearful of spending time with her father. Before his visits, she would hide behind the couch and say "I don't want to go." More recently, she had started crying and screaming before his visits. Then, after last weekend, she told her mother "Daddy touched me down there. It hurt." I cringed to hear this. I had counseled adults who were molested as children, and some had used almost the exact same words, in describing how sexual abuse had changed their lives forever.

The judge admitted the Child Protective Services letter into evidence, which said Frank should have no contact with his daughter while an investigation was being completed over the next few weeks. The judge agreed and made a "no contact" order until the investigation was completed.

Frank was furious and adamantly denied doing anything inappropriate with his daughter. I knew such denials were typical for child abusers. But as an attorney, I knew I was supposed to give him the benefit of the doubt. My stomach was in knots. I didn't want to represent a child molester, but I also knew that in the 1990's a lot of innocent day care center workers were being released from prison because of false allegations of child sexual abuse. Repeated and aggressive interviews with the children had produced "tainted" and extreme statements.

A few days later, I heard from Frank. "Guess what!" he exclaimed. "There's a whole book written on this type of problem. Now I understand why Patti was starting to resist spending time with me. Her mother was purposely alienating her from me to block my effort to increase my parenting time at court. It's called 'Parental Alienation Syndrome' and the book is by Richard Gardner, a psychiatrist who handles child custody cases."

While I had never heard of Parental Alienation Syndrome before, I had heard of Richard Gardner. He was a psychiatrist who developed the "Talking, Feeling, Doing" game that I used as a therapist in the 1980's with young children to get them talking about their lives. I thought it was helpful. It's not easy to just sit down with a child and get him or her talking about life, feelings, and new ways of doing things.

Initially, I thought there was a lot of logic to Parental Alienation Syndrome. Now that I was an attorney, I was appalled at what some people would purposefully do to win in court. Lying, manipulating, and blatantly harming people, was behavior I was not used to as a therapist. I used to believe that everyone was well-intentioned, but sometimes confused and mis-communicating.

In family court, I started learning about all kinds of bad behavior that people do. Even though all statements made in family court are supposed to be "under penalty of perjury," I knew that there was more lying going on in family court than anywhere else I had ever been. It was as if "under penalty of perjury" really meant "lie here!" I had met Frank's ex-wife, Christina, at court and wondered if she was intentionally making false allegations? Frank was convinced, but I just didn't know.

For four months, Frank had no contact with his daughter. A police investigation and a psychological evaluation proceeded slowly. Finally, after a new judge was on our case and Christina had a new attorney, I was able to convince the court that Frank should be allowed to have supervised parenting time. Christina's attorney, of course, opposed this request, saying the Patti had great fear of her father and could be traumatized by any contact before a full investigation had been completed.

When Frank first saw his daughter in a small visitation room at a local supervised visitation center, Patti ran up to him, put her arms around him, and said: "Daddy, where have you been!" The visitation supervisor put these comments in her written report. The visit was a warm occasion, as Patti wanted Frank to pick her up, share a toy with her, and expressed her sadness at his absence from her life. The visitation supervisor indicated that during the whole two hour visit there was never any expression of fear or inappropriate behavior by Patti or her father.

Chapter 2: Child Alienation

When Frank described this joyful visit, he was quite relieved and encouraged. "Now we have proof that I never hurt her or touched her inappropriately."

"I'm relieved to hear that too," I said (and I really was). "But you need to know that some sexually abused children show no fear or negative feelings toward an abusive parent – especially a young child who doesn't know that what has happened to her is inappropriate and abusive. Let's just see how this goes. But I'm happy for you and quite relieved to hear this report."

A week later, at the beginning of her second supervised visit with her father, Patti was tentative and fearful. She did not run up to Frank, but instead avoided eye contact with him and went directly to play with the toys. Frank was surprised, but took his time to re-establish conversation with her. In about 5 minutes, she was as open and friendly with him as she had been the prior week, the supervisor explained in her notes.

Why did she behave so differently at the beginning of the first and second visits? I decided to ask Christina this question when I took her deposition a few weeks later.

"What, if anything, did you say to Patti about her first visit with her father after four months of no contact?"

"I didn't tell her anything," she replied. "In fact, I didn't even tell her that she was going to see her father."

"Okay," I said. "And what did you say before you brought her to her second visit with Frank?"

"I told her she would be seeing her father again, and that she should tell the supervisor if she ever felt worried that her father was frightening her or he wanted to do anything that might hurt her."

"Okay," I said. I wondered: Did Christina's comments make Patti cautious and fearful? If so, did Christina intend to have that effect, or was she truly concerned? If she was purposefully trying to make her daughter fearful of her father, why didn't she "warn" her to expect danger at the first visit? Or did she assume that her daughter would be truly afraid on her own? But she wasn't.

After four months of no contact, then three months of supervised access, and a psychological evaluation, the psychologist said: "The chances that she has been sexually abused by her father – or anyone - are less than one in a million, in my opinion."

So she wasn't sexually abused! And she wasn't alienated! The judge said there was no reason to require supervised parenting time, and there was no evidence that Christina had done anything wrong either. The case was over. Of course, Frank's original plan to increase his parenting time was permanently brought to a halt.

As often happens, I lost track of Frank after his case was over. But, ten years later, he happened to call me about an unrelated legal question. I asked how it was going with his daughter, who would have been about 14 by then.

"Oh," he said. "We live in different cities now. I see her for a week or two every summer. But Christina never let me have a real relationship with Patti after the court case was over. She always found one reason or another that I shouldn't see her."

"Were there any further allegations against you? About anything, sexual or otherwise?" I asked.

"No," Frank said. "There's never even been a hint of allegations against me. She just finds reasons that it's inconvenient for her or for Patti."

"How does she respond to you when you spend time together now?" I asked.

"Oh, she wants to keep it short. In fact, she said this coming summer she would rather spend it with a friend. She's learned that she doesn't want to spend time with me. Now Patti doesn't see the point in having a relationship with me at all. It's no longer her mother's influence. Now it's Patti's own opinion. I have lost any meaningful relationship with my daughter."

So maybe this is an alienation case after all. But it doesn't fit Gardner's Parental Alienation Syndrome. There's no court hearings. No advantage for Christina in a custody battle. The battle's over. She won ten years ago. Why would she intentionally keep it going? The alienation all occurred after the court process was over.

Court Case Examples

Today's reality is that there is no "Parental Alienation Syndrome" in most family courts. It fails the "Frye test," which came out of a federal court case in 1923. The Frye test mandates that all courts, state and federal, must determine whether a new scientific principle has been generally accepted by the relevant scientific community before it can be used in making a court decision. Parental alienation syndrome has not been generally accepted among most mental health professionals and is not in the Diagnostic and Statistical Manual used by mental health professionals. Therefore, with a few exceptions, the syndrome has not been generally accepted by the courts.

The courts instead address the issue in terms of "alienating behavior." In 2007, two decades after PAS was coined, a computer search of family law court of appeals cases around the United States showed 105 cases which included the phrase "parental alienation syndrome." Just three years later, in 2010, the same search turned up 142 cases – a 26% increase. This subject is getting a lot more interest these days. However, the consistent pattern is that the courts of appeal avoid recognizing a "syndrome," while still looking at specific parent behavior, as the following cases demonstrate.

C.L.J. v. M.W.B.

In this case, the trial court ordered a change of custody from the mother to the father, with the mother having only supervised access. The mother appealed the decision. The court of appeals agreed with the trial court (the judge is called the "trial court" by courts of appeal), explaining as follows:

> [The psychologist, Dr. Kirkland, stated that the mother] has consciously or unconsciously chosen the path of alienating the children's affection from their father. Regardless of whether we label it a particular syndrome, the alienating and destructive behaviors are obvious, persistent, chronic, and pervasive.... In my opinion, the degree of alienating behavior on the part of the mother in this case is significant enough to warrant the recommendation of a change in custody.
>
> ....
>
> [The court of appeal stated that the mother] argues that PAS, which she says Dr. Kirkland used in making his evaluation, does not meet the Frye test for admissibility because it is not generally accepted in the scientific community....
>
> We instead conclude that Dr. Kirkland's written custody evaluation and his testimony at trial were not based on a diagnosis of PAS as much as they were based on the mother's repeated and admitted inability to promote, or to at least be neutral concerning, the father's role as parent.
>
> ....

Although we might, if faced squarely with the question whether evidence concerning an actual diagnosis of PAS as admissible under Frye's 'general acceptance' test, be inclined to agree with the mother and find that PAS had not been generally accepted in the scientific community, we do not need to make that decision in this case. The trial court was presented with a myriad of evidence that the mother desired to end all contact between her children and their father — even to the point of expressing a desire for termination of his parental rights....

C.L.J. v. M.W.B. (2003), Ct of Civ App Alabama, 879 So. 2d 1169, 1176-78.

Pearson v. Pearson

In this case, the judge denied a change of custody to the father, which the father had requested. The father appealed the decision. The court of appeals agreed with the judge, explaining as follows:

The trial court concluded that Sara is 'the parent most capable of allowing an open and loving relationship with the other.' But Mark argues that the trial court erred when it concluded that Sara was not trying to alienate him from their children's lives.

To support his argument, Mark asserts that the trial court erroneously disregarded the evidence he presented regarding parental alienation syndrome. He cited a long list of cases from states and Canadian provinces sustaining decisions to admit evidence of the syndrome. But this authority is not relevant because the trial court did admit Mark's proffered evidence. Instead, we read Mark's argument as a challenge to the trial court's factual conclusion that the children did not suffer from parental alienation syndrome.

The trial court's findings regarding parental alienation syndrome are not clearly erroneous. Although the syndrome is not universally accepted, the trial court heard evidence from two experts, Dr. Weinstein and Dr. King, who both believe that it may occur. But the experts disagreed as to whether the syndrome was present in this case. The trial court analyzed both experts' testimony, concluding that Dr. King based his testimony on more objective observations and was more helpful to the court. Because 'assessment of witness credibility is left to the discretion of the superior court,' we will not overturn the trial court's conclusion that Sara was not deliberately alienating Mark and his family.

Pearson v. Pearson, (2000) S Ct of Alaska, 5 P. 3d 239, 243.

Concerns About Parental Alienation Syndrome

There is much I agree with about the parental alienation theory. From my experience, there is no doubt in my mind that many children are alienated from a parent, and it is not the result of something the rejected parent did – such as being abusive, inadequate, inappropriate, over-reacting, or otherwise justifying "realistic estrangement" from a parent. Over the past 17 years as a family law attorney and divorce mediator, I have seen many cases in which alienation exists and it was not "caused" by the rejected parent.

In 2005 and 2006, I did a survey of family lawyers in San Diego County, including questions about Parental Alienation. In the first survey of 47 Certified Family Law Specialists (who had lots of experience and passed a difficult exam), only one said they did not believe in parental alienation. In the second survey of 131 family lawyers, all of them said they believed in it.

However, I also agree with the criticisms of parental alienation. I don't believe it is a syndrome – you shouldn't assume that the favored parent has "intentionally" alienated the child, as Gardner said, and there are real cases of child abuse.

I also don't see alienation as only occurring in divorce or custody disputes. As a family therapist in the 1980's, I had many cases in which a child was aligned with one parent and in conflict with the other parent – in families that were not divorced. And, while many rejected parents in divorce had not done something to justify estrangement, I saw that they still acted in ways that reinforced the alienation. It wasn't just "the alienator."

To their credit, many proponents of parental alienation now agree that many mothers – not just fathers – are the victims or "targets" of alienation. They also agree that there are many cases that do not involve a "syndrome." They also recognize that there are real cases of child abuse. But they still haven't given a satisfying explanation of why this alienation occurs.

I don't see alienation as a "strategy" or "campaign of denigration" or the result of intentional behavior. I disagree with them about calling one parent "the alienator" and the other parent "the good, loving parent." I don't think it's that simple. Such all-or-nothing thinking has led to many disastrous court orders and parenting results.

Many father's rights groups believe strongly in Parental Alienation Syndrome. I have had many clients who were fathers, who told me their cases were the result of PAS, and that was the end of it in their minds. I had to tell them that this is not the case in today's family courts. Many rejected fathers (and rejected mothers) are very disappointed to learn this. It's just not that easy. If you think that way, you will be unprepared for the realities of this dispute.

As Justice R. James Williams (2001) of the Supreme Court of Nova Scotia has written:

> In my view the foregoing [analysis of the issue] demonstrates that the concepts of Parental Alienation Syndrome and/or Parental Alienation face considerable difficulty if examined critically with respect to principles of admissibility. Courts have been less than vigilant in exercising their 'gatekeeper' role. The admissibility of Parental Alienation Syndrome and/or Parental Alienation should not be benignly taken for granted. (p. 279)

Concerns About the Child Abuse Presumption

Many advocates against child abuse and domestic violence reject the concept of Parental Alienation, either as a Syndrome or even just the term parental alienation. It still implies blame of the favored parent. I agree with them. I have represented several parents who were blamed for being "the alienator." Yet from my work with them over the years, it became clear to me that they were being unjustly blamed and inappropriately humiliated in court.

Child abuse is real and increases during economic hard times. Many people are in denial about the extent of child abuse in our society, including child sexual abuse. Even though recent research shows a reduction in child abuse rates from 1993 to 2006, including a significant reduction in child sexual abuse (44%), it is generally recognized that half or more of child abuse cases are never even reported, let alone addressed in court. Also, between 2001 and 2007, the rate of child murders increased 35%. Advocates against abuse have had a hard struggle for decades getting society in general and professionals in particular to recognize this problem. These are serious problems.

However, in divorce cases I think many advocates have a child abuse presumption – that when a child refuses contact it must be because the rejected parent is "the abuser." When courts order changes in parenting time to increase time or change custody to the rejected parent, advocates oppose those decisions and often refer to that parent publicly as "the abuser" and to the parent who is losing custody as "the protective parent."

I am just as disturbed about publicly labeling a parent "the abuser" as I am about labeling a parent "the alienator." We shouldn't be publicly saying that someone is an alienating parent and we shouldn't be publicly saying that someone has sexually abused their own child, with no credible evidence to support it. Remember, these are almost always cases with no criminal court involvement.

Yet I can understand how this presumption happens. As a social worker in the 1980's, I counseled children and adults who had been abused as children. I had child sexual abuse cases that were very disturbing. It's not unusual to develop a gut-wrenching reaction to the idea that someone may be sexually abusing a child. I have had that feeling in true cases and in false cases of child sexual abuse allegations in divorce. As a social worker-advocate, it's tempting to believe in a child abuse presumption. It operates on a gut level after you've seen enough true cases.

The high-conflict cases are stoked by opinions in the absence of evidence.

However, in the 1990's, there were many cases of false allegations of child sexual abuse in daycare centers. Psychological research showed that the way the children were interviewed caused them to say things which weren't true. After courts of appeal threw out many long-term sentences against men and women daycare workers, there was a greater skepticism about child abuse allegations. Child Protective Services agencies refined their interviewing techniques and became more discriminating in their determinations of founded and unfounded cases of abuse.

Today's family court judges, lawyers and counselors know that children can be affected by the tensions in a divorce. Symptoms such as bed-wetting, aggressive behavior, withdrawn behavior – even running away from a parent – are more often believed to be reactions to high-conflict divorces rather than child abuse. There are no clear symptoms associated with child sexual abuse. Only about 30% of true cases have physical evidence of abuse. This makes them very difficult to assess.

Yet, even today, many mothers in divorce assume that they will be the primary parent or the only parent after a separation or divorce. When a child hints at abusive behavior from a father, these mothers believe that the courts will automatically support their concerns and affirm their control of the child. I have represented many mothers who seemed truly shocked to have their parenting skills questioned. I have had to explain that it's not that simple. There is no "Child Abuse Presumption" in the law either.

Where Are We Now?

The problem in most cases of child resistance or refusal is the lack of any real evidence of abuse or alienating behavior. The cases that become high-conflict are not usually the cases with a conviction in criminal courts. Those are clearly resolved. The high-conflict cases are stoked by opinions in the absence of evidence. The dispute is often over the meaning of children's statements and behavior, with presumptions by both sides about the causes.

Child sexual abuse is alleged in approximately 2-5% of divorce custody disputes, whereas alignment with one parent and rejection of the other is alleged in approximately 20-27% of divorce custody disputes. Abuse and alienation are two very different problems. Also, in many cases of domestic violence, the perpetrators of the violence engage in alienating behaviors with the child. In other words, the victim of abuse may also be the victim of alienation. So these two theories do not fit neatly into an "either/or," "abuse vs. alienation" analysis.

Allegations of parental alienation seem to be increasing. Anger at family courts about parental alienation versus child abuse also seems to be increasing. When I go to family court and see protesters outside, I get a sense of how frustrating this is for everyone. One day, a father's rights group is protesting: "Family courts are biased against men." Another day, advocates for mothers accused of alienation are protesting: "The courts are biased against mothers. They're giving children to their abusers."

From my experience, the courts are working hard to be fair and laws continue to be refined. I have represented mothers and fathers about equally, and I believe today they are more equal than ever before in family courts. In my experience and in my seminars for judges, I have not met a more sincere group of people. They really do want to help families and do the right thing.

I don't think the problem is gender bias, stupidity nor lack of concern. I believe the problem is something quite different. I agree that some children are abused by a parent. I agree that some children become alienated against a parent. I generally agree with the concept of "child alienation," as described by family researchers Joan Kelly and Janet Johnston.

Child Alienation

Kelly and Johnston (2001) acknowledge that some children are alienated. They just make no assumptions about who is "at fault," so they don't use the phrase "parental alienation," as that implies that one parent is the cause. They have "reformulated" the issue from one of parental alienation to one of an "alienated child."

> An *alienated child* is defined here as one who expresses, freely and persistently, unreasonable negative feelings and beliefs (such as anger, hatred, rejection, and/or fear) toward a parent that are significantly disproportionate to the child's actual experience with that parent. From this viewpoint, the perni-

cious behaviors of a "programming" parent are no longer the starting point. Rather, the problem of the alienated child begins with a primary focus on the child, his or her observable behaviors, and parent-child relationships. (p. 251)

Family law professionals now frequently refer to this "reformulation" as the best way to approach alienation cases. In many ways, it has calmed the conflict between professionals who were advocates against abuse and professionals who were advocates against parental alienation.

In their article, Kelly and Johnston describe a range of possibilities in family relationships, including: an "affinity" with one parent over the other, an "alignment" with one parent and some resistance to the other, "realistic estrangement" in response to a rejected parent's abusive or undesirable behavior, and "alienation" with intense rejection of a parent without a reasonable basis.

However, for simplicity's sake in this short book, I am using the term "child alienation" to include all of the above possibilities. I favor the general dictionary meaning of "alienation" as "alienation of affection" from someone close – regardless of the reason.

Johnston and colleagues (2009) have emphasized a multi-factor, family systems approach in understanding and treating child alienation.

> The main problem with the PAS theory is that it focuses almost exclusively on an alienating parent as the etiological agent of the child's alienation. Our research shows that a singular focus on the aligned parent as being primarily responsible for the child's alienation is overly simplistic and not supported by available data. Rather, the problem of a child's rejection of a parent is a family system's pathology exacerbated by an adversarial legal system, not an individual psychiatric disorder. PAS cannot properly be considered a "diagnostic syndrome" ac-

cording to customary psychiatric nomenclature because there are no "commonly recognized, or empirically verified pathogenesis, course, familial pattern, or treatment selection for the condition." Hence the label "PAS" does not add any information that would enlighten the court, the clinician, or their clients, all of whom would be better served by a more specific description of the child's behavior in the context of his family.

....

...Rather, the problem of the alienated child begins with a primary, neutral, and objective focus on the child and his or her observable behaviors and expressed feelings and invites a broad search among multiple factors that might help explain the parent-child relationships. (pp. 363-364)

You can see how some parents and professionals can become focused on Mom as the "all-bad" parent or Dad as the "all-bad" parent. This all-or-nothing approach adds many bricks to the Wall of Alienation. The child's resistance is a problem with many factors to be understood, as Kelly and Johnston explain. Therefore, throughout this book, I refer to the problem of "child alienation" without any assumptions that it's Mom's fault or Dad's fault. In fact, that's where the next theory begins.

Short Summary

Parents: It is important for you to know that today's courts do not generally recognize Parental Alienation Syndrome. Instead, they look for alienating behavior. Also, courts do not assume that there is child abuse when a child resists a parent. Instead, they look for abusive behavior. So if your child is resisting contact with one of you, don't assume it is all the other parent's fault. Seek objective assessment if there is a problem. Get consultation with professionals before making statements at court that could alienate your judge from you.

Family and Friends: It's easy to get caught up in the distraught emotions of a loved one who is involved in a high-conflict divorce, especially with allegations of abuse or alienation. Help your loved one get information from more than one source. Make no assumptions. Ask if he or she is sure, when emotions run high. On the other hand, don't discourage him or her from raising concerns and providing descriptions of concerning behavior to the court. Just avoid jumping to conclusions and promoting emotional opinions without facts.

Professionals: Avoid making assumptions about a child's resistance to one of the parents. If you are known as an advocate against abuse or against alienation, it will be very important to focus on facts and specific behavior, otherwise your advocacy and opinions may hurt your client. Explain the doubts that many professionals have about allegations of child abuse and allegations of parental alienation in a divorce. On the other hand, don't disregard the possibility that your client it accurate regardless of the emotions involved.

1000 Little Bricks

In this chapter I explain a theory of child alienation that I have developed called "1000 Little Bricks." It's based on three Cultures of Blame and the little behaviors (bricks) that children absorb from them. When these three cultures reinforce each other, it is a "perfect storm" which can build alienation. This is in contrast to what cultures are supposed to do by protecting children and building their resilience for the future. If any one of these stopped being a Culture of Blame, I believe there would be much less child alienation.

1. A family Culture of Blame, when a high-conflict parent is involved.

2. Today's family court Culture of Blame, which pits parent against parent in an unnecessary contest over who is the "all-good" parent and who is the "all-bad" parent in a divorce, and which involves many family members and professionals who become emotionally "hooked" and feed the escalating conflict.

3. Our society's increasing Culture of Blame, which turns complex problems into the simple blaming of individuals, with lots of all-or-nothing commentaries, unmanaged emotions and extreme behaviors repeated endlessly through the news media, entertainment and politics, which feed alienation on a larger scale and influence children's personality development.

I will also introduce the brain science which explains more about how children learn and absorb these Cultures of Blame, without anyone intending it or even realizing it. It is similar to the way that children learn prejudice.

Cultures define desirable behavior, what is undesirable but tolerated, and what is unacceptable. Cultures define values, status, and punishments for their people. This is all learned, but without anyone specifically teaching it. Everyone absorbs their culture every day through thousands of comments, jokes, images, whispers, styles, gossip, accusations, praise for heroes, disparaging remarks for villains, and social punishments for those who violate the values or the power structure of the culture.

High school students and college students study world cultures, but at the same time they are learning about their own culture – who's in, who's out. Adolescence is when you learn where you fit in your family status, your peer group status, and develop your goals for your career and marital status. When children and adolescents try out thousands of behaviors, they get feedback from everyone around them – positive and negative. They absorb most of it unconsciously and it trains them to fit into one culture or another – sometimes even a "counter-culture." Children have to fit somewhere, and they learn the rules of the game – as defined by their culture. Child alienation in divorce appears to develop more in early adolescence than in any other age group.

Many cultures are peaceful and many are warlike – for a while. Most have rules about groups of people – who you're supposed to hate and who you're supposed to love and die for, if necessary. Today's modern urban cultures have become much more individualized, so that you are not automatically part of a secure group with clearcut enemies anymore. Instead, you are always vulnerable as an individual and anyone could be blamed as an individual for today's complex problems – even you. So there is a pressure today to focus the blame on someone else, so that it doesn't come back to focus on you.

A Family Culture of Blame

Let me start with two examples in which children grew up in a family Culture of Blame that focused on one parent for years, then on the other parent.

[As reported by Tracey Tyler, January 25, 2009] "In a stunning and unusual family law decision, a Toronto judge has stripped a mother of custody of her three children after the woman spent more than a decade trying to alienate them from their father. The mother's "consistent and overwhelming" campaign to brainwash the children into thinking their father was a bad person was nothing short of emotional abuse, Justice Faye McWatt of the Superior Court of Justice wrote in her decision.

…McWatt stipulated that K.D. [the mother] is to have no access to the children except in conjunction with counseling, including a special intensive therapy program for children affected by "parental alienation syndrome." The mother must bear the costs. Harold Niman, the father's lawyer, said the decision serves as a wake-up call to parents who, "for bitterness, anger or whatever reason," decide to use their children to punish their former partners. "Maybe if they realize the courts will actually step in and do something and there is a risk of not only losing custody, but having no contact with their children, they'll think twice about it," Niman said in an interview.

… The judge said awarding A.L. [the father] sole custody was the children's only hope for having a relationship with their father, given their mother's long-running transgressions. These include ignoring court orders, shutting the

door in A.L.'s face when he came to collect the children and refusing to answer the phone when he called to say goodnight. (He was granted telephone access to say good night on Monday, Wednesday and Friday). At times, she also arranged for police to show up when her daughters had overnight visits with their father.

...Nicholas Bala, a Queen's University law professor who specializes in family law, said "badmouthing" or negative attitudes by one parent toward another is quite common among separated couples. But in recent years, the justice system has begun to understand the harmful effects of the worst form of this behavior. In most cases, the problem is resolved through counseling, where parents are encouraged to accept they'll both always be in their children's lives, said Bala....Having said that, there are some people – and I think some of them are suffering from personality disorders – who will not respond to therapy and will not respond to directions from judges."

...Bala said courts are unlikely to take such a drastic step without hearing expert testimony about what's happening in the family. A child may be avoiding a parent for legitimate reasons such as physical or emotional abuse. McWatt heard testimony from Barbara Fidler, a Toronto mediator and clinical psychologist who predicted eight years ago the three girls were at risk of becoming alienated from their father. The Office of the Children's Lawyer argued the family dynamics could not continue. Fidler says research points to long-term damage in people alienated from a parent in childhood.

...Early intervention is best, Niman said. "Really, parental alienation is a process. If you can nip it in the bud, that's the best advice I can give to clients. Because the longer it goes on, the more difficult it can be to undo." (A1)

"Save Matthew!" the signs said as a handful of protesters stood in front of family court. "Stop the court from giving Matthew to his abuser!"

In this case, the mother said that the boy had been sexually abused by his father, based on a vague, dreamlike incident that the boy reported to his mother after Matthew and his brother spent a weekend with their father. Matthew was six when this incident occurred. It was investigated by Children's Protective Services (CPS) and a psychological evaluation was ordered.

His interview with CPS was videotaped and unremarkable. The boy and his father got along okay. The psychologist said that the mother was overbearing and that the father was fine. The court shifted custody from primarily with mother to equal parenting time. The boys seemed to do well at each parent's home.

But the mother was adamant that abuse had occurred, even though there was no evidence that the court found credible. She proceeded to interfere with the father's parenting, until the court received a recommendation to award primary physical custody to the father from a lawyer representing the child. Just before the judge heard the matter, the mother disappeared with the boys. They were on the run for a couple years.

Upon her return, the court ordered the boys into the sole legal and physical custody of the father. Then the boys started running away – to the mother's house. The court then ordered no contact with the mother, and one boy went back to live with the father and Matthew went to live with someone else. In both cases, they were to have no contact with their mother for at least 3 months.

At family court, the protesters brought their signs in support of the mother. They freely said that the father was a child sexual abuser, even though no professional had found that to be true. As evidence of his abuse, the protesters emphasized that the boy had run away from his father's house to his mother's house. However, it didn't seem to matter that the boy had not done that after the alleged abuse occurred two year earlier, when he appeared to get along fine with his father. Running away from his father only happened after his mother ran away with the boys herself and then returned.

These examples show how tragic and escalated child alienation cases can become over time. One family member – one parent – got singled out as a monster for months or years. Then the other parent became identified as the monster for months or years. The hostilities increased, rather than decreased. And in each case, many other people got involved – professionals and others – and they all became very frustrated and angry as part of the family's Culture of Blame.

A Culture of Blame from Day One

High-conflict parents (especially borderlines and narcissists, as described in Chapter One) naturally split people into "all-good" and "all-bad." From birth, children of HCPs learn about this. For example, Aunt Mary has been the HCP's favorite sister for many years. But then she goes on a trip and doesn't invite the HCP. The HCP is offended and sees Aunt Mary now as "all-bad." The children learn to take the HCP's side against Aunt Mary, and this calms down the HCP parent.

Then, the HCP gets in a dispute with the neighbor. The children know what to do. It's automatic. And the other parent, who may not be an HCP, has also learned that you don't argue with an angry HCP when he or she is splitting people into all-good or all-bad. If you do argue with splitting, then YOU become a target and treated as all-bad too.

So the children have learned the family Culture of Blame: The HCP parent is unpredictable and frightening. This parent's intense anger and blame can flare up at any moment. The family solution with an HCP parent is usually to tolerate and adapt to this inappropriate behavior – until it becomes intolerable.

Most families don't have this Culture of Blame *within* the family. But for HCPs, it's all about family – the hated people are usually those they used to love, because of splitting. The people they are preoccupied with the most are usually close family members, such as the other parent, one of the children (often HCPs treat one child as "all-good" and another as "all-bad"), one of the grandparents, or other relatives. The children are used to disliking and criticizing one or more of their family members.

So it's a natural progression to absorb the HCP's emotions about the other parent in a divorce. The child doesn't have to be given any instructions. The whole family culture has been doing this for years – including the HCP's relatives. And the non-HCP parent has learned to tolerate it, so the children learn to tolerate it too. It's contagious and mostly non-verbal.

Right and Left Brains

The human brain is divided into a right hemisphere and a left hemisphere. Each of these "brains" process different information at the same time. The left hemisphere is active in processing language, words and details. When the left hemisphere is working on solving a problem, you may be conscious of thinking about it. The left brain is more active with problem-solving tasks and planning for the future.

The right hemisphere is more focused on the big picture, non-verbal behavior, and people's moods. It is very attentive to other people's tone of voice, facial expressions and hand gestures. If someone in your environment is especially angry or fearful, your right brain will pick up this anger and fear, and your body may tense up before you consciously know why.

For the first three years of life, children's right brains are dominant and developing rapidly, in comparison to their left brains. This means that they are learning everything based primarily on their parents' tone of voice, facial expressions, hand gestures and the emotional messages they are constantly sending out. They become highly familiar with their parent's regulation of their own emotions and their general level of peacefulness or anxiety.

They learn what triggers anxiety in their parent and what calms them down. This is all learned before they really understand language. Their parent's body language is really all they need to know. They learn the family's Culture of Blame very quickly and thoroughly – and nonverbally and unconsciously.

With an HCP parent, blaming someone becomes natural. Children quickly learn who's powerful and who's not in their family culture. They learn whose moods dominate everyone else's behavior. It's natural to want to be on the winning side – for survival. Children are on the road to becoming alienated against several people in their lives well before their parents split up. They are also at high risk of becoming HCPs themselves.

Why Parents Cling to One Child

Why would each of the parents in the above examples with primary physical custody engage in such extreme behavior – which was almost guaranteed to cause them to lose custody? Even if a parent believed that their child had been sexually abused, but there wasn't credible evidence to convict the alleged perpetrator, wouldn't they be in a better position to do something about it in the future if they continued to be the primary custodial parent or had at least 50% of the parenting time?

I have had clients concerned about child abuse who have taken that strategic and moderate approach, and they still have primary physical custody or 50-50 parenting years later. The abuse appears to have stopped, or may never have occurred. In either case, the situation has been contained and the conflict has reduced. They still have 50% or more of the parenting time.

In child alienation cases, however, it appears that there is a parent who cannot take a strategic and moderate approach, but instead appears driven to cling to at least one child and to eliminate the other parent one way or another – even at great risk to their future parenting relationship. In other words, they are splitting. They see the other parent as "all-bad" and view their own behavior as "all-good" and blameless – even though it appears from the outside to be extremely bad and self-defeating.

In the first case above, the mother's "consistent and overwhelming" campaign to brainwash the children into thinking their father was a bad person was nothing short of emotional abuse, the judge wrote.

In the second case above, the mother disappeared with the children rather than lose 50% custody; but then she did lose custody upon her return.

I believe there is a logic to this behavior. By understanding this logic, we can prepare for it, prevent it from reaching this point, and respond to it better.

Early Childhood Attachment

Over the past 60 years, there has been a lot of research about "attachment" in early childhood. Even as early as 12 months of age, a child can be observed by researchers to have a "secure attachment" with his or her parent(s) or an "insecure attachment." There have been some studies which suggest that this can be a contributing "risk factor" for developing a personality disorder – including the behavior we see in child alienation cases.

A "primary attachment" relationship starts at birth, usually with one or both parents. It is necessary for survival at first, but then it is necessary for growth and building a foundation for all future relationship skills. A child "turns on" his attachment behavior of seeking his primary attachment figure (usually Mom or Dad) through eye contact, getting closer (grabbing legs, crawling) and trying to communicate his needs. If there's no response, then he will shift to extreme behavior (screaming, tantrum) until he gets the attention he needs.

This primary attachment relationship is the foundation of all of a child's close relationships in life – primarily learned the first year, but especially the first five years, and to some extent through all of childhood into adulthood.

The primary attachment relationship is most often with the child's mother, but others in the child's life may also form a meaningful "attachment" relationship, including the child's father, siblings, grandparents and others. Sometimes it's the father with whom the child has the most secure attachment relationship. While relationships throughout life will come and go, what happens through an early childhood attachment relationship is necessary for human survival and growth.

There are many important lessons a child must learn in their early childhood attachment relationship(s) that a child is not born knowing (many people don't realize this):

A sense of security that her/his basic needs will be met

Confidence that problems can be solved one way or another

Awareness of what s/he is feeling inside

Awareness of other people's feelings

Learning to "read" other people's moods

Learning to "read" other people's intentions

Learning that s/he can manage her/his own emotions

Learning that s/he can manage her/his own behavior

Learning that s/he can be flexible in new situations

Learning that s/he and others can be different and still be okay

Learning that s/he can influence others and be influenced by others

Learning that s/he can reflect on her thoughts, feelings, behavior

Learning that s/he can change her thoughts, feelings, behavior

Learning that people have a combination of good and bad qualities

Much of this is learned by mirroring parents – their facial expressions, tone of voice, hand gestures, and so forth. But much of this is also learned by having parents mirror the child. When a parent (or other attachment figure) mirrors the child's facial expressions, tone of voice, hand gestures, and so forth, the child becomes aware of herself/himself. It is only through others that s/he can develop a sense of herself/himself – by being responded to in a satisfying way and specific way (now you seem sad, now you seem angry, now you seem hungry).

These lessons cannot be taught like a lecture or a class. The lessons are learned by how the parent and other attachment figures **respond** to the child's behavior. So it is only when a baby cries that a baby can learn that her cries will get sympathetic attention from her attachment figures. It is only when a baby laughs, that she learns that other people like it when she laughs. You don't teach a baby to cry or to laugh. You respond!

Attachment Behavior

As soon as a babies are born, they "turn on" attachment behavior: eyes look to meet the eyes of those around them. They look at people when they cry. They look at people when they laugh. For the first six months, they don't really care a lot about who holds them, feeds them and changes them – they just need to get it done.

But starting at about six months, attachment behavior becomes very picky – who the child wants to be held by, fed by and changed by: Mom, Dad or another attachment figure. Ordinary strangers suddenly become frightening, unless Mom or Dad is present. This is a very important time in the child's life, as he or she begins to form the most important attachment relationship(s).

By twelve months, the child should have formed at least one primary attachment relationship from which to learn the close relationship skills described above. Now, the child can start taking some risks. Playing Peek-a-Boo is really a very serious game of testing this attachment relationship: "Will Mom or Dad still be there if I hide for a minute – or if they hide for a minute?" Of course, this isn't a conscious thought. Testing the attachment relationship happens automatically – it's part of the child's development.

Exploring Behavior

In the 1950's and 1960's, researchers John Bowlby and Mary Ainsworth developed "attachment theory," which explains the importance of very early childhood learning. They found that most children have a secure attachment relationship with at least one person by the time they are 12 months old. This can be observed by those trained in attachment research.

Children with a secure attachment show an equal balance of "attachment behavior" (crying, clinging, seeking to be held by the parent, seeking reassurance) and "exploring behavior" (ready to turn away from the parent, look around, explore their environment, show the parent new toys). When a parent responds effectively (paying full attention, talking to child in soothing manner, feeding, changing or otherwise responding to child's needs), the child feels confident to "turn off" his attachment behavior and "turn on" his exploring behavior.

In a common attachment experiment, known as the "Strange Situation," a 12-month-old child can be observed demonstrating their attachment style.

A researcher meets with the parent and child in an unfamiliar room, with toys and other items for play. First, all three are in the room. Then, the parent leaves and the child stays behind with the stranger (researcher) in this unfamiliar room for a few minutes. Studies show that the child's heart rate speeds up and cortisol (the stress hormone) is released in his or her mouth. Here's what they often observe about the child's attachment behavior when the parent returns:

Secure Attachment: The child runs to the parent, possibly cries a little bit, and wants to be picked up by the parent. The parent holds the child and speaks softly, trying to soothe the child. Pretty quickly, the child stops crying and starts looking around the room. Then the child wants to be put down and begins to play with the toys, possibly showing them to the parent. Their heart rates quickly return to normal and the cortisol level in their mouths quickly subsides.

Here's how one attachment researcher, David Wallin (2007), describes it:

> In the secure [attachments], the infant clearly expressed his need for comfort after separation, his relief at being soothed during reunion, and his consequent readiness to resume play. The mother accurately read his nonverbal cues (his tearful approach with upraised arms, his molding to her body when held, his eventual restlessness) and responded accordingly (picking him up, holding him tenderly, and releasing him to play). This sequence reflected a kind of attuned communication that has been described as collaborative and contingent: One party signals while the other answers with behavior that says, in effect, I can sense what you're feeling and respond to what you need. (p. 21)

This balance of "attachment behavior" and "exploring behavior" was missing in those interactions where a child did not have a secure attachment.

Insecure Attachment Styles

The attachment researchers have seen that some children do not have a secure attachment with their parents, and instead have the following three "insecure attachment" styles:

Dismissive Attachment Style (also known as Avoidant)

Preoccupied Attachment Style (also known as Ambivalent)

Fearful Attachment Style (also known as Disorganized)

Dismissive Attachment: When the parent is gone, this child looks independent and confident, but really is not – their heart rate and cortisol level are just as high as the first child. However, when the mother returns, the child keeps playing with the toys. He or she does not seek reassurance and appears not to expect this parent to be able to provide it. Their heart rate and cortisol level remain high. When the parent reaches out, the child is dismissive of the parent.

Preoccupied Attachment: When the parent is gone, this child goes into a panic. Sometimes they have to quickly bring back the parent, because children with this attachment style are so extremely distressed in the absence of the parent. When the parent returns, the child runs to the parent and clings and won't let go. Often the child is unable to be soothed and just cries and cries, clings and clings. Nothing the parent does seems to calm the child down. Their heart rate and cortisol level remain high. When the parent tries to put them down, the child resists and insists on continuing to be held.

Fearful Attachment: These children are not sure what to do. While the Dismissive and Preoccupied style children have a consistent strategy (avoiding or clinging), these children have an inconsistent mix of seeking and fearing their parent. When the parent returns to the room, these children have been observed to approach and then back off. Some burst into tears in the middle of the room, just sitting down, lying down or curling up with themselves. Their parent seems to be both the source of reassurance and the source of fear – both at the same time. These parents often have a history of depression, drug use, anger problems, or other causes for inconsistent behavior. These children don't know what to expect anymore – yet they desperately need reassurance.

Researchers have seen children do well who didn't have a secure attachment relationship until they were 2 or 4 or even older.

If children grow up with one of these insecure attachment styles, they will lack the secure foundation to fully develop the skills described above. They may not learn that problems can be solved, that emotions can be managed and that moderate behaviors can succeed. The good news is that they can still develop a secure attachment relationship even after 12 months old. Researchers have seen children do well who didn't have a secure attachment relationship until they were 2 or 4 or even older. Sometimes the secure attachment figure is a grandparent, adoptive parent or a counselor. Sometimes it's a therapist or a spouse in adult life.

Once they develop that secure attachment relationship, they can learn how to better manage themselves, their thinking, their emotions and their behavior. But the older they are when they first experience a secure attachment relationship, the harder it gets to learn these skills and gain a sense of confidence about close relationships.

Unfortunately, these insecure styles can become rigid patterns of relationship behavior for some that extend into adulthood and remain stuck throughout the person's life. Unless they sincerely work on trying to change a dysfunctional relationship style, they will bring it into all of their romantic relationships and other close relationships – usually without even realizing it. Research suggests that these early childhood insecure attachment styles can be risk factors for developing personality disorders.

>**Dismissive** may develop into Narcissistic Personality Disorder
>(Ever felt constantly dismissed by an arrogant parent or professional?)
>
>**Preoccupied** may develop into Histrionic or Borderline Personality Disorder
>(Ever felt that someone was constantly clinging to you with phone calls, emails or drama?)
>
>**Fearful** may develop into Borderline, Paranoid or Antisocial Personality Disorder
>(Ever felt someone was highly inconsistent, constantly manipulative, suspicious, or potentially dangerous?)

These personality patterns of behavior may date back to their first year of life. This also suggests that people with these disorders may still be seeking the secure relationship that they never had growing up. It also helps explain why some people react so strongly in a divorce. The person divorcing them may have been the most secure person they ever had in their lives.

Adult Relationships

By the time a child grows into an adult, he or she should have experienced sufficiently secure primary attachment relationship(s) to be able to manage close relationships with a *balance* of seeking behavior and exploring behavior. However, if they grew up with only insecure attachments, they still have attachment needs. They may *still be looking* for an out-of-balance preoccupied relationship that's incredibly close or an out-of-balance dismissive relationship with lots of disdain – because feeling close would feel too threatening but they still want a relationship. These are the only relationships that *feel secure* by the time they reach adulthood – but they are not secure attachments. They cause the creation of out-of-balance relationships, as the other party usually discovers, sooner or later.

If an adult love relationship is a substitute for an early childhood secure attachment relationship they never had, it may truly feel like they will die if their partner leaves. That may explain why so many high-conflict people "can't just let go." They have to have a partner they can cling to or a partner they can treat with disdain – or both. If you don't understand this, you won't be able to realistically prepare for their reactions during a separation or divorce. All of that seemingly strange behavior (excessive clinging, manipulation, threats) makes sense if you picture the person as a 12-month-old desperate for survival.

While it doesn't seem to make sense that an adult would hurt a spouse or child they love, it may be that they are acting out the abandonment fear or rage that an infant feels and never learned to manage. If you picture a 3-year-old hitting his mother or crying on the floor to get attention, you may have an accurate picture of what some 20- 30- 40- 50- 60-year-olds are doing, who never had a secure relationship and are now facing the loss of the closest thing to it they ever had.

Insecure attachment may explain why a parent could cling so desperately to one or more of their children, and put so much effort into eliminating the other parent after a separation ("this child is mine, all mine"). This could explain why the parent's behavior doesn't change, even over ten years, because the insecure attachment issue hasn't changed – even though this behavior may have extreme consequences. This is a key characteristic of personality disorders. They don't change over time. They are stuck in the past and not working in their own present self-interest – or that of their children. They're trying to establish a secure attachment relationship.

This could explain why a parent would run away with a child – to protect their primary attachment relationship. This could also explain why, in so many alienation cases, only one child is alienated. The parent only clings to that one child and that one child is the only one who rejects the other parent. In many of my alienation cases, the other child or children stay neutral about both parents or at least do not reject one parent even if they favor the other.

Insecure attachment behavior could explain why so many of the cases I've seen where *both* parents appear to have high-conflict personalities don't have an alienation issue. The children's attachment behavior is "turned on" much of the time with both parents. The child or children are busy keeping both of them calmed down, as little diplomats, without rejecting either parent – but sacrificing their own sense of self and not learning the relationship skills they need.

If a child learns that one parent can truly provide a secure attachment relationship (balance of reassurance and freedom to explore), then the child doesn't need to be in fear about that parent's moods. They can just be kids with that parent. But the kids know that they better be allies for their HCP parent. I have seen several of these reasonable parents do everything right, but the child becomes alienated and enmeshed with their HCP parent – because such a relationship requires all of their attachment behavior and energy.

For the HCP parent, the people (professionals, friends and family) who support this attachment obsession of the parent will be viewed as the "all-good" people. Those who try to force the HCP to share their child with the other parent, will be seen as the "all-bad" people. Understanding this may help us design our responses as professionals and reasonable parents. Otherwise, we get split and remain split.

Understanding all of this does not justify violence or alienation. But if we don't understand it, we will be doomed to repeat it through the generations. This may be what the children are learning and carrying into their adult relationships, if we don't break the cycle of insecure attachments.

Attachment and Splitting

During the first 18 months, a child does not realize he or she is a separate person from parents and others. The child is simply aware of having needs and getting them met (or not). But starting around 18 months, the child begins to develop a separate sense of himself or herself. Here's how psychiatrist Jerold J. Kreisman (1989) describes it:

> The ages of eighteen to thirty months, when the child begins the struggle to gain autonomy, are particularly crucial. Some parents actively resist the child's move toward separation and insist instead on a controlled, exclusive, often suffocating symbiosis. At the other extreme, other parents offer only erratic parenting (or are absent) during much of the child-raising period and so fail to provide sufficient attention to, and validation for, the child's feelings and experiences. Either extreme of parental behavior can eventuate in the child's failure to develop a positive, stable sense of self and may lead to a constant, intense need for attachment and chronic fears of abandonment.
>
> ....
>
> A further complicating factor during this time is that the developing infant tends to perceive each individual in the environment as two separate personae. For example, when mother is comforting and sensitive, she is seen as "all good." When she is unavailable or unable to comfort and soothe, she is perceived as a separate, "all bad" mother. When she leaves his sight, the infant perceives her as annihilated, gone forever, and cries for her return to relieve the despair and panic. As the child develops, this normal "splitting" is replaced by a healthier integra-

> tion of mother's good and bad traits, and separation anxiety is
> replaced by the knowledge that mother exists even when she is
> not physically present and will, in time, return... (pp. 48, 50)

In other words, it's inborn for a child to start "splitting" around 1 ½ years
old, as a step on the way to developing into a separate individual from his
parent. But then, with ordinary secure attachment, the child learns to integrate people's good and bad traits by about the age of 3 years old.

However, if the child does not have a secure attachment to build on, or has
some kind of attachment trauma, such as child abuse, then this learning
process may be seriously disrupted. The child may not learn to cope with
the temporary absences or negative emotions of a parent. Instead, a parent's frequent anger or absence may feel overwhelming and the child will
experience these temporary moments as "all bad." Without regular soothing and security from the parent, a child will have great difficulty learning
to contain or regulate his or her own emotions.

Here's how a neuroscientist, Louis Cozolino (2006), describes it, particularly in terms of borderline personality development and brain development:

> People with borderline personality disorder live on an emo-
> tional roller coaster....They experience criticism, shame, and
> abandonment from all directions as they hang on for their
> emotional lives. When confronted with even a hint of criticism
> or rejection, these people become emotionally overwhelmed
> and catapulted into drastically fluctuating moods, unstable
> perceptions, and rocky relationships. Friends and family suf-
> fer with them: they are targets of rage, accused of sadistically
> causing pain, and bewildered by unpredictable shifts in mood
> and behavior. Borderline personality is truly an interpersonal
> disorder, created in a social milieu, triggered by close relation-
> ships, and destructive to social connectedness.

What we witness in the lives of borderline clients is the result of a profound disruption of the development and integration of social brain systems and the ability to regulate emotion. The histories and symptoms of borderline clients strongly suggest that early attachment was experienced as highly traumatic and sometimes life-threatening (Fonagy, Target, & Gergely, 2000). Attachment trauma can result from physical and/or sexual abuse, neglect, or profound misattunement between parent and child....Whatever the cause, the child is unable to utilize others in the development of secure attachment and to regulate overwhelming anxiety and fear. The result is that real or imagined abandonment triggers a state of terror, similar to what any young primate experiences when physically abandoned by its mother. (pp. 256-257)

Dr. Cozolino mentions several important points about attachment which relate to splitting:

- Without secure attachment, the child cannot learn to regulate anxiety and fear.

- A hint of criticism, shame or rejection sends such a child into extremely overwhelming emotions.

- Such children develop "targets of rage" and accuse others of causing them pain.

- When feelings are triggered, that's all there is at that moment. Any slight problems or negative feelings will be experienced as intensely "all bad" in this all-or-nothing world. Any good experience or feeling will be "all good" – but just briefly. People who are splitting are only able to experience the feeling of the moment, so they must keep secure people (even children) close to them at all times, in order to have any good feelings.

Adult splitting appears to be the result of insecure attachments. The person apparently has not yet learned flexible thinking, managed emotions, and moderate behaviors, because these are learned in a secure attachment relationship. Parents with insecure attachments from their own childhood are still searching for a secure attachment relationship and may turn to their children after an intimate adult relationship ends.

Of course, most divorcing parents do this to some extent – they give their child too much information about the divorce, they have an emotional outburst that's overheard, and they may say or do something extreme on occasion. It's all a matter of degree and balance. Most parents catch themselves and quickly change their behavior and make "repairing" comments about the other parent.

For HCP parents, insecure attachments can be quite powerful. Their desperate drive to find a secure attachment relationship may help explain the life-or-death energy HCPs have and pass on to their children. It is automatically extreme, because it truly feels like survival is at stake.

In their quest for a secure attachment relationship, insecure parents may use splitting as a means to get their child to "take their side" against the "all-bad" parent. However, the close bond between a parent and child that is based on splitting is artificial and lacks the balance of a secure attachment for the parent or child.

The intense closeness based on splitting also requires an evil enemy. This bond often breaks down when the child discovers that the favored parent isn't "all-good" or that the evil enemy isn't "all-bad." Therefore, it requires extreme behavior by a parent to hold on to even a little sense of security from a parent-child bond that is based on splitting.

The Family Court Culture of Blame

Family courts are not designed to understand the hidden dynamics of parent-child relationships. This makes sense when you consider that family courts have the same basic structure of all courts, which are focused on individuals. There is a plaintiff (someone who has been injured) and a defendant (the one who is accused of causing the injury). Since 1970, all states have adopted "no fault" divorce laws, which say that it is improper to even consider who is to blame for the divorce. It has become a hybrid structure – it's designed for two sides to blame each other proving or defending against the finding of fault. However, you are not allowed to find fault for the reason for the divorce. Therefore, other issues become the focus of fault-finding.

When the issues of child support and spousal support first were getting decided in the no-fault system, the parties would argue over how each other spent money. But then states adopted a system of guidelines, which eliminated most of the blaming arguments about how each parent spent money.

Property division rules were established without fault in many states. Approximately ten states use "community property" rules, which just split everything 50-50 for most items, regardless of wise or poor decisions during the marriage in regard to property. Other states have "equitable division" rules, which allow a little bit of wiggle room in dividing property in a divorce, but not a lot. This has mostly been eliminated as an area for blaming behavior.

Parenting, on the other hand, is a wide-open potential battle ground over who is "all-good" and who is "all-bad." With the court's modern concern to prevent or reduce child abuse and domestic violence, allegations of abuse get a lot of attention and influence almost every aspect of the case. The court can decide temporary property allocation and support based on where the children live and what percent of time each parent has.

The result of all of this is that family courts still model, tolerate and often encourage high-conflict behavior. Family courts have a Culture of Blame, unless the professionals involved work hard to overcome it. This can include lawyers, counselors, mediators and judges. Ways to overcome this Culture of Blame for each of these professionals will be addressed in Part 2 of this book.

What is important to note here is that the blaming behavior of family law professionals is contagious when it comes to HCPs. Parents know very little about the realities of family court. Movies, TV shows and the news give a distorted view of how family court judges make decisions and the procedures that are involved. Therefore, parents follow the professionals' lead in managing their cases. Even when many parents do not have lawyers, they still observe the behavior of all the professionals at court and absorb their behavior. They are role models of high-conflict or low-conflict behavior.

When HCP parents become involved in the family court process, they are extremely vulnerable to the thinking, emotions and behaviors around them. As HCP parents, they generally have difficulty managing their own emotions, especially under stress, often because they never had secure attachments from which to learn this. Further, their unmanaged emotions are easily hooked by other people's anger, criticism, blame, sadness and anxiety. Their emotional controls and boundaries are weak. This means that when someone blames them for misbehavior, or gets angry at them or shares intense fear with them – they pass it directly on to their children.

This emotional contagion can also go directly from the child to parent to professional, as reports are made of inappropriate behavior with the child, large or small. If the professional cannot contain his or her own upset emotions, then he or she gets emotionally hooked and passes anger, fear, frustration, hatred, and so forth right back at the parent, who passes these emotions directly back to the children. It is right brain emotions transferring to right brain emotions, without either person realizing it. This emotional feedback loop easily drives blaming behavior and splitting.

The longer a high-conflict case goes, the more people involved, the more frustration there is without resolution, the more likely it is that the professionals' frustration and the HCP parent's extreme stress, fear and anger will pass directly to the children. It's as if the children were there in every room with their HCP parent during every conversation about the court case with every other professional. The child absorbs the judge's angry statements, the lawyers' angry statements, the other professionals' angry statements, family and friends' angry statements. The entire family court culture usually blames someone – and when it's one of the child's parents, it seems to become an irresistible force which almost no child has the ability to resist.

HCP parents often raise allegations of abuse or alienation at the beginning of a case. This parent often requests that the court restrict the other parent's involvement with the children. This escalates as legal professionals attack one parent, then the other. Unfortunately, the family court structure allows this "all-bad" parent and "all-good" parent contest, with lots of emotion and many extreme behaviors – all justified by what the other parent "has done." This immediately escalates the case into high-conflict, lots of anger and emphasis on determining which parent is to blame for the child's abuse or alienation. Deciding which parent is to blame fits right in with the court Culture of Blame. But this adversarial process of deciding which parent to blame is not the solution - it's the problem! It helps build a Wall of Alienation.

Our Society's Culture of Blame

This "1000 Little Bricks" theory goes even further to include the increasingly negative and blaming culture of today's news and entertainment industries, which bombard children with images of fear and blame every day. They promote the idea that children live in an incredibly dangerous world surrounded by "all-bad" people everywhere they go.

In her research about the effects of our modern culture on children, Jean Twenge (2006) describes some significant changes:

I was stunned by the size of the changes I found. Anxiety increased so much that the average college student in the 1990s was more anxious than 85% of students in the 1950s and 71% of students in the 1970s. The trend for children was even more striking: Children as young as 9 years old were markedly more anxious than kids had been in the 1950s. The change was so large that "normal" schoolchildren in the 1980s reported higher levels of anxiety than child psychiatric patients in the 1950s. (p. 107)

Developing an absolute fear of a parent fits easily into this Culture of Blame. After all, when something goes wrong, the headlines scream "Who do you blame for this sorry situation?" The constant message is that it's all one person's fault and we just need to eliminate that person from the planet. These industries teach children to be in a constant state of fear and over-reaction, and to seek extreme solutions to problems.

This Culture of Blame has filtered down to our court system, with numerous TV shows now about using the courts for blame and vindication. Many HCPs now come to court expecting a stage for parents, family, friends, and professionals to blame others. There's all-or-nothing thinking, unmanaged emotions and extreme behaviors: "It's ALL her fault! She's an unfit mother!" or "It's ALL his fault! He's an abusive father."

Rather than trying to change real behavior problems, the focus has become "Who do you blame?" and then trying to eliminate that bad parent from the children's lives. That's what high-conflict divorce is often about. It's not about problem-solving – it's mostly about attempts to eliminate parents and cling to children.

In today's modern world, we have 24-hour news cycles which focus on extreme behavior and "who do you blame" for it. Extreme behavior sells. TV, movies and news media know that the more extreme the programming, the better it is at getting viewers' attention. Our brains are wired to pay attention to extreme behavior. And viewer attention is important in order to sell the advertiser's products.

With more competition among TV stations, cable and the internet, companies that aren't extreme in their programming will go out of business. Therefore, what sells is all-or-nothing thinking, unmanaged emotions, and extreme behavior – the key ingredients for developing personality disorders. This competition is increasing, as journalist Ken Auletta (2010) says in a recent article about the news cycle:

> As media outlets multiply and it becomes easier to disseminate information on the Web and on cable, the news cycle is getting shorter—to the point that there is no pause, only the constancy of the Web and the endless argument of cable. This creates pressure to entertain or perish, which has fed the press' dominant bias: not pro-liberal or pro-conservative but pro-conflict. (p. 38)

This is all role-modeling for children who already live in a shaky world. This isn't all it takes to build anxiety and alienation, but it appears to be a contributing factor when combined with a family Culture of Blame and a family court Culture of Blame.

Our society cannot survive with this type of unchecked conflict behavior by so many people. We must learn to restrain ourselves – to restrain our blaming instincts. Our brains appear to be wired for intense blaming and splitting to give us energy and group cohesion during wartime. But our families, family courts and larger daily lives shouldn't be war zones. Today they are, in many cases.

Children's Right to Choose?

In addition to anxiety and constant conflict, add to this Culture of Blame a child's right to choose. More than ever before in history, children get to decide: what they wear, where they eat, how they spend their time – and with whom they spend their time. Society has changed. You can't blame this on one parent. As author Twenge (2006) states:

> Parental authority also isn't what it used to be. "Parents are no longer eager to be 'parents.' They want to love and guide their children as a trusted friend," says family studies professor Robert Billingham in a recent Chicago Sun-Times article. Chicago-area parent Richard Shields says that his 17-year-old son is his best friend. He prefers them to have fun together rather than impose strict rules or discipline. "It's better for them to see our values and decide to gain them for themselves," he says.
>
> This also means that children play a much larger role in family decisions. The kids who chose their own outfits as preschoolers have grown into teenagers who help their parents choose which car to buy or even where to live. The Sun-Times article interviewed a large group of teens and their families, finding one where a teenage daughter helped her father decide on a new job, and another where the two teenage kids make all of the home-decorating and electronics-purchasing decisions. Forty percent of teens see their opinions as "very important" in making family decisions. (pp. 30-31)

Today is it not surprising that parents feel helpless when a child says that he or she doesn't want to spend time with the other parent. This is true, even in non-divorced families. Children feel empowered to make decisions about their relationships with their parents, and our culture blames the parents for this.

There seems to be less support for parents by the general culture than ever before. Parents have to compete with the internet, movies and TV in setting the styles and attitudes for their children. Then, when their children don't do what they say, it's all the parent's fault. It's not surprising when kids absorb all of this. Our society's Culture of Blame has added many bricks to the Wall of Alienation and, if trends continue, is likely to be adding many more in the future.

Comparing Theories

I don't want to leave you feeling overwhelmed by these cultural influences. I believe they can be changed, and that we *can* set boundaries protecting the kids from them.

The next three chapters more specifically explain each of the three bricks which build this problem of alienation. Then, the second half of this book explains how parents and professionals can apply the three bricks for building a Foundation of Resilience instead: *flexible thinking, managed emotions,* and *moderate behaviors.*

To sum up these three theories, the following chart may be helpful.

Three Theories of Child Alienation

PARENTAL ALIENATION	CHILD ABUSE	1000 LITTLE BRICKS
It's all the alienator's fault!	It's all the abuser's fault!	Many contribute in little ways
It's intentional alienation	It's intentional abuse	It's mostly unconscious behavior
The child has been coached	The child has been abused	Child has been influenced by all
Remove child from the alienator	Remove child from abuser	Protect child and relationships
Order alienator into counseling	Order abuser into counseling	Teach both parents new skills
All or nothing solutions	All or nothing solutions	Teach flexible thinking skills
Hatred of alienator is reasonable	Hatred of abuser is reasonable	Teach managed emotions
Treat alienator as all-bad person	Treat abuser as all-bad person	Treat both parents with respect
Treat "target" parent as hero	Treat "protective" parent as hero	Treat both as needing support
Extreme behavior is justifiable	Extreme behavior is justifiable	Teach moderate behaviors
Focus on other's past behavior	Focus on other's past behavior	Focus on your future behavior
Advocates are always helpful	Advocates are always helpful	Some advocates are a problem
It's all the family's fault	It's all the family's fault	It's a social, cultural problem

Closing Tips

If you are a parent or someone helping a parent, avoid making assumptions about the cause of your child's feelings and behavior. Avoid making assumptions about the court and how professionals (lawyers, counselors, mediators) think about this issue today. Many parents have read a lot and/ or associated a lot with those on just one "side" of this issue. Many still assume that the court and professionals will automatically restrict or eliminate the other parent from the child's life, if allegations of child abuse or child alienation are made. This is no longer true in many, possibly most, of today's family courts.

If you are concerned that your child has been abused or alienated by the other parent, avoid extreme certainty, extreme emotions and extreme requests that indicate you want to eliminate the other parent. Instead, as I will describe in Part II of this book, present your concerns and willingness to work with professionals without making assumptions. Seek assistance from open-minded and experienced professionals, who have a reputation for objectivity and respect. Abuse and alienation do occur, and concerns need to be assessed and protections considered.

Be open to the possibility that many factors have influenced your child. Let the decision-makers know that you are open to sharing the problem and being part of the solution, such as getting counseling and supporting your child's contact with the other parent – even if there are some restrictions. When thorough and objective decisions are made, they are usually much more stable than extremes that have to keep being argued.

In today's courts, many professionals believe that parents making extreme allegations have personality disorders. Instead, the more that you can show that you have flexible thinking, managed emotions and moderate behaviors, the more likely it is that you will be taken seriously, and treated with flexibility and moderation in response.

I have learned (the hard way) that the best way to avoid building a Wall of Alienation is to manage your own anxieties. This goes for parents and professionals. In many cases, you will be wise to make reasonable compromises and stay out of court all together, thereby avoiding the intense blaming that could be passed on to your child. You can also avoid the larger Culture of Blame by turning off the television, limiting the internet, and doing what you can to offer your child a flexible, managed and moderate lifestyle – thereby using your bricks for a Foundation of Resilience instead.

Short Summary

Parents: There are many contributing factors to the Wall of Alienation, including three Cultures of Blame: 1) A family Culture of Blame, in which everyone adapts to a high-conflict parent who views some people as "all-bad" and others as "all-good." Often the HCP parent is seeking to fulfill their own early childhood "attachment" needs through the child. 2) A family court Culture of Blame, in which some professionals demonstrate unmanaged emotions and all-or-nothing thinking. 3) A larger Culture of Blame, in which there are repeated images of "all-bad" people which frighten children and reinforce rejecting some people completely.

Family and Friends: In supporting your friend or family member, try to provide a secure relationship (but not a deep "attachment" relationship), with a balance of supportive listening and encouraging him or her to learn skills for dealing with the situation. Notice if you or anyone else close to the situation is adding to a Culture of Blame, and see how you can change the focus to one of problem-solving. Encourage finding out-of-court solutions as much as possible. Encourage protection and stability for the child, while avoiding efforts to eliminate the other parent. Instead, help the parents focus on providing secure attachments for their child.

Professionals: Help your client(s) understand that there are several Cultures of Blame which may be contributing bricks to the child's Wall of Alienation, rather than simply agreeing that it is all one parent's "fault." Avoid escalating conflict unnecessarily by emotionally blaming the other parent and reinforcing all-or-nothing thinking in your client. Educate your client(s) about attachment issues, and how to provide a secure attachment even during the divorce, by providing a balance of reassurance and encouraging the child to learn skills for coping. Discourage efforts by either parent to cling to the child or deny all contact with the other.

Emotions are Contagious

"I WISH YOU WOULD F--ING DIE!" Olivia screamed at the top of her lungs, as her husband Colin loaded their tearful 10-year-old daughter, Samantha, into his car for their day together. The neighbors could easily hear Olivia as she stood at the front door of the house they used to share just a few weeks ago.

They had been a stable family with undercurrents of unhappiness. Olivia tended to feel frustrated that she was a successful businesswoman and Colin had a job working at an auto parts store. Then Olivia discovered that Colin was an internet pornography addict – adult pornography. She immediately told him to move out and the marriage was ended. She only allowed him to see Samantha one day a week, without any overnights, because she was concerned he would molest their daughter. There were no allegations that Colin had ever previously abused her, and he was the one who had cared for Samantha the majority of the time when Olivia was away on business trips.

Over the next few years, Olivia was very careful not to tell anyone, including Samantha, the reason that she was divorcing her father. But she freely shared her emotions with Samantha. By the time she was 14, Samantha refused to have any contact with her father. When the court ordered her into counseling with her father, Samantha told him "You destroyed my life!" But she couldn't describe what he had done to destroy her life. She just knew that she hated him with all her heart and considered him an inferior person. The counseling failed and she still refuses to see him.

Emotions are contagious! The more strong the emotions, the more likely we are to catch them – good and bad. As human beings, we're hard-wired to be influenced by each other's emotions. The closer the relationship, the more easily we absorb what each other is feeling – mostly without even realizing it. Recent brain research has discovered how this seems to happen.

The Amygdala

The amygdala in our brain is like a smoke detector. What we see, hear and feel is always being *immediately* checked for signs of danger by the amygdala, much faster than we can *consciously* think. Once the amygdala senses danger, it can *instantly* shift all of our attention to protecting ourselves by setting off the "fight, flight or freeze response" in our brains – within a fraction of a second!

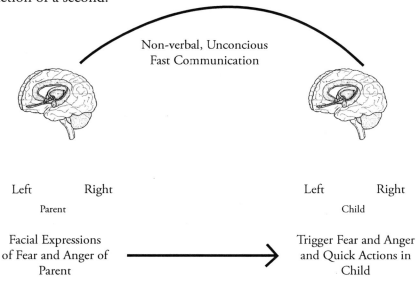

Non-verbal, Unconcious
Fast Communication

Left   Right   Left   Right
Parent   Child

Facial Expressions   Trigger Fear and Anger
of Fear and Anger of   ⟶   and Quick Actions in
Parent   Child

You actually have two of these almond-shaped amygdala – one in the mid-brain area of your brain's left hemisphere and one in the midbrain area of your right hemisphere. Remember, the right brain is the side that is more responsive to non-verbal information (facial expressions, tone of voice, hand gestures) and more active with negative emotions.

Therefore, it's not surprising that research shows the right amygdala is extremely sensitive to other people's facial expressions of fear and anger - more so than any other emotions. When someone else's face looks extremely angry or extremely scared, it instantly sets off your amygdala and your brain drops whatever you were thinking about and focuses all of your attention on whether you need to fight or flee the situation – unless your brain is used to the threat and used to over-riding it with its higher functioning prefrontal cortext. This is the part of the brain that's just behind your forehead and includes more complex thinking, and which can over-rule the amygdala.

But the brain remembers! When you face a new event that *reminds* the amygdala of a previous fearful event, the amygdala triggers the fight, flight, or freeze response. It primarily remembers the *emotions* associated with the prior experience – especially if fear was part of the memory.

Anger is Contagious

When Samantha heard her mother screaming at Colin, you can imagine that her amygdala remembered danger! How many times did it take for her to associate her father with danger triggered by her mother's angry emotions?

But Samantha wasn't initially refusing to see her father. In fact, she seemed to enjoy her visits with him on Saturdays. As long as he didn't ask for more time with Samantha, Olivia seemed to calm down. Of course, Olivia wouldn't let him have Samantha for any overnights.

For about a year, Colin accepted this situation. Then he went to court to increase his parenting time with Samantha. He asked for a 50-50 shared parenting schedule, since he had had more than 50% sometimes before their separation, when Olivia was away on business trips.

Olivia was absolutely furious that he would make such a request. She insisted on an evaluation of his sexual behavior and risk to their daughter. The result of these evaluations was that he clearly had no sexual interest in children, and no history of any abusive behavior in the ten years he had cared for her. In fact, there were indications that he had been the more emotionally nurturing parent, while Olivia was more driven and focused on her career.

But throughout the evaluation process, which dragged on for six months, Olivia was furious that Colin was persisting in asking for 50% of the parenting time and Samantha started to emotionally withdraw from Colin. At first he noticed that she didn't want to discuss as much with him about her school activities – which Olivia had forbidden him to attend (as a potential child-molester in her mind).

Then, Samantha also started getting angry with Colin during their visits, telling him to stop pressuring Olivia for more time. He tried to avoid discuss their parenting dispute with Samantha, but apparently Olivia was discussing it with her. Was she mostly fearful for her daughter, because of his sexual addiction? Or was she mostly angry with her ex-husband for humiliating her with his problem? It seemed that Samantha was mostly absorbing her mother's anger.

Once, when there was going to be a court hearing, Samantha angrily confronted Colin on their Saturday together: "Why are you taking us back to court?"

Colin brought this issue up in court. The judge asked Olivia what she told Samantha about her father.

"She doesn't know anything about his problem. I just told her that he has a problem that I don't have, and that I can't tell her about it until she's 18," Olivia said.

The judge responded: "Don't you think that would get her thinking that there's danger associated with her father?"

"No," she responded. "Any fear she has of him is caused by his insensitivity to her – and who knows what else. She tells me she doesn't want to see him any more than one day a week, but he won't listen to her. And she's starting to complain about that. He brought this all on himself. He has only himself to blame."

The judge told Olivia not to tell Samantha anything about court hearings – not even saying when they were occurring. When they went back to court the next time, Colin said Samantha didn't seem to know about it. Olivia had changed a bad behavior. She had removed a brick from the wall.

But Samantha started asking to skip a Saturday, here and there. She would call Colin up and ask him to let her miss a visit, explaining she had homework or a friend she needed to see. At first Colin was angry with her.

"What do you mean, you don't want to see me. Did your mother tell you to say that?"

Samantha was angry back: "Stop blaming mom for everything. Now you've really made me angry."

Colin felt caught in a bind. If he said "No" to her request, then Samantha would be angry with him for "forcing" a visit with him. If he said "Yes," then he wouldn't see her and couldn't try to strengthen his fading relationship with her.

By age 14, she stopped visiting him altogether. He would call her and she would talk to him on the phone. But she refused to spend any time with him. After the failed counseling sessions described above, Colin gave up trying to get her to spend time with him.

They still lived in the same neighborhood. One day he happened to see her walking home from school with a friend as he drove by. Maybe she missed him by now, he thought. But when she saw him driving by, she raised her hand and gave him the finger!

Samantha seemed to have caught her mother's unrestrained anger, and perhaps a bit of her father's as well. It was hard to tell if her mother's anger was mostly based on protecting her daughter, or mostly based on her anger at Colin for embarrassing her with his adult sexual addiction. In either case, it appears that Samantha picked up her mother's anger more than any other emotion.

But are other emotions also contagious? Brain research indicates that anxiety (fear) is the most contagious of all. When you are anxious is when you are most likely to pick up other people's emotions. The stronger the fear shown in someone else's face, the more intense your amygdala's response will be. Researchers explain that this makes sense as a human survival mechanism. We are much more able to survive as a group if we can instantly pick up each other's warning signs and take immediate action – often without a word even being spoken.

Fear is Contagious

After Jennifer remarried, Jeremy became extremely anxious about his sons' care in her home. Since he was allowed to call them every other night, he would spend a lot of the time asking the boys (Nathan, age 11 and Braden, age 8) questions about their new stepfather. He would tell them that they didn't have to listen to their stepfather, ironically causing many behavioral problems that otherwise may not have happened.

Jeremy professed that the stepfather was being too harsh about homework and abusive with his sons. He told the boys that Jennifer was not protecting the children from the stepfather, because "she didn't want to lose her husband" and "valued him more than her own sons." So Jeremy called Child Protective Services several times.

Each time, a social worker came out and each time said that there was no evidence of the stepfather being abusive. Jeremy's allegations were "unfounded." In fact, after the last such visit, the social worker wrote in her report a concern that Jeremy was emotionally abusing his sons with his obsession about the mother and her new husband's care of the children.

Eventually, there was a psychological evaluation, which suggested that Jeremy had paranoid personality traits. He was consumed by fear – with no basis in reality. This fear obsession mixed with his other high-conflict traits (abusive and dominating personality) to create a toxic effect. Each year, for many years, Jeremy went to court seeking primary physical custody, based on vague allegations of inadequate parenting by Jennifer and her husband. He would discuss the court case in depth with his young sons (against all psychological advice and in violation of court orders), while Jennifer was very careful not to. She didn't even let them know when there was going to be a court hearing.

At court, Jeremy was visibly anxious about all aspects of his sons' lives. He made the children the focus of his day – even though they lived primarily with their mother. He sent emails criticizing her about how she managed doctor's appointments, about sports activities, about studying for school. At the same time, the oldest son was getting into conflicts with his teachers and classmates at school, and Jeremy told him he was right to stand up to them and not let himself be "pushed around." He seemed as paranoid about his son's treatment at school as at their mother's house. He advised Nathan in detail about how he should handle his teachers and classmates at school.

Nathan picked up his father's anxiety and blame of others and started seeing everyone as hostile and not to be trusted – except his dad. The teachers said he seemed to have a chip on his shoulder. He was constantly over-reacting to normal interactions with the other children. He felt picked on by his teachers, when they had just given him ordinary feedback. Instead of encouraging him to make constructive use of his teacher's feedback, Jeremy told Nathan that teachers can't be trusted to look out for his interests and to protect him. Only his father can do that, he said.

There was a court order that said that Nathan and Braden were to play sports in their mother's community, as she had the majority of parenting time (70%), and playing in her neighborhood would bring the boys social stability. For years, Jeremy complained that he should be able to be his sons' coach in their sports. Jennifer understandably did not want this, and the court agreed, as Jeremy had physically abused her when they were married. But when Jeremy simply showed up at his sons' soccer practices to coach, she did not complain, but physically removed herself from the practices.

Nathan started telling his mother that he wanted to play in his father's community, against the clear court order. Jeremy became very anxious and demanded that Jennifer allow their son to do what he "wanted," which was to play soccer with his father and in his father's community. He said he was very worried about what would happen if Nathan didn't get to do what he so desperately "wanted." He insisted that he had nothing to do with Nathan "wanting" to play soccer in his father's community. He kept going back to court seeking an order allowing Nathan to play soccer in his neighborhood, with Jeremy as his coach. Jeremy insisted that his mother was uncaring and insensitive, because she wouldn't let Nathan play in his neighborhood. He said it would harm Nathan's development, not to be able to do what he "wants."

On the surface, it may have looked like Jeremy was a very caring and committed father. But under the surface, he was emotionally obsessed with his sons in a way that most people would say was unreasonable. He could not let them deal with life without his constant advice and involvement – even though he only had 30% of the parenting time.

Eventually, Jennifer got a court order stopping Jeremy from having phone calls with the boys while they were at her house. She hoped this would stop his influence over their lives. However, Jeremy secretly bought them a cell phone to call him if they ever felt in danger from their mother and stepfather. He got Nathan his own web email address and taught him how to email him from the school and library computers. He also taught them how to take the bus to come to his house directly from school, or from the mother's house, if they ever were in fear of their mother and stepfather.

Eventually, the boys "ran away" to their father's house one day on the way home from school, using the bus just as they were taught. Jennifer eventually gave up, because she could see that the escalating conflict was hurting her boys. Now they live at their father's house. Nathan rarely sees his mother, although Braden regularly spends alternate weekends with her.

Jeremy was extremely absorbed in his anxiety and his belief that only he could protect his sons from a hostile world. In the process, he passed a belief to his sons that the world was hostile. Jennifer did not seem to be passing intense emotions to the boys. In fact, she was very careful to avoid involving them in any of their parenting disputes. Ironically, this left the field open to Jeremy, who couldn't stop himself from involving Nathan in his obsessive anxieties. You either agreed with him or avoided him. Unfortunately, he made it impossible for his sons to avoid. So they ended up agreeing with him and sharing his anxieties.

Children's Emotions are Contagious Too

In the above examples, the parents' fear (anxiety) and anger spilled over onto their children, who became fearful and angry as well. But this also goes the other way. Parents can catch their children's fears and anger as well.

An example is with Jeremy above. Nathan said he "desperately wanted" to play soccer in his father's neighborhood and "desperately wanted" his father to be his coach. Jeremy became absorbed in desperate pleas at court and to the mother to let Nathan do as he "desperately wanted." He became highly concerned that if Nathan didn't get what he wanted, it would somehow harm Nathan for life. Jeremy had no recognition that Nathan may have been reflecting back Jeremy's own anxiety about controlling Nathan's life.

Furthermore, Jeremy had no idea that "feelings are not decisions." Sometimes, children are better off if they learn to delay getting what they want. And sometimes what children really need is the opposite of what they "desperately want," as the next example demonstrates.

School Refusal

Recent research on "school refusal" shows that it is a very similar problem to child alienation. Instead of refusing to go with a parent, the child refuses to go to school – also for vague reasons that don't fit the situation.

Bridget, age 13, started refusing to go to school because she developed a fear that she would throw up in front of her classmates. Her parents were afraid that her anxiety would harm her, and when it was intense enough they let her stay home from school. They tried to convince her to go. When she went, they would text message with her all day at school to help her stay, and they would pick her up when she felt sick or too anxious.

Finally, after Bridget missed several weeks of school, her parents sought some help from a clinic associated with Brown University in Rhode Island. A psychologist with the program, C. Sloan Alday (2009), explains their approach to school refusal.

> Commonly, parents believe that the school refusal is 'just a phase' that will pass. They may worry that experiencing extreme anxiety is somehow harmful to their child or fear that forcing their child to experience something unpleasant will permanently damage the parent-child relationship. Finally, parents often believe that anxiety is untreatable and permanent.

....

Because parents' anxiety feeds children's anxiety, an important step in treatment is helping parents manage their own anxiety....[F]or parents who worry about harming the parent-child relationship by forcing the child to experience something unpleasant (such as attending school), family therapy must supplement any form of intervention. Parents need a safe and supportive place for exploring their concerns and understanding how their worries affect their child. [Bold added]

The clinic took a step by step approach to helping Bridget and her parents, starting with education about school refusal. Then, the parents were taught ways of setting firm limits for school attendance, Bridget was taught relaxation methods to manage her own anxiety, and they had family therapy sessions together.

After learning that anxiety was not dangerous or harmful to her and that anxiety would remit over time, they were more comfortable setting firm limits with her regarding school attendance. Through... visualizing school scenarios...and learning relaxation techniques, Bridget became more willing to attend school. The family learned cognitive behavioral techniques together, and Bridget's parents began emphasizing that becoming sick at school was not in itself a catastrophic event.

....

Family therapy sessions focused on helping members feel secure in their relationships and accept negative feelings states, such as anxiety and anger, as tolerable parts of every family's experience. Today Bridget attends school regularly with some periods of anxiety that she and her family are able to manage. (pp. 6-7)

Fortunately, Bridget and her parents found professionals who understood this problem. Fortunately, it wasn't in the context of a divorce and the parents were working together to help their daughter.

This example addresses the exact same issue which often escalates anger and fear in divorce cases – the issue of "forcing" a child to do something he or she doesn't want to do. In high-conflict divorce cases, it's very common to hear parents, counselors and even judges saying "I won't 'force' the child to spend time with the other parent." I hear it so often that I have written handouts for parents and professionals about it. (See Appendices)

After learning that anxiety was not harmful and would remit over time, they were more comfortable setting firm limits with her.

In one case, a counselor for two daughters who were seeing their father, but very little time each week, told them in their first session that he would "try to persuade the parents not to 'force' them to spend more time with their father." I understand that he was trying to form a "therapeutic alliance" with them by starting where they were "at." However, even after a year, he had not changed his position – nor had they. Eventually, the older daughter refused any visits with her father.

I suggest that it's better to use the word "expect," rather than the word "force." We *expect* children to go to school, we expect them to go to the dentist, and we expect them not to take drugs and not to have sex. We find ways to make these things happen or ways to prevent them. Children need adults to look out for their best interests, which sometimes are different from what they "desperately want."

Sadness is Contagious

All feelings can be contagious. I have had cases (even in mediation, when parents are mostly supportive of each other), with one parent who is overwhelmingly distressed by sadness about the divorce – even a year after the parents have separated. Sometimes the sad parent is the mother and sometimes the father. They aren't openly angry. They're tearful – constantly tearful. When I see this, I can generally predict that sooner or later one parent will say that the children or oldest child no longer wants to spend time with the other parent. These are parents who want the children to visit, but feel helpless to make it happen.

One woman described her parents' divorce several decades earlier. She said that her father was devastated and depressed. When she would spend weekends with him, she absorbed his sadness and felt really distressed. Then, when she went back to her mother's house, where she primarily resided, she remembers being very angry with her mother about how her dad felt. "I told her it was all her fault!" She doesn't remember much about those days, but decades after their divorce she still remembers how her father was sad and depressed.

Professionals' Emotions are Contagious

In the examples above, one or both parents are expressing fear, anger and/ or sadness around the child – so much that the child "catches" their emotions. In all of these cases, it doesn't seem to be what the parents are *saying* to the child that is the major problem, but what emotions are spilling over to the child – repeatedly. It would be easy to blame one or both parents for this problem. But is it their problem alone? What about the culture they live in? And what about the family court Culture of Blame, which may influence parents and professionals?

The family court Culture of Blame is highly emotional in high-conflict cases – especially disputes over the children. In Jeremy and Jennifer's case,

Sadness is Contagious

All feelings can be contagious. I have had cases (even in mediation, when parents are mostly supportive of each other), with one parent who is over-whelmingly distressed by sadness about the divorce – even a year after the parents have separated. Sometimes the sad parent is the mother and some-times the father. They aren't openly angry. They're tearful – constantly tear-ful. When I see this, I can generally predict that sooner or later one parent will say that the children or oldest child no longer wants to spend time with the other parent. These are parents who want the children to visit, but feel helpless to make it happen.

One woman described her parents' divorce several decades earlier. She said that her father was devastated and depressed. When she would spend week-ends with him, she absorbed his sadness and felt really distressed. Then, when she went back to her mother's house, where she primarily resided, she remembers being very angry with her mother about how her dad felt. "I told her it was all her fault!" She doesn't remember much about those days, but decades after their divorce she still remembers how her father was sad and depressed.

Professionals' Emotions are Contagious

In the examples above, one or both parents are expressing fear, anger and/or sadness around the child – so much that the child "catches" their emo-tions. In all of these cases, it doesn't seem to be what the parents are *saying* to the child that is the major problem, but what emotions are spilling over to the child – repeatedly. It would be easy to blame one or both parents for this problem. But is it their problem alone? What about the culture they live in? And what about the family court Culture of Blame, which may influence parents and professionals?

The family court Culture of Blame is highly emotional in high-conflict cases – especially disputes over the children. In Jeremy and Jennifer's case, here is what the judge said after several hearings over Jeremy's request for a change of custody and request to have Nathan play soccer in his neighborhood:

The judge was visibly angry. "ALL I SEE IN FRONT OF ME ARE TWO PIG-HEADED PARENTS WHO DON'T CARE ABOUT THEIR SONS!" he said sternly to Jeremy and Jennifer, and their attorneys. "There's no good reason for me to change custody to you, Dad. Mom's doing fine as the custodial parent. You already have lots of time – with 30% of the time. And you, Mom: I see no good reason that you won't just agree to letting the boys play soccer in their father's neighborhood. I won't change any of my court orders without a compelling reason. But I don't see why you just don't agree to it yourself."

Jennifer knew why she wouldn't give in on that: she was trying to protect the boys from their father's obsessions and to let them have some independent activities.

After this hearing, Jeremy angrily confronted Jennifer in the court hallway and said: "See, the judge says it's both of us. You're not so great. He's says you're a problem too! Why don't you just agree to let me have the boys play soccer in my neighborhood."

I can think of a million reasons, Jennifer thought to herself. But she tried to avoid him and walked away, frustrated. They both were angry now. They had caught the judge's contagious anger. Jeremy was angry at Jennifer, and Jennifer was angry at the judge, for making a comment that opened her up to more of Jeremy's obsessive thinking and demands. He brought the judge's comments up to her on a regular basis for weeks after that.

Positive Emotions Are Contagious Too!

Hopefully, it is obvious that I believe that contagious emotions are far more powerful in children's lives than anything that a parent or professional could say. These emotions are passed back and forth between parents and children, and professionals and parents throughout high-conflict family court cases. It is amazing that more children don't catch these emotions – or maybe they do.

But there's also good news. Positive emotions are also contagious! A smile. A laugh. A friendly hug. This is the stuff that helps give children resilience. The big issue is finding ways to give children more positive emotions about the other parent than negative emotions.

Marriage researchers, John and Julie Gottman, say that even in healthy marriages people say negative things and show negative emotions. But they are far outweighed by positive statements and positive emotions – perhaps 5 to 1. So when a parent, or a professional, or anyone says something intensely negative about a child's parent, it is very important to balance it with many more positive statements and emotions.

Parent-Child Interaction Therapy is a program for parents who have been physically abusive with their children. Their research shows that abusive parents generally don't say more negative comments to their children. The difference is that they don't say positive comments and express positive emotions. The program (PCIT) teaches parents how to say positive comments on a regular basis, which helps the children improve their behavior a lot.

Here's what some adult children said mattered to them in looking back on their parents' divorce, in follow-up research by Constance Ahrons (2004):

> Get rid of your hostility, or mask it if you can't. Don't cut your spouse down. Don't attack the other parent's treatment of the children. Also don't talk poorly about your exspouse no matter if it kills you. Your children lose a lot of respect for you if you do that.

....

Put yourself in your kids' shoes. For your children's sake, bite your tongue, don't say anything bad about the other parent. Keep the problems away from the children.

...As a child, I really looked up to both my parents, and when one of them would say something bad about the other, it would put me in the position of agreeing and thinking something bad about the other parent, or disagreeing and putting me in conflict with the parent. That's hard for parents to do, but I think it's really important. (pp. 229-230)

It's all a question of the bricks we are using, since they are all contagious. Are we mostly using the bad "wall" bricks of unmanaged, negative emotions? Or are we balancing out the occasional bad brick with many more positive, managed emotions? It's up to all of us in the children's environment. They may absorb it all!

Short Summary

Parents: Remember that emotions are contagious. Make your best efforts not to expose your child to your intense anger, fear, hurt, sadness and other negative emotions about the other parent – even about an HCP parent. When you do (because no one's perfect), make positive comments about the other parent to keep things balanced. Avoid believing that feelings are decisions. If your child is anxious, remind him or her that feelings are not harmful and reduce with time. This is part of resilience.

Family and Friends: Be careful not to absorb the contagious emotions of those involved in a potentially high-conflict divorce. Check yourself to see if you are getting "hooked" by negative emotions. Acknowledge that these are upsetting times and that emotions can reduce and heal. Be reassuring, while gently focusing back on problem-solving when your family member or friend is ready. Let the children know that you understand these are stressful times, but feelings aren't decisions and reduce with time.

Professionals: Teach your clients that emotions are contagious – your client's and your own. Watch out for getting emotionally "hooked" by your client's pain, fear, and anger. Also, watch out for passing your frustration on to your clients, who may pass them on to the children. Educate other professionals and the courts about emotional contagion, so that they understand that everyone's expressed emotions may be even more important than what they say.

All-or-Nothing Thinking

On her 15th birthday, Hailey Harris ended her relationship with her father. She wrote him a letter telling him that she no longer wanted to have contact with him, as she felt uncomfortable with him. He could send her a birthday card once a year and she might send him one back. But that was all.

Her mother said that she should have a relationship with her father and should see him according to their schedule of alternate weekends with the father. However, her mother also told her that she was not going to force Hailey to spend time with her father if she refused to go.

Of course, her father was upset about this. After he received the letter and spoke with the mother, he decided to return to family court to seek an order requiring the mother to send their daughter for the normal alternate weekend parenting time. If the mother didn't do this, he was going to ask for a change of custody of Hailey to him.

The parents had separated and divorced five years earlier. It was a high-conflict divorce, with a major dispute over the parenting of Hailey. The mother thought that the father should have very little parenting time, because he had not been very involved with Hailey before the divorce and because she thought he was a creepy person. On the other hand, the father insisted on having 50/50 parenting time. He indicated he would settle for nothing less and that the mother was a bad influence on Hailey.

They went back and forth in family court for two years. There was a psychological evaluation and each parent was criticized for letting their disputes spill over onto the child. They settled on a common parenting plan of alternate weekends and Wednesday overnights with Dad and the rest of the time with Mom. However, over the years, Hailey stopped going to Dad's on Wednesdays, but she kept going on the weekends – until her 15th birthday.

It's no surprise that Hailey took an "all-or-nothing" position in dealing with her parents. We see that all the time in child alienation cases. It was her solution to feeling "uncomfortable." There were no allegations of any inappropriate behavior by the father. But there was a history of tension between the parents – low-level tension. The mother in this case was a highly-anxious woman and the father had taken a generally passive approach.

All-or-nothing solutions to relationships were common in this family. For years, the mother had ended relationships with friends and relatives when things got too tense. She said that she just couldn't handle the frustration and tension. Years ago, she had stopped talking with her own mother. The father had generally accepted this characteristic of his wife, until it applied to him. Then he fought her for two years in family court, but eventually gave up. She was no longer talking to him. But she supported her daughter's relationship with him, primarily because she had been ordered to by the court several years earlier.

Now, Hailey's decision to end her relationship with her father was really her own decision. Neither parent disputed that – neither the mother nor the father. Hailey was doing well in school and was a very rational, logical person – beyond her years in understanding people and communicating with them.

Cognitive Distortions

People with personality disorders – including many HCPs – have a lot of cognitive distortions in their close relationships. This has nothing to do with intelligence. Their brains unconsciously distort or "spin" information to view things very negatively.

I was trained as a therapist in treating cognitive distortions in the 1980's for people with depression and anxiety. One of the handbooks I used was The Feeling Good Handbook in which the author, David Burns, listed ten forms of "distorted thinking," a few of which I have summarized here:

- **All-or-Nothing Thinking**
   Seeing things in absolutes, when little is absolute in reality

- **Overgeneralization**
   Drawing huge conclusions from minor or rare events

- **Discounting the positive**
   Rejecting positive experiences as minor or unimportant, compared to negative experiences

- **Jumping to Conclusions**
   Interpreting things negatively without basis; predicting things will go badly without the ability to know the future

- **Personalization and Blame**
   Blaming oneself entirely for events beyond your control; or blaming others entirely for problems that are really shared

The treatment for these cognitive distortions was slow and step by step, but highly successful with people who were depressed or anxious. The techniques I learned to teach my clients were so successful that I used them on myself when I was going to law school. When classes or exams looked hopeless or overwhelming, I would do cognitive therapy writing exercises and feel a lot better. I ended up doing better than I expected.

These same principles have been used in treating people with personality disorders. In short, cognitive distortions involve a negative, self-sabotaging view of the world, a view that is not accurate. These distortions may be acquired as a person grows up, based on life experience and on the interpretation of life experience. We all have cognitive distortions some of the time. They just pop up automatically. But most people check to see if they are accurate, based on current information.

In many ways, cognitive distortions are fast, defensive thoughts that may help us act quickly in a crisis to protect ourselves. Our brains are hard-wired for quick reactions to life-or-death crises. But in modern life, most situations are not life or death. We have to get good at knowing the difference between a crisis and a routine harmless event. We have to check the situation in more depth before we respond. High-conflict people are constantly over-reacting, because it feels like a crisis and they don't check it out to see if it really is – they just assume it is.

For persons with personality disorders, the negative comments and experiences of their lives can be so strongly imbedded in their thinking that little new information can get in. Rather than challenging their distortions, they seek confirmation of their distortions. While this might be momentarily reassuring, it keeps the person off-track and over the long run triggers more distress.

Cognitive distortions are contagious. All-or-nothing thinking is particularly contagious. It especially doesn't work in close relationships. Yet if one or both parents use a lot of all-or-nothing solutions to personal problems, children will learn to do this as well.

All-or-Nothing Court Solutions

Family court is structured around all-or-nothing solutions, just as all other courts:

- The defendant is guilty or not guilty

- The plaintiff is all innocent, because the case is about the defendant

- The lawyers cannot be criticized for their behavior in court, because they are zealously advocating for their clients

- The judge cannot be blamed, because he or she is the judge

So, only one person can be at fault in court – the defendant. In family courts, while technically there are no defendants, in reality it is one parent or the other. In order to avoid being the "all-bad parent," parents fight hard to identify the other parent as all-bad – really, really bad. This is what happened in Hailey's case.

The judge entirely blamed the mother. When they got to court, the judge said that he was not going to allow such an end to the father-daughter relationship. He ordered the father, at the father's request, to have father- daughter counseling sessions with a highly experienced local psychologist.

Three weeks later, the father, mother and their attorneys returned to court. The father said he was withdrawing his request to oppose Hailey's decision, because she was so adamant in the counseling that this was what she wanted. He had decided to just accept it. The judge accepted the father's decision, but he was furious with the mother and told her it was all her fault. Then he gave up and the case ended – along with the end of the father-daughter relationship.

As described in Chapter One, this is a common case of "splitting" – where the judge viewed the mother as the "all-bad" parent and the father was the "all-good" parent. With such all-or-nothing thinking, little could be done to solve the situation. Hailey absorbed her parents' splitting and the judge absorbed this splitting as well.

In fact, family law professionals regularly become engaged in such splitting, out of exasperation. They become "emotionally hooked." But it doesn't have to be this way, if they become educated about this. This problem has been well-known for years for mental health professionals working with personality disorders.

Professional Splitting

When this type of all-or-nothing thinking is combined with intense emotions, it can be highly contagious. In fact, "staff splitting" is a common problem when someone with a personality disorder is in a drug treatment program or psychiatric hospital. Some staff members see the patient as helpless and needing lots of support and understanding, while other staff members see the patient as much more capable and needing to shape up and work harder at getting well.

These staff members get emotionally upset with each other and become "split" over the best treatment plans. They have absorbed the all-or-nothing thinking of the patient, with some taking the soft and supportive extreme (the "all-good" staff in the patient's eyes) and others taking the harsh and demanding extreme (the "all-bad" staff in the patient's eyes).

Unless staff members know about "staff splitting," they can easily get stuck hating each other over which approach is correct, as this unresolved conflict gets worse and worse. The resolution is to realize that the patient is "splitting" and that the patient needs to recognize and deal with *both* sides of the split: to get staff support and expectations for growth. Teaching the patient how to integrate both sides of the split is the solution, not just picking one extreme or the other for the patient.

Unfortunately, in the court context, the solution is usually to pick one extreme or the other. When there is someone with a high-conflict personality involved in the case, legal professionals (judges, lawyers, counselors) often become intensely emotional – and very angry with each other. I have given seminars to legal professionals on "professional splitting" in legal disputes, to help them understand this dynamic. It is virtually identical to the problem of staff splitting. As I tell legal professionals, the dynamics are:

- It's personal

- It's hostile

- It's about attacking personal competence, ethics, intelligence, etc.

- Positions are polar opposites, all-or-nothing

- One or more professionals may be splitting

- One or more professionals may have a high-conflict personality (but more often it's reasonable professionals getting emotionally hooked and not realizing it)

An easy example of professional splitting among legal professionals was in the criminal murder trial of O.J. Simpson for killing his wife Nicole Brown Simpson. The prosecution and defense lawyers grew to despise each other and frequently threatened to bring ethical complaints against the other lawyers. Each side saw the other as being "all-bad." Spectators to the case often picked sides, favoring the prosecution or the defense – and seeing the other side as all-wrong.

In family courts, families are often treated as having one "all-good" parent who is generally treated as a helpless victim who needs gentle support and understanding, and one "all-bad" parent who is seen as a perpetrator of abuse or alienation and needs to be harshly criticized. The real resolution is to recognize that each parent has strengths and weaknesses and to have both parents work on their own problems and skills, whatever they are, rather than to make it a competition between the parents.

If trained professionals in psychiatric hospitals and drug treatment programs, and trained professionals in our legal system can get "split," it's not at all surprising that children become "split" when they live with a parent with a high-conflict personality.

Not only do children learn that all-or-nothing solutions are normal and appropriate for their parents, but that the culture at large supports this type of thinking. After all, the judge has made all-or-nothing decisions. And Mom's or Dad's lawyer argues that the other parent is a piece of dirt. Since adolescence is when you primarily learn your adult social skills, this thinking could last a lifetime.

Family Court Focuses on One Parent

Ironically, family courts often slip into this all-or-nothing thinking from the start of a case. The very definition of the case is often made at the first hearing. Suddenly, it is about whether Dad is all-bad or not; or whether Mom is all-bad or not. Just one parent's bad behavior is usually the focus — and the attack-defend cycle begins.

Father as Target of Blame: When a mother has "primary custody" or simply the majority of parenting time, and the father wants to increase his access time somewhat at court, he will be the focus of attention. Why does he want more time? Is he really qualified to have more time? What has his parenting history been? What's wrong with him that he doesn't respect the mother's successful role as primary parent. Many fathers are totally frustrated by this, and much of the time their requests are denied.

As Abraham Lincoln used to say: "If you look for the bad in people expecting to find it, you surely will."

Mother as Target of Blame: When the father wants to have primary custody or the majority of parenting time, then the focus is on the mother to prove that she is not "unfit." What has she done that she should not have the majority of parenting time? Is she a drug addict? A pill addict? Depressed? Borderline? There must be something wrong with her for the father to think that he could have the majority of parenting time. Once again, Lincoln's saying applies: "If you look for the bad in people expecting to find it, you surely will." Many mothers are totally frustrated by this, and much of the time the father's requests are approved and "custody" is awarded to him.

I may be wrong in this observation from my 30 years' experience with divorcing families – in fact, I hope I'm wrong. If I'm correct, the unfortunate moral of this story is that if a father wants to increase his parenting time, he may have a better chance by requesting primary custody than by requesting to just increase his parenting time a moderate amount. And if Mom wants to have the majority of parenting time, she better have something bad to say about Dad. All-or-nothing thinking, all-or-nothing arguments and all-or-nothing requests seem to be the theme in the adversarial court culture – unless everyone works hard to overcome it.

All-or-Nothing Stereotypes

This all-or-nothing thinking has been studied in young children. In the 1990's, there was a lot of concern about children reporting horrible sexual abuse by their daycare center workers. In fact, based on their reports, several day care center workers were initially given long-term jail sentences. Then, research on how children are interviewed showed a surprising problem: if you interview children and suggest that the person is a "bad man," the children will actually make up facts that fit a "bad man."

For example, researchers had a man named "Sam Stone" come into a few preschool classrooms for 2 minutes. He only said "Hello" and "Goodbye" and didn't do anything except look around and walk around, and then leave without touching anything. One group of children was told nothing before the visit and afterward they accurately described what they saw.

But another group of children was told in advance that Sam Stone was clumsy and often breaks things. When they were asked about the visit afterwards, the interviewer suggested he had ripped a book and soiled a teddy bear. Many of the children agreed and some even embellished on the story by describing how they *saw* him throw the teddy bear in the air, soak it in water and use a crayon on it.

The researchers concluded that children can make something out of nothing, if they are given a negative stereotype and "suggestive" questioning about someone. Rather than just confusing details of events, they concluded that children can totally fabricate events and come to believe them, even though they never occurred.

We know this happens with children who are in high-conflict divorces: Mom or Dad questions the child about the other's behavior. That was true in the case of Jeremy and Jennifer in the previous chapter. Jeremy could not stop questioning Nathan about his Mom and her new husband. Nathan quickly came to dislike her new husband for being "abusive" toward him, even though there was never an incident of abuse that he could describe. But his father repeatedly suggested that he was abused.

Parent Prejudice?

All-or-nothing thinking about racial groups has existed for centuries and may have some relevance here. Brain research recently has also shown that racial prejudice occurs on two different levels. One is "explicit," in which a person knowingly dislikes someone because of their racial group. But the other is "implicit," which is unconscious, so the person doesn't even know that they are having racist feelings. The researchers explain that we may be surprised by our own prejudicial feelings and spontaneous outbursts, because we don't even know that we have them.

This dynamic is very common with alienated children, who describe intense dislike for one parent without even knowing why and they have spontaneous outbursts of anger based on these feelings. This reminds me of Samantha in Chapter Four, giving her father the finger in front of her classmate as he drove by. She believed that he had ruined her life, but she couldn't say why.

Brain researchers indicate that implicit prejudice comes from many unconscious "cultural factors" like jokes, catchphrases, overheard taunts, and so forth, from peers, parents and the media. It is not hard to imagine an angry parent making off-hand comments and making gestures about the other parent in the presence of the child, without consciously being aware of it. It's not hard to imagine the child absorbing all of this without being consciously aware of it as well.

Very recent research indicates that implicit racism is learned by children by the time they are 6 years old and that it remains in place as a filter through which the children view others the rest of their lives. In other words, children learn racism from those around them — emotional responses, off-hand comments by anyone in the child's environment, negative facial expressions — before they are old enough to have any logical understanding of racial history and cultures. Yet as they grow up, this affects their choices of friends, hiring decisions, medical decisions and many other discriminatory behaviors — without even realizing it and truly believing one is not prejudiced. Social psychologist Siri Carpenter (2008) explains this unconscious process.

> Whatever the neural underpinnings of implicit bias, cultural factors — such as shopworn ethnic jokes, careless catchphrases and playground taunts dispensed by peers, parents or the media — often reinforce such prejudice. Subtle sociocultural signals may carry particularly insidious power. [In a study of 72 white families in Italy] they found that young children's racial preferences were unaffected by their parents' explicit ra-

cial attitudes (perhaps because those attitudes were muted). Children whose mothers had more negative implicit attitudes toward blacks, however, tended to choose a white over a black playmate and ascribed more negative traits to a fictional black child than to a white child. Children whose mothers showed less implicit racial bias on an implicit bias test were less likely to exhibit such racial preferences. (p. 35)

No Disparaging Remarks

In alienation cases, the problem is very similar. Most family courts have a standard court order that says something like this: "Neither parent shall make disparaging remarks about the other parent while in the presence of the child, nor shall a parent allow others to do so." This is a good court order to address *explicit* alienating behavior.

I think the problem isn't *explicit alienation* – the problem seems to be *implicit alienation*. They can't see it and we need to understand that, rather than lecturing them on their bad behavior, as though they know why they act badly and chose all of their behavior carefully.

Implicit attitudes, beliefs and non-verbal behaviors about the other parent are much harder to recognize. In most cases, parents and professionals are not even aware of their own implicit biases and how they pass them on to the children. This seems to fit the old song about prejudice from the musical *South Pacific*, about World War II:

> You've got to be taught to hate and fear,
> You've got to be taught from year to year,
> It's got to be drummed in your dear little ear –
> You've got to be carefully taught.
>
> You've got to be taught to be afraid

Of people whose eyes are oddly made,
And people whose skin is a different shade –
You've got to be carefully taught.

You've got to be taught before it's too late,
Before you are six or seven or eight,
To hate all the people your relatives hate –
You've got to be carefully taught!
You've got to be carefully taught!

Few people are consciously aware of being taught this. Before you are six or seven or eight, your learning appears to be mostly non-verbal, emotional messages absorbed by your right brain from your family and culture – relatives, friends and the media. The brain research is helping us understand how subtle this can be.

How could a court make an order against *implicit disparaging emotions*? Perhaps parents and professionals should be required to learn about how emotions are contagious and this unconscious *implicit bias*. Then, parents could be required to state how they are going to protect the children from their upset emotions during the divorce process, and professionals could be required to state how they are going to protect their clients from their upset emotions. I explain more about this in Chapter Twelve.

Tribal Warfare

In her book, *In the Name of the Child*, Janet Johnston and colleagues write that high-conflict divorce cases are often characterized by "tribal warfare." Family, friends and professionals all gang up on one parent, who then gets a "tribe" of family, friends and professionals to gang up on the other parent. This term seems highly appropriate, when you think of how high-conflict cases escalate and involve more and more people and their family cultures.

Sadly, Dr. Johnston recognized this problem over 20 years ago, when her book was first published, yet tribal warfare continues today more than ever.

For a child to avoid getting caught in this "split" would seem almost impossible – especially if one parent and his or her tribe had negative attitudes toward the other parent for years, even before the separation or divorce.

As I suggested in Chapter 5, being "carefully taught" starts at birth when you live with a high-conflict parent. All-or-nothing stereotypes, splitting, implicit prejudice, and tribal warfare rarely start with a separation or divorce for an HCP parent. The groundwork has been laid for years. The child learns that people are all-good or all-bad, and that all-bad people are to be rejected – even if the child used to love them.

A reasonable parent may have learned to walk on eggshells around this behavior, which may have inadvertently implied to the child that the reasonable parent supported the HCP parent's way of thinking and way of handling emotions and behavior. Then, when the HCP turned on the reasonable parent, it was too late. The child already had been trained to reject someone the HCP rejects – and the child expects the reasonable parent to tolerate that, as he or she has always tolerated this all-or-nothing behavior.

Our society's all-or-nothing media Culture of Blame also doesn't help. Any child who watches television these days is constantly reminded, through fictional characters and real people in the news, that voting people off the island or killing off bad guys is reasonable and ordinary behavior. It's not surprising that a child would come to believe that eliminating a parent is a reasonable and ordinary event in our culture's daily life.

All-or-nothing bricks add up quickly in building the Wall of Alienation. It is one of the most striking aspects. There seems to be no gray area for an alienated child. Their brains respond to the most emotionally intense messages. For HCP parents, the power behind their all-or-nothing messages may be one of survival – drawing from insecure attachment issues rather than true danger from the environment.

For family court professionals, all-or-nothing thinking comes in the pressure to "win" the case. For our society's Culture of Blame, this shows up in endless dramas of good versus evil. It's not surprising that kids become alienated.

On the other hand, there may be specific concerns of abuse which still must be investigated. With alienation and abuse, we must be careful to keep an open mind and not succumb to all-or-nothing thinking in either direction. Of course, don't expect to be perfect at this or anything else. You know what that would be!

Short Summary

Parents: It is normal to have all-or-nothing thinking some of the time. Just make sure to "check yourself" for its accuracy in dealing with your child, dealing with others involved in your divorce, and in dealing with the courts. Children absorb all-or-nothing thinking just like they absorb emotions – without being aware of it. Teach your child about all-or-nothing thinking, and to "check yourself" to see if it's appropriate to the situation. Be careful to avoid negative stereotypes and correct your child when he or she uses them. Understand that prejudices are both explicit (we're aware of these) and implicit (these prejudices are hidden).

Family and Friends: Be aware of all-or-nothing thinking and "check yourself" regularly to see if you have any all-or-nothing thinking in regard to your family member's or friend's divorce. Remind those involved to avoid all-or-nothing thinking – in either direction: that the HCP parent's behavior is totally bad or totally okay. Also, share this information about negative stereotypes and about explicit and implicit prejudice.

Professionals: Be aware of your own all-or-nothing thinking, as you think about both parents, the children, family members and friends involved in the case. Watch out for professional splitting – intense all-or-nothing thinking in regard to other professionals involved in the case. Educate the courts and other professionals about avoiding all-or-nothing thinking, professional splitting, negative stereotyping, explicit and implicit prejudice.

Mirroring Bad Behavior

Jeremy liked to tell jokes about women – very disparaging jokes about women. Nathan, age 11, learned that this was cool. After a weekend with his Dad, Nathan told his mother one of these jokes. She was shocked and angry. Nathan was surprised. He thought that everyone made jokes like that. He became angry at her, and called her a name she had never heard before from her son. She told him to go to his room, which he did, as he mumbled the name again.

Albert painfully recalled being beaten by his father – and his mother. He was in a batterer's treatment program now for beating his former Wife, and he had supervised contact with his children. He had punished them using his belt and a wooden spoon. They said he had also withheld food as a punishment. He was in family counseling now to try to improve his parenting. As he recalled his own history of being abused, he also remembered how guilty he felt when he left home at 15 years old, because he left his younger siblings behind. Overwhelming guilt and overwhelming anger were automatic, daily experiences for him. He admitted that his children were afraid of him.

Children learn what they live. This has been known for centuries. But very recently scientists have begun to explain how this may work, with the discovery of "mirror neurons." Mirror neurons occur in many parts of our brains. They are some of the 100 billion neurons we have in our brains – little microscopic "wires" that form connections which help us think, feel and act.

Mirror neurons replay in our brains what we observe others do, as if we were doing the exact same action. For example, while you are watching someone playing baseball, you are also at the exact same time playing baseball in your brain in the exact same way. Since these mirror neurons are often right next to action neurons ("motor neurons") in your brain, they appear to be helping you get ready to do what you see other people doing. If you had never played baseball before and the baseball suddenly came in your direction, you might automatically catch it and throw it back the same way – because your neurons had already been practicing and getting ready to do the exact same actions.

Apparently, this is how children learn much of what they do. This is good news and bad news. As the examples of Nathan and Albert above show us, bad behavior is easily learned and repeated by children. It is much worse than we thought. When a parent is violent against another parent, their child isn't just seeing what's happening. Their child is also mirroring in his or her brain the exact actions of the violent parent and the victim parent, as if their child was committing the abuse and being abused. Someday, this child may play out the role of being the abuser or being abused or both – automatically without realizing why.

Restraining Ourselves

But are children helpless observers, doomed to do all of the bad behaviors they have seen? No. This is what child "raising" is all about – raising children above their automatic impulses, in order to become rational and successful adults. Parents, professionals and our culture have a huge influence over which behaviors are acceptable and which are not. If children learn that a behavior they have just seen is bad in the eyes of those closest to them, they are much less likely to do it themselves. But if the people they are closest to are doing the bad behavior, they are much more likely to do it themselves.

Children learn social rules from their many environments – their family culture, community leaders and the media. In most modern families, violence, sexist jokes and running away are discouraged or strongly forbidden. But in some families, these are tolerated or even encouraged.

Ironically, television drama, movies and the news repeatedly show bad behavior and in many cases treat it as acceptable, funny or even desirable. They do this to get your attention, so that you will watch their programs and buy the products they advertise.

Unfortunately, while adults may think the extreme behaviors they see on the screen are funny or good drama, children are seeing them as role-modeling. After all, children's brains are not fully developed until they are about 25 years old. What's entertainment for adults will become part of children's repertoire of socially-acceptable behavior – since television, movies and the news are given such high status in our modern society. And this is all happening unconsciously.

Violent Impulses

A tragic example of this mirroring was recently reported in the news. An Indiana boy, Andrew, age 17, allegedly killed his brother Connor, age 10. Andrew was said to have had the desire to kill someone since he was in 8th grade. He apparently said he identified with the main character in the popular television show "Dexter." Part of this TV drama is showing Dexter in his youth, when he starts killing. This character is a serial killer who also works for the police department as a blood spatter specialist on crime investigations. The show can be quite graphic about the steps to take when you're killing someone.

As part of child raising, children are supposed to be taught by their culture how to restrain such impulses – otherwise we would have a society filled with chaos and murder. Children have to be carefully taught how to restrain themselves. Bad thoughts and impulses are fine – we all have them – but actions require restraint. We don't do most of what we see, because our culture tells us it's not okay. Or is that changing?

A sign of cultural change may be children's behavior immediately after watching a violent television program. Since the 1970's, studies have shown that boys will commit an aggressive act within minutes after watching a violent TV show. Curiously, the studies 30 years ago showed that girls did not have such a response at all. Apparently, cultural restraints kept them from acting on possible violent impulses that they may have mirrored in their minds. However, current studies show that there is no difference anymore between the TV responses of girls and boys. Today, girls equally engage in aggressive behavior within minutes after watching violent TV shows as boys.

What's changed? Cultural values. The images of violence have always been there. Now we see these images of violence so much more often and they include images of girls perpetrating the violence. These images are often accompanied by an air of acceptability and attention. For example, after the Virginia Tech shooter killed 30 people on his campus, TV news programs played his video tape justifying his actions. How are children to understand that this was not a reward for this behavior, when getting yourself on TV is the goal for so many young people in today's society? Children learn what they live.

Why Don't High-Conflict Parents Restrain Themselves?

High-conflict parents can't seem to stop themselves. They are repeatedly told to behave, by counselors, lawyers and judges. Yet they keep behaving badly, and often behave worse. Why is this?

HCP parents are naturally defensive. They feel at war with the world. They take things personally, they over-react emotionally, and they often blame someone else for all of their problems – what I call their Target of Blame. In other words, "the issue's not the issue." You pick an issue, and they'll take things personally, over-react emotionally, and blame their Target of Blame. You help them solve a problem, then there will be a new issue – which they'll take personally, over-react emotionally, and blame their Target of Blame. The problem is their personality-based difficulty in resolving conflicts and solving problems.

High-conflict parents are not self-aware. They do not see the effect of their own behavior on others, including their children. It is as if they are blind. You can't get them to see, even if you yell, say it softly, or give a long explanation. They just won't get it, because they don't have the ability to get it - yet.

Bridge Between Right and Left Brains

One explanation of why HCPs are not self-aware is based on brain research about the bridge between the right and left hemispheres of the brain – known as the corpus callosum. This bridge of about 300 million neurons helps the different types of thinking of each hemisphere work smoothly together. As I mentioned in Chapter Three, the right hemisphere processes mostly nonverbal emotional information (especially negative emotions) very quickly, while the left hemisphere mostly processes language, a slower detailed analysis of things, and logical problem-solving.

Allan Schore, of the University of California at Los Angeles (UCLA), talks about "right brain to right brain" communication between parents and children. He explains how the eye contact and positive emotional responses of parents and children (right brain activity for both) help strengthen the child's corpus callosum as the child learns to connect upset emotions (right brain) with problem-solving (left brain).

He explains how a secure attachment is built on this right-brain-to-right-brain process and how a secure attachment is necessary to build the child's own connections between right-brain and left brain functioning – with lots of repetition. Through this process, the child slowly develops connections for self-awareness and self-control (the right brain has more brain cell connections with the body) and planning (the left brain has more cells for planning how to deal with the outside world).

This strengthening seems to be based on the saying by neuroscientists that "neurons that fire together, wire together." This means that when two things happen at once (such as a child's upset emotion combined with a parent's calm response and problem-solving behavior), neurons in the brain react ("firing" chemicals) and actually grow little branches (dendrites) to form connections between the parts of the brain dealing with both issues. So after many learning experiences, when the child is upset he or she will think of the problem-solving behavior that goes with it – and eventually solve the problem himself or herself without needing the parent's help.

For example, suppose a child named Caitlin might get upset and pick up a block and hit her brother. Caitlin's mom or dad steps in and says "We don't hit in this family. Let's use the blocks to build a house." Caitlin learns to build things instead of hitting – after lots of repetitions. Connections between being upset and building with blocks are being made, and (over time) Caitlin's upsets get briefer and briefer as she learns that it's more fun to build than to hit.

But what about a parent who hits the child back with the block and doesn't teach problem-solving? Martin Teicher at Harvard University and others have been studying the effects of child abuse on brain development. They have discovered that all types of abuse (physical, sexual, emotional, verbal and neglect) can cause hormones to saturate the brain in a way that actually damages the corpus callosum and makes it smaller after enough repeated abuse.

How does this happen? Apparently, when a person is stressed, cortisol – also known as the stress hormone – is released. At first, this can be a good thing. Cortisol sharpens the brain's problem-solving abilities and memory, while also triggering an increase in energy for the muscles to prepare for intense fight or flight. This is supposed to help us quickly deal with the problem. However, if our brains and bodies are awash with cortisol for longer than about thirty minutes (constant, repeated stress), then it interferes with our brain cells replenishing themselves and with enough continued exposure to cortisol they can actually shrink or even die.

So if Caitlin's mom or dad, above, hits her with the block or yells repeatedly or engages in other abusive behavior a lot, Caitlin won't grow useful connections between upsets and problem-solving. But even worse, if she repeatedly is stressed enough, it may trigger too much cortisol for too long on her brain, and may shrink or even kill some of her brain cells. The long-term effects of this can lead to an adult personality disorder, with an inability to manage her own emotions and an inability to solve problems consistently.

Based on the results of research by Teicher and several other scientists, they found that the corpus callosum for abused boys actually had a significantly smaller middle part, especially if they had been neglected. The corpus callosum for abused girls also had a significantly smaller middle part, especially if they had been sexually abused. They found that the stress of any type of abuse, including repeated verbal and emotional abuse, could have a harmful impact. This could lead to long-term inability to manage emotions and relationships.

Teicher (2002) explains the effect of this damage to the bridge between hemispheres:

> Reduced integration between the right and left hemispheres and a smaller corpus callosum may predispose these patients to shift abruptly from left- to right-dominated states with very different emotional perceptions and memories. Such polarized hemispheric dominance could cause a person to see friends, family and co-workers in an overly positive way in one state and in a resoundingly negative way in another – which is the hallmark of the disorder. (p. 72)

The result of this research is that there may actually be a physical barrier to self-awareness, self-control, and problem-solving for many high-conflict parents. This doesn't mean that all were abused growing up, but they may not have developed these skills sufficiently. The good news is that counseling and training that emphasize learning skills appear to help some people overcome these problems.

For example, Marsha Linehan, is a clinical and research psychologist at the University of Washington who has developed a method of treating those with Borderline Personality Disorder called Dialectical Behavior Therapy. As part of this therapy, clients repeatedly practice new skills for managing their upsets and solving problems. Results show that many are able to outgrow their diagnosis of Borderline Personality Disorder after a few years with this overall approach (DBT usually includes an individual therapist and a skills-building group). Perhaps they are strengthening their corpus callosum neurons and dendrites to overcome earlier damage or lack of skills training in childhood.

Cycle of High-Conflict Thinking

Keeping the above in mind, we need to reconsider how we respond to high-conflict parents. We need to shift our thinking from shame and blame

– which just reinforces the problem and doesn't build stronger connections – to teaching skills. We need to understand that the logic of their behavior is fear-based rather than evil – but still needing restraint. They are stuck in a Cycle of High-Conflict Thinking.

The following diagram shows how this cycle appears to happen for high-conflict parents:

Cycle of High-Conflict Thinking

1. M.A.D.

Mistaken
Assessment of
Danger

2. B.A.D.

Behavior
that's
Aggressively
Defensive

3. N.F.

Negative

Feedback

This cycle shows that they are constantly having a Mistaken Assessment of Danger. Because of this M.A.D., they think (or just react) that they must take extremely aggressive action to protect themselves – and their children. As high-conflict people, they believe that the source of all of this danger is their Target of Blame (usually the other parent, but potentially lawyers, counselors, or others). Therefore, their Behavior that's Aggressively Defensive is directed at their Target of Blame, to somehow cause the Target to change their behavior or disappear as the solution to the problem.

However, because the problem isn't really their Target of Blame, but rather their Mistaken Assessment of Danger, nothing changes after their aggressive attack. Instead, they get Negative Feedback (from the other parent, lawyers, counselors and/or the judge). This, in turn, they take personally, over-react to, and blame on their Target of Blame. This increases (or at least doesn't reduce) their Mistaken Assessment of Danger, and the cycle continues and continues.

Thus, it's important to realize that their extreme behavior is a defense against something, rather than just being stupid, crazy or evil. It's actually seen as a solution in their distorted thinking. Remember, this has nothing to do with intelligence. So if you respond with extreme behavior of your own – in an effort to stop their extreme behavior – you will usually make things worse.

Aim for Moderate Behaviors

For this reason, it is very important to respond to their high-conflict behavior with moderate behaviors instead, as I will explain in the second half of this book. In other words, you must be careful NOT to mirror their extreme behavior. Instead, be aware of this temptation and use all of your own skills to think rationally and respond moderately.

This does not mean that their extreme behavior should be tolerated. Quite the opposite. Their extreme behavior needs to be restrained or stopped, since they can't stop themselves. However, personal attacks won't stop it – that will escalate it (or at least not reduce it). And ignoring it won't stop it.

Only a moderate, assertive response generally works – a response that doesn't personally attack them and redirects them toward positive future behavior, which may include some appropriate and immediate consequences. The focus is on new behavior, rather than Negative Feedback.

Remember, if bad behavior can get mirrored, good behavior can also. Once you're aware of that, you can influence people to calm down and respond more positively by responding positively yourself.

How Mirroring Helps Self-Control

The last point about brain development and behavior is that children need the modeling of emotional containment by a parent in order to wire their own brains for future moderate behavior. They learn to connect their own upset emotions and impulses for extreme behavior to the parent's behavior that they are mirroring. This helps strengthen the connections between left and right hemispheres. I'll try to explain this.

When children are born, they have lots of extreme impulses, but they are not organized. They yell, they fidget, they kick. The way they learn behavior is mostly by mirroring those around them. If their extreme behavior is responded to with moderate behavior, then they mirror the moderate behavior. They start to learn that when they are extremely upset, the appropriate response is a moderate behavior. Since moderate behaviors get you more of what you want in the modern world, the child learns to use moderate behaviors.

For example, if Dad is coming over to pick up the child for his parenting time and Mom is anxious about it, then the child will become anxious too. A 3 or 4-year-old child may start screaming, because feelings are contagious and she is absorbing Mom's anxiety.

But if Mom calms herself and says: "It's going to be okay. You're going to have a fun time with Dad. I'm just a little nervous, because this is all so new. But my feelings are my feelings and I can manage them. Even if I'm nervous, I can get your things together and be ready when he arrives. Isn't that neat, how we can pull ourselves together, even while we're a little bit nervous. There, I feel better already. I think you're all set now."

That's a moderate response to upset feelings. Children learn a tremendous amount by mirroring their parent's methods of managing upset emotions with moderate behaviors. This is often called "containment" of emotions.

Children exposed to abusive parenting are not only physically hurt, but they also don't learn this important ability to contain normal upset emotions and to restrain extreme behaviors. However, even if only one of their parents is able to do this, the child is much more likely to learn this skill and grow up healthy. If both parents react to each other with extreme behaviors, then the child is much less likely to learn this.

Avoid Extreme Responses to Alienation

An example of overreacting with extreme behaviors comes up often in alienation cases. Many of my clients who were the rejected parent in alienation cases have said the following at some point: "I might as well give up. Maybe I should just stop trying to see my child. Or maybe I should move across country." These are extreme behaviors in response to extreme behaviors by the other parent or child. I talk them out of that approach by explaining that it teaches the child the wrong message – it's a tempting solution, but it's an "all-or-nothing" solution.

While I can certainly understand the feelings underneath those ideas, I instead encourage the parent to act confidently and moderately for the child's benefit. The message to convey is that it is not reasonable for a child to reject a parent and that this parent will make appropriate efforts to maintain contact – for the child's benefit, painful as it is for the parent to keep feeling rejected.

In short, children learn more from what we do than what we say. They will mirror the behavior of everyone around them in their brains. But teaching them skills for managing their own behavior will help them build resilience for the rest of their lives. The way they see their parents resolve their separation and divorce will lay the groundwork for how they manage conflicts in their own marriages, jobs and communities.

Children need to learn that they can respond moderately to the most absurd behaviors of others. It's not today's decisions that matter most to children. It's the skills they learn for a lifetime about the behaviors that their parents used in making these decisions.

Be the Reasonable Alternative

As I have said, I wrote this book primarily for reasonable parents and professionals. When we are dealing with a high-conflict parent, we need to be role models of flexible thinking, managed emotions, and moderate behaviors – for them to mirror. This will help the children develop skills for coping with a high-conflict parent. Even if just one parent is demonstrating these positive skills, the children will mirror them and absorb them.

But no one's perfect, so don't be surprised that you will occasionally get hooked and mirror the HCP parent's behavior. Demonstrate for your child how you can catch yourself and change your responses back to reasonable ones as soon as possible.

Remember, it's not about who's an all-good parent and who's an all-bad parent. It's about a thousand little behaviors and interactions. Whether you're a parent or a professional, don't let an HCP parent hook you into helping build that Wall of Alienation.

Build a Foundation of Resilience instead. You can start building this at any time, regardless of what you or anyone else has done up to now. How to build this Foundation of Resilience is the focus of the second half of this book. Some of the ideas may surprise you. They are often the opposite of what you feel like doing.

Short Summary

Parents: Recent research shows that we have mirror neurons in our brains that prepare us to do the exact same actions that are performed by those around us. This means that we have to be much more careful about exposing children to our extreme behavior, because they may do the exact same actions someday. It also helps to tell children that extreme behaviors are not socially tolerated, so that if they see a bad behavior they will also learn that they should not do it. Try to limit your child from seeing bad behavior as much as you can, as it's the sights and sounds that get mirrored. This could include the people around you, as well as TV and the internet.

Family and Friends: Be a positive role model. Be careful to avoid behaving in a manner that you would not want your divorcing family member or friend, or their children, to behave. Explain mirror neurons to those who might benefit from this information. Encourage positive activities, especially with people who would be good role models for the children, as well as for your friend or family member.

Professionals: Be professional and civil with everyone involved in the case. Act as if everything you do will be mirrored by your clients, and then by their children. Teach your clients strategies for providing positive behavior in response to negative behavior by the high-conflict parent. Educate the court about how children learn from everything they see and hear, but don't use this as a reason to try to eliminate the other parent. Encourage the use of moderate coping methods for dealing with HCPs in the divorce process.

PART 2:

Building a Foundation of Resilience
(What to Do)

Children are born kicking and screaming, with all-or-nothing thinking, unmanaged emotions and extreme behaviors. Then, parents and cultures "raise" their children to refine these powerful abilities into skills of flexible thinking, managed emotions and moderate behaviors which work in their culture. These skills give children, their families and communities the resilience to manage almost any unpredictable event in the future, because these skills help people work closely together despite stress, loss and change.

Today, more than ever before, children face rapidly changing times in a rapidly shrinking world. Conflict and change will be inevitable, over longer and longer lifespans. The children who will be most successful in the future will be the children who grow up with the most solid Foundation of Resilience, built with the strongest bricks of flexible thinking, managed emotions and moderate behaviors.

Teaching Resilience

Lauren and Ethan started out with a high-conflict separation. This included calling the police a couple times because of conflicts during parenting exchanges. However, after two years, the parents reached an out-of-court divorce agreement which included approximately equal parenting time.

Ethan was highly distressed by the finalization of the divorce. He never wanted the divorce and he had a hard time managing his emotions about it, even two years after the parents had separated. He was alternately tearful and angry, as the date to sign the final agreement was coming up.

Just before the agreement was to be signed, their 4-year-old son, Wyatt, started having extreme emotional responses to leaving his father during their parenting exchanges. Wyatt would cry and cling to his father, and resist going to his mother.

Ethan became very distressed by Wyatt's clinging and fearful behavior. He insisted that something must be wrong at Lauren's house and insisted on reducing Lauren's parenting time, as this is what appeared to him to be upsetting

Wyatt. It seemed to be a logical plan to him. Reduce Lauren's time and Wyatt's upsets would reduce.

So Ethan presented this idea to Wyatt's therapist, who also became very concerned that there was a problem at Lauren's house.

But Lauren was resilient. She had a divorce coach who gave her suggested responses to Wyatt, to Ethan, and to the therapist. Lauren learned to say things to Wyatt such as:

"I know this is an upsetting time. But you're just 4 years old and shouldn't have to worry about how I feel or how your father feels. It's okay for you to just be a kid and think about what you want to do today. You're going to spend a lot of time with each of us, and it's our job to handle our own upset emotions." Wyatt usually calmed down right away at her house, after absorbing how calm Lauren was about the whole thing.

Lauren also spoke to Ethan, saying: "Remember our feelings aren't decisions. Just because we're upset right now doesn't mean that anything needs to change with Wyatt's schedule. He does just fine at my house, after he calms down from the exchange. It usually takes him just a few minutes. He tells me he's upset, then we play. I suggest that we have someone with us during our parenting exchanges who can make it feel more neutral, and see if Wyatt does better."

Lauren also suggested this "exchange supervisor" idea to Wyatt's therapist, who thought it was a great idea.

After 3 parenting exchanges with the exchange supervisor, Wyatt was having no problems with the exchanges. The divorce agreement had been signed, and Ethan seemed to calm down too, as it became clear that their marriage was over.

One day, Wyatt said he didn't feel like going to his father's house for his scheduled parenting time. Lauren said: "I understand, but you'll have a good time with your father. Remember, feelings aren't decisions." And Wyatt would go and usually have a good time.

But occasionally, Wyatt would be upset at his father's and Ethan would call Lauren and say: "Wyatt's upset. He wants to go back to you right now. Can you pick him up? Or should I bring him back?"

Lauren said: "Remember, feelings aren't decisions. We shouldn't teach Wyatt that just because he's upset, everything changes. I already have other plans for today. Let me talk to him." And she explained the same thing to Wyatt.

Lauren told her coach: "Sometimes it feels like I'm raising two children. But it seems to be working out."

Resilience is not automatic. It's mostly learned from life experience, although children have some of it built in at birth. Reasonable parents generally raise resilient children. But this resilience can be extremely impacted by the conflicts and emotions of a divorce. What may be a difficult time in a parent's life may become part of the child's personality, since high-conflict thinking, emotions and behavior are so contagious.

The most important part of teaching resilience is for a parent to provide a secure attachment for the child—a secure base for the child's problems while growing up, especially when the child is under stress. This means providing a two-step response to the child's upsets. You can think of these two steps as "Love and Skills."

1. **Love** – This means reassuring your child when he or she is upset, by mirroring and showing caring for his or her feelings.

AND

2. **Skills** – This means encouraging your child to explore the world, and
learn new ways to manage and solve problems.

These are the two most basic ingredients for a secure attachment. Many parents just do one of these two steps over and over again. Some are constantly showing love to their child, soothing their child, and showing concern for

the child, but not teaching their child skills to become more and more independent. Others are focused on pushing the child to learn skills and be independent, without showing much nurturing and soothing when the child
is upset. Parents tend to do what they learned to do as kids.

Too much of just one of these steps and a child will feel insecure and won't
gain the *confidence in others* that he can connect with them, or the *confidence in himself* that he can explore and solve his own problems. The goal
is to respond with both steps in most upset situations.

Teaching by Responding

Children learn resilience mostly from how their parents *respond* to their
children's problems and upsetting emotions. It's a different kind of teaching. You can't really plan to teach resilience and then instruct your child
with today's lesson. It's how you routinely *respond* when your child presents
you with her or her *own* problems and upsets. The bigger the problem or
upset, the more important the balanced response. The key is to practice responding with *flexible thinking*, *managed emotions*, and *moderate behaviors*.
This doesn't mean being perfect, but regularly practicing these skills as each
new mood or problem arises.

In a secure attachment, the parent mirrors the child's emotions to build the
child's self-awareness and sense of growing up to be a separate person. This
includes mirroring upset emotions. But then the parent shifts to a managed
emotional response, which the child then mirrors and thereby learns to
manage his or her own emotions. The parent shows love by *connecting* with
the child's upsets and mirroring them. When ready, the parent *redirects* the
child to problem-solving skills. With a secure attachment, the child will let
you know when he or she needs love (reassurance), then when he or she
is ready to automatically be interested in exploring again (learning skills).

Mirroring and Cooling Hot Emotions

It's like a hot brick: The child has a hot brick and can't handle it, so he tosses it to his parent. The parent then holds on to it for a moment and cools it down (because the parent has hot pad holders and has learned how to hold it). Then the parent returns it to the child, who can now manage it and wants to build something with it (learn skills).

If the parent just throws it back as is, without cooling it down, then it burns the child and upsets the child even more – and the child doesn't learn any skills for dealing with hot bricks. If the parent holds onto it but doesn't cool it down, then it burns the parent and the child feels bad or frightened that he caused his parent some pain – and didn't learn any skills for dealing with hot bricks. And the parent may eventually learn to avoid the child and his hot bricks, because he or she can't handle them.

Here's how psychologist David Wallin (2007) describes it:

> From the moment they are born, babies are subject to feelings of distress that they are utterly unequipped to manage on their own. To experience the "felt security" that has been described as the set goal of attachment, babies depend on the attachment figure [parent] to help them modulate [manage] their overwhelming affects [emotions]. (p. 48)
>
> ....
>
> Such emotionally attuned mirroring is absolutely critical, for it is through "resonating with, reflecting on, and expressing the internal state which the infant displays" that the parents allow the child to gradually discover her own emotions as mental states that can be recognized and shared – a discovery that

lays the foundation for affect regulation [managed emotions] and impulse control [moderate behaviors]. (p. 49)

A Secure Response

An example of a secure response could be the following. Suppose that a child, Josh, spent the weekend at his dad's house. Now he's just returned to his mom's house.

"Josh, you look upset," she says. "Did something upsetting happen this weekend?"

"Oh, Dad made me do my homework instead of letting me watch Alien Creeps yesterday. Now all my friends have seen it, and I feel left out," says Josh.

"That sounds frustrating," Mom said, scrunching up her face with a brief frustrated expression. "I know what it's like to feel left out sometimes. [She's mirroring his feelings and reassuring Josh.] Next time, maybe you can ask your dad to help you get your homework done at the beginning of the weekend. [She's suggesting skills for solving this problem, namely planning ahead.] What do you think of that idea?"

"Oh, Dad just sucks!"

"Well, I know you're upset right now, because you didn't get to go with your friends. [Mirroring, reassuring] But let's not talk about your dad that way. He means well and wants you to succeed, just as I do." [Teaching skills of "understanding it's not personal" and not speaking "that way."]

"Can we stop talking about this?" Josh sighs.

"Sure."

In this example, Mom showed love by mirroring Josh's feelings by scrunching up her face with a brief frustrated expression and saying: "I know what it's like to feel left out sometimes." This was reassuring to Josh, although he didn't let on that it was.

Next, Mom shifted to skills by encouraging Josh to deal with the world — his father in this case. Love and skills.

A Preoccupied Response

Let's look at what happens when a parent has a preoccupied relationship with the child and doesn't provide this balance of Love and Skills:

"Josh, you look upset," she says. "Did something upsetting happen this weekend?"

"Oh, Dad made me do my homework instead of letting me watch Alien Creeps yesterday. Now all my friends have seen it, and I feel left out," says Josh.

Mom's response: "Oh, your father is such a creep! I hate when he does that. He has no respect for you and how important it is to feel part of the group. He should have asked if you had any homework and made sure you did it so you would have time to see the movie. If he can't think about your homework like a responsible parent, then maybe I should go back to court and reduce his parenting time." [Mom is trying to connect or show love by splitting the parents and being the "all-good" mom.]

"Yeah, Mom. I'd rather spend my weekends at your house. You totally understand me. You would have let me go with my friends."

"You're right! Your father will never understand you like I do." [Mom continues to try to connect by splitting some more and being the all-good mom.]

In this example, Mom held on to Josh's upset feelings and added to them. (Like putting a hot brick in the oven to make it hotter!) She was splitting, by criticizing Dad to Josh *with strong emotions and words* – like "creep" and "I hate when he does that" and saying he had "no respect for you" and saying he should have acted "like a responsible parent." Four bad bricks just like that. She was building a wall to help her feel loved and secure with her son.

Rather than redirecting Josh with some problem-solving skills, she engaged in more splitting by creating a competition with Dad as a parent: She said how he "should have" dealt with the situation, and "Your father will never understand you like I do."

She also shifted immediately to an extreme behavior: "Maybe I should go back to court and reduce his parenting time."

In one very brief interaction, Mom has demonstrated All-or-Nothing Thinking, Unmanaged Emotions and Extreme Behavior. Is this contagious? You bet it is. Look at Josh's response to Mom's response:

"Yeah, Mom. I'd rather spend all my weekends at your house. You totally understand me. You would have let me go with my friends."

Now, does Josh really mean this? Or is he just trying to calm down his mother? It depends on how preoccupied his mother is with him and how preoccupied his attachment is with his mother. If he has a preoccupied attachment, then he probably believes his statement that she totally understands him and wants to spend all his weekends at her house. While this might seem like a strong relationship, it will backfire because his attachment with her is insecure. It's out of balance – he will have a hard time dealing with the world when he has to, sooner or later.

She has tried to connect, but has not redirected Josh and given him skills for dealing with the world. She has not taught him flexible thinking, managed emotions or moderate behaviors. She has unknowingly sacrificed teaching skills for a temporary feeling of love and security from her child which can't last because splitting creates an artificial attachment, not a secure attachment. What often looks like a "strong" attachment, is really a preoccupied insecure attachment.

A Dismissive Response

Let's look at what happens when a parent has a dismissive response to the child, and the child has a dismissive attachment with the rejected parent.

"Josh, you look upset," she says. "Did something upsetting happen this weekend?"

"Oh, Dad made me do my homework instead of letting me watch Alien Creeps yesterday. Now all my friends have seen it, and I feel left out," says Josh.

"Well, you knew your Dad was an idiot before you went over there. Why did you even go? When are you going to get it? You know you're old enough to decide where you live, now that you're 14. [This isn't legally true, but many parents think it is.] You know I won't force you to go see the idiot. Unless you want to follow in his footsteps." [Mom is trying to connect and put Josh down at the same time – a typical dismissive response.]

"Don't worry, Mom. I know he's a fool. I know he's not worth wasting my time on. But I go sometimes, just to keep him off your back."

"Well, aren't you the hero? Thanks. Now let's go shopping."

In this example, you can feel the disrespect and disdain that Mom has for Dad, which she puts on Josh as well. Josh has also picked up this disdain for his Dad, and doesn't want it to land on him. Mom does not redirect Josh into problem-solving skills. She shows no encouragement for dealing with the world – it's probably full of "idiots" in her mind. Josh is quickly learning to relate this way too. Yet Josh also doesn't really get any reassurance from this Mom, does he? She's disrespectful to him also, by saying "Why did you even go? When are you going to get it?" "Unless you want to follow in his footsteps." "Well, aren't you the hero?"

Josh agrees with Mom and tries to impress her with his excuse for seeing his father as based on protecting her. He joins in the dismissing comments: "I know he's not worth wasting my time on." Mom throws the hot brick back at Josh, so he has to throw it at his father.

There's no cooling down of bricks in either of the Dismissive or Preoccupied examples. Josh's ongoing relationship with the dismissive Mom and the preoccupied Mom are both "insecure attachments." They lack the balance that reassures a child and teaches a child that he or she can go into the world with confidence that hot emotions can be cooled down and problems can be solved. Without this secure attachment, it is less likely that Josh will learn flexible thinking, managed emotions, and moderate behaviors.

Risk Factors

Attachment researchers emphasize that the parent's behavior can lead to the child learning to feel either secure or insecure. If there is an established pattern of insecurity, there is a risk that it can lead to personality problems later on.

Responding appropriately means containing the child's emotions in a balanced manner. Wallin (2007) explains the problems when this response is out of balance, with reference to correspondence he has had with attachment researcher Peter Fonagy.

> In effect, we become what the child needs us to be. This is the
> process at the core of the child's emerging individuality. And

if the caregiver is unable to do that—if the caregiver is either too much themselves [just holding on to the hot emotions] or too much the child [immediately throwing back the hot emotions]—the child cannot develop a sense of separateness in the same kind of effective way. (Fonagy, personal communication, 2006) (pp. 49-50).

....

Fonagy suggests that particular kinds of psychopathology may be associated with particular failures of attunement and mirroring. When the parent's affective mirroring is not [contained] it can lead the child to feel overwhelmed by the **contagious nature of his distress**—for his upset seems only to provoke an **identical emotion in the parent** [hot emotions burn the parent]. Repeated exposures to [uncontained] mirroring are thought to reinforce the psychic equivalence mode because the child's internal experience seems regularly to be matched by his external experience, and there may appear to be no way out. Fonagy theorizes that this may be part of the genesis of **borderline pathology**.

Secure attachment... is a balance of Love and Skills – reassurance and encouragement to explore

---

In contrast, mirroring that is [non-responsive to the child's emotions] can result in a sense of internal emptiness and variations on the false-self theme—because what the child is invited to internalize is an **image not of his own emotional self** but rather the **emotional self of the parent**. Because the links here are severed between the child's internal experience and its reflection in the responses of the external world, [non-responsive] mirroring is thought to reinforce the use of the pretend mode. Thus, according to Fonagy, the child who is regularly exposed to mirroring that is not [responsive] may be vulnerable to **narcissistic pathology** in which imagined grandiosity functions as [a coping method] for the empty self. (Fonagy et al., 2002)" (pp. 50-51) [Bold added]

Finding the Balance

So parents need to find this balance of mirroring the child's emotions as a respected separate person, while responding with confidence to the child with suggested skills and room to explore other relationships. The effect of this is a balance of Love and Skills - reassurance and encouragement to explore:

Love Your Child by Providing Reassurance:

- that your child has a name for what he or she is feeling – angry, afraid, etc.

- that it's different from what you are feeling right now

- that it's okay that your child has this different feeling

- and that it doesn't upset you (or not too much) that your child feels this way

Teach Your Child by Encouraging Learning Skills:

- that it's not okay to act in certain ways when you have the above feeling

- that you believe your child can manage this feeling/situation (managed emotions)

- and that he or she can go on to the next activity (a moderate behavior)

BUILDING RESILIENCE

HIGH CONFLICT PARENT	+	REASONABLE OTHER PARENT	+	REASONABLE FAMILY, FRIENDS AND PROFESSIONALS	=	RESILIENT CHILD
All-or-Nothing Thinking		**Flexible Thinking**		**Flexible Thinking**		**Flexible Thinking**
Seeing other parent as "all-bad" with no redeeming value		Seeing other parent as having a mix of good and bad qualities and behaviors		Seeing other parent as having a mix of good and bad qualities and behaviors		Seeing both parents as having a mix of good and bad qualities and behaviors
Seeing himself or herself as "all-good" with nothing to change or improve		Seeing himself or herself as having a mix of good and bad, and working to improve self		Reminding others that both parents have good and bad qualities		Not worrying about own relationship with each parent, or parents' relationship with each other; focusing on own age-appropriate issues
Demanding no contact with the children for the other parent		Supporting best relationship possible with the other parent		Supporting best relationship possible with the child and other parent, even if limited		Learning skills and gaining strengths from each parent; learning weaknesses to avoid of each
Demanding 50-50, with no flexibility		Proposing shared parenting, with flexibility		Proposing shared parenting, with flexibility		Learning not to take HCP's behavior personally
Having only one solution to each problem		Proposing several solutions to any problem		Proposing several solutions to any problem		Able to see several solutions to any problem
Unmanaged Emotions		**Managed Emotions**		**Managed Emotions**		**Managed Emotions**
Yelling at other parent or making threats during exchanges of the children		Containing his or her angry emotions around children at exchanges and at home		Containing his or her angry emotions around children, around parents and professionals		Learning to contain his or her angry emotions around parents, friends and professionals
Sudden outbursts of anger when discussing problems and solutions with other parent		Taking a break when discussions of problems get heated; avoiding bad times to talk		Taking a break when discussions of problems get heated; avoiding bad times to talk		Learning to take a break when emotions get too hot; learning when others' emotions are too hot
Intense blaming of the other parent, to children, friends, family and professionals		Regularly making positive statements about other parent to child, family, professionals		Regularly making positive statements about other parent to child, family, and professionals		Comfortable mentioning each parent's strengths and weaknesses to other parent
Intense or prolonged crying in front of the children about divorce and other parent		Containing his or her own sad emotions around children; getting counseling to help		Containing his or her own sad emotions around children; getting counseling to help, if needed		Learning to manage own sad emotions by talking to someone; use counseling, if needed
Trying to make children feel anxious or guilty while they are with other parent		Telling children about positive benefits of spending time with other parent		Telling children about positive benefits of spending time with both parents		Feel empathy for other people's joy and pain, including both parents, friends and strangers
Extreme Behaviors		**Moderate Behaviors**		**Moderate Behaviors**		**Moderate Behaviors**
Not exchanging the child as scheduled, including hiding child, disappearing with child		Sticking to the schedule, even when it's inconvenient, until schedule is changed		Supporting parenting schedule, even when it's inconvenient, until parents make new schedule		Comfortable spending time with each parent; learning how to set boundaries and assert self
Interfering with other parent's time, such as scheduling appointments or fun activities		Not scheduling competing events, activities		Not supporting competing events, activities		Learning methods for dealing with HCP parent;
Hiding money or withholding or threatening to withhold payments of financial obligations		Making agreed payments, even when it's inconvenient, until schedule is changed		Gathering information and discussing options, without working harder than the parents		Comfortable requesting changes to parenting schedule to fit activities and friends
Threatening to eliminate the other parent from children's lives through the court		Actively supporting other parent's relationship with the children, even if limited		Actively supporting both parents' relationship with the children, even if limited		Comfortable sharing school information, activities, big events with both parents
Domestic violence: hitting, shoving, threatening to hurt other parent and/or child		Taking breaks when upset		Taking breaks when upset		Considering behaviors of each parent and seeing benefits and consequences of each
		Practicing respectful communication at all times		Practicing respectful communication at all times		

DON'T ALIENATE THE KIDS! © 2010 Bill Eddy www.HighConflictInstitute.com

This type of balanced message can be communicated very quickly and mostly by your attitude and nonverbal behavior. It is a very secure message to your child (even if he doesn't act appreciative) and strengthens your relationship, while strengthening your child's sense of confidence in him- or herself. You took your child's hot brick, cooled it off, and gave it back for constructive use. This brick will help build your child's Foundation of Resilience.

But it's just one brick. There will be thousands more. And even though there will be a few hot bricks you don't handle so well, there can be so many cooled down bricks in his or her Foundation of Resilience that a few hot bricks won't matter much.

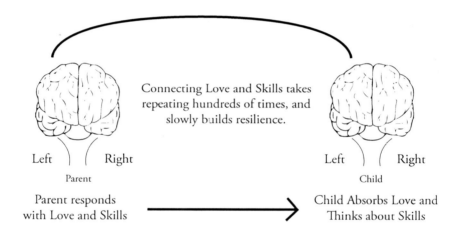

Connecting Love and Skills takes repeating hundreds of times, and slowly builds resilience.

Left) (Right

Parent

Left) (Right

Child

Parent responds
with Love and Skills

Child Absorbs Love and
Thinks about Skills

Lauren and Wyatt are a good example of this. She acknowledged his upsets and said she could understand them. This helped Wyatt understand and accept himself. Then she stretched beyond the upset to saying what they could do instead (playing; going to his dad's to have a good time) and saying that feelings aren't decisions. She held his hot bricks, then gave them back to him at a manageable temperature.

Reasonable Parents, Family, Friends and Professionals

It should be clear by now that the people in the child's environment make a huge difference in whether a child grows up with a Wall of Alienation or a Foundation of Resilience. The following chart shows in a nutshell how everyone involved can help build resilience, even if there is a high-conflict parent involved.

Professionals and Parents

To help parents teach resilience to their children, professionals need to take the same approach. Rather than showing the love that only a parent can show, professionals can "Connect and Redirect," by finding the balance between reassuring their clients AND encouraging them to stretch their skills and solutions. If they just agree with their client, the client will stay stuck. If they pressure their client to change without being supportive, the client will stay stuck and possibly become more upset.

For example, suppose a client says the following to a lawyer:

Father says: "My 13-year-old daughter tells me that my wife is really annoying and controlling. I would like to have sole physical custody of my daughter, and her mother should only have parenting time when my daughter wants to see her."

Lawyer says: "Has there been any events that she described to you that would cause her to want restricted contact with her mother?"

Father: "Nothing specific. Her mother's just constantly being bossy and keeping her from having any fun. She wants to live with me."

A Resilient Response

Lawyer: "Well, it sounds like you're concerned and I can understand you wanting to restrict contact with her mother, when your daughter says those things. [Connecting] I also want to inform you that the court's policy is that both parents have significant time with the children, and that the preferred parent for physical custody is the parent who most supports the other parent's contact with your child. [Redirecting to skills of supporting the other parent.]

"So there will be some risks to proposing that the mother has no contact except when your daughter wants to see her. You might be seen as trying to be too controlling of contact with the mother. An alternative might be building regular time into the schedule for them to spend together, so that it's not up to your daughter whether it happens. She needs both of you and the courts want neither parent to seem controlling of contact with the other parent, except in cases of abuse."

Father: "Well, that's a dumb policy. Won't you just do what I ask you to do?"

Lawyer: "Well, I understand your frustration. But that's what I find is most effective for clients – to take a balanced approach. And I want to help you. [Connecting] It's less likely to backfire on you. Why don't you think about it for a few days. We don't have to decide right now. But what you ask for often determines whether the case will escalate into a high-conflict case for months or years. I'm just trying to protect you from that." [Redirecting to skills of moderating "what you ask for."]

With this response, the lawyer is reassuring the client by saying that the lawyer can understand the father's frustration. Then, the lawyer encourages the father to consider the consequences if they make this request in dealing with the real world. The lawyer hasn't added heat to the situation, and hasn't split the parents into all-good and all-bad. By calming the parent and giving realistic information, the parent may be more realistic about telling the child what to expect.

An Alienating Response

Lawyer: "Sure, whatever you want. I will fight for you. We'll make a list of all the worst things that her mother has done. Maybe you can ask your daughter to tell you things that are critical of her mother, but don't tell anyone I suggested that you do that. I will do whatever it takes to represent your position." [Trying to connect by splitting and being the "all-good" professional.]

This lawyer is completely holding on to the client's position, without question or feedback. His client will like this in the short-run, but agreeing with a client's strong emotions and extreme position may backfire – as the client AND the lawyer may appear to be high-conflict people to the court. The lawyer may even get in trouble for appearing to have advised his client to pressure the parties' daughter to get more information against the mother.

If the father is a high-conflict person, the lawyer's feedback will likely be shared directly with the daughter – because HCPs have weak emotional boundaries and often share everything with their children as extensions of themselves, especially "bad" information about the "all-bad" parent. The daughter may believe that taking sides with one parent against the other is an appropriate and, perhaps, necessary behavior in a divorce, with the lawyer's stamp of approval.

Domestic Violence

Soon after Don and Bobbie Jo separated, Don came back to the house to pick up some of his papers and clothes. Bobbie Jo questioned him about a bank account and he grabbed for the paper and Bobbie Jo fell down and broke her glasses. Don was extremely apologetic and left immediately.

Bobbie Jo went to her counselor and asked what she should do.

A Resilient Response

Counselor #1: "You must have felt pretty shaken up. I'm glad you're okay. Let me give you some brief background about domestic violence. There are different kinds of domestic violence. One kind is when one person – often called the batterer – has a pattern of behavior that includes using violence to have power and control over the other person, and the other person – often called the victim – lives in fear of the batterer, but is afraid to leave. That's typically called "battering.""

"Another type is called Situational Couple Violence, where there isn't a history of abuse and the parties are fairly equal in decision-making and problem-solving. No one is regularly fearful of the other person, but sometimes they get into a fight that becomes pushing and shoving. They may equally contribute to the conflict and the physical fight.

"A third type is called Separation-Instigated Violence, where there's no history of violence, but there's one or two incidents at separation.

"So which type do you think you are dealing with?"

Bobbie Jo: "I think it's the third type. There's no history of this happening before, and Don seemed really surprised and ashamed when I fell down and broke my glasses. He was in a hurry to leave after that."

Counselor: "Without a history of this problem, you might want to think about whether a restraining order would be necessary to protect you and the children in the future, or whether you want to wait to see if he becomes threatening in the future. If you decide not to get the restraining order right now, then I'd suggest that you still write down exactly what happened, so that you can be ready to file for a restraining order if anything else causes you concern. If you decide to get a restraining order now, I can give you the names of some lawyers who can help you. What do you want to do?"

This counselor gave Bobbie Jo empathy for her experience. [Connecting] Then she gave her balanced information with an informed choice. This is the same balance that parents give to their children in secure attachment relationships. The counselor respected Bobbie Jo enough to give her information and options, rather than all-or-nothing answers. In the long run, this will help Bobbie Jo learn to deal with this problem and other problems —especially if Don has a high-conflict personality. [Redirecting to learning skills of flexible thinking and moderate behaviors.]

An Alienating Response

Counselor #2: "That's horrible. You've been abused. You should get a restraining order and ask for Don to have no contact with the children."

Bobbie Jo: "Oh, okay. If you really think that's what I should do, then I'll do it."

Or:

Counselor #3: "That's not domestic violence. That's called 'mutual combat' and you'd never get a restraining order based on that. I'd say just tell Don to stay away. There's nothing you can do."

Bobbie Jo: "Oh, I didn't realize that. Okay, if that's what you think."

In these alternate responses, each counselor took a splitting position – all-or-nothing. In both responses, the counselor did not help the client think it through and did not give much information. While the counselor was trying to reassure the client in both responses [connecting], in neither response did the counselor help the client explore options with good information. [No redirecting to learn and use skills.]

While these counselor alternatives may seem like unlikely "all-or-nothing" responses for a professional, they are not unusual in high-conflict cases and often contribute to increasing the conflict.

Conclusion

As described in Chapter 3, children start splitting when they are around 1 ½ years old, to help them become a separate person. Splitting is inborn, but resilience is mostly learned. Teaching resilience to children is mostly about how you respond to their upsets and problems. Resilience is built on a secure attachment with a parent, which is best promoted by responding with a balance of: 1) Love - reassuring the child by mirroring or identifying the child's emotion with facial expressions of empathy and words; and 2) Skills - encouraging the child to deal with the world by solving problems and calming his or her own emotions.

A good way to remember this is to picture a child with a hot brick, who tosses it to the parent, who cools it down and returns it to the child at a manageable temperature and helps the child use it to build something positive. This balance of reassurance and encouraging problem-solving is the secure base for building a Foundation of Resilience.

This balance is also important for professionals who work with families going through a separation or divorce. If one parent has a high-conflict personality, it is very likely that the way the professional treats the parent is the same way that the parent will treat the child. HCPs have weak emotional boundaries with their children, so that negative or positive statements and emotions by professionals directed at an HCP parent will be passed directly to the children, as if they were present.

The next chapters explain ways that everyone in the child's environment can provide the child with the "Foundation" bricks of *flexible thinking, managed emotions* and *moderate behaviors* while going through a separation or divorce with a high-conflict parent.

Short Summary

Parents: A child's Foundation of Resilience is mostly built upon a secure attachment with at least one reasonable adult. A secure attachment includes a balance of Love and Skills: providing caring and reassurance, AND allowing and encouraging the child to explore the world and learn skills for solving problems. When your child is upset or has a problem, it's like a hot brick you can cool down by using flexible thinking, managed emotions and moderate behaviors. Even if the other parent is an HCP, the child can still learn from you. Even if you mishandle some hot bricks, you can still build a strong Foundation of hundreds of cool bricks.

Family and Friends: You can be a positive role model of providing Love and Skills to your family member or friend. When he or she is upset, provide reassurance AND encourage learning skills to deal with the situation. If you have contact with the children, provide this balance of reassurance AND learning skills to them as well. Avoid the temptation to just agree with your family member or friend as a way of calming them. Avoid the temptation to push skills without providing some reassurance. Your efforts may make the difference between building a Wall of Alienation or a Foundation of Resilience for the children – using your cool bricks of flexible thinking, managed emotions and moderate behavior.

Professionals: You can contribute to building a Foundation of Resilience for the children by providing your clients with a balance of Connecting and Redirecting. Connect by providing empathy and encouragement. Redirect by pointing them toward skills they can learn to deal with their situation – whether it's taking a parenting class, anger management, or learning relaxation techniques. Resist the urge to totally agree with your clients' upsets about the other parent, and resist the urge to tell them to just "get over it." Your efforts to calmly provide flexible thinking, managed emotions and moderate behaviors may make the difference in whether the parents build a Wall of Alienation or Foundation of Resilience for their children.

Reasonable Parent's Dilemma

When Jacob and Sarah separated, their children were 3 and 5. Several months after they separated and were getting ready to go to court, Sarah said that Jacob touched their 3-year-old son inappropriately and she made a child sexual abuse report to Child Protective Services (CPS). Sarah and her attorney obtained temporary custody of the children with Sarah, and Jacob had supervised parenting time for a few hours per week while CPS investigated the case.

CPS found no credibility to the allegations and closed their case as "unfounded." After that, Jacob was given unsupervised parenting time for a day and a half each week.

Six months later, Sarah again made a report of child sexual abuse against Jacob. She told parents and teachers at their son's pre-school and at their daughter's kindergarten that Jacob was a child molester.

CPS investigated this new report and again determined it to be unfounded. Jacob and his attorney went to court seeking sole legal and physical custody of the children. At court, a full evaluation with a psychologist was ordered and the judge temporarily gave Jacob alternate weekends and one night per week – exchanging the children at their son's preschool and their daughter's school.

While the evaluation was going on with the psychologist, Sarah would show up at school to give things to the children just a few minutes before Jacob was going to pick them up. Then, when he arrived, they were upset and confused about which parent to go with.

When they were in his care, she would call to tell them good night and described how upset their stuffed toys were about missing them. Sometimes their son would cry himself to sleep at his father's house after these calls from their mother.

Sarah believed that the children would be better off without their father in their lives, to protect them from his sexual abuse. Jacob believed that the children should have very little contact with their mother, to protect them from her extreme thinking and interference with his role as a father.

What should Jacob do? What should Sarah do?

Reasonable parents are faced with a serious dilemma when separating from or divorcing a high-conflict parent. On one hand, it might seem best to totally exclude an HCP parent from the child's life, in order to protect the child from the extreme thinking and behavior of that parent. On the other hand, that approach itself will teach the child extreme solutions to relationship problems. What should you do?

Efforts to exclude the HCP parent usually escalate the HCP's extremely defensive and aggressive behavior. Once you get to court to fight for excluding the HCP parent, the HCP may turn on the charm and blame so strong that YOU may be seen as the HCP parent. This behavior that's aggressively defensive is what often drives high-conflict divorces and custody disputes.

But if you don't fight to put some limits on the HCP parent's behavior with the child, he or she may feel free to abuse the child or have a highly negative influence on the child's development and may actually alienate the child against you. You don't want this to happen either.

The Assertive Approach

The solution that I have arrived at (after 30 years) is what I call "The Assertive Approach." This is an alternative to being overly aggressive and trying to eliminate the other parent – and an alternative to being overly passive and adapting to whatever the HCP parent does. This approach is very hard to do as one person, while everyone else around you is being aggressive or passive. That's why I hope that many of the people in your situation use an assertive approach as well. But you can use it regardless of what others do.

An assertive approach seeks objective information, provides objective information to decision-makers, and seeks restrictions on "bad behaviors," rather than the elimination of "bad people." An assertive approach sees the good and bad in everyone, rather than seeing one person as all-good and the other as all-bad. While one person may be behaving much better than the other, we all have things we can learn. An assertive approach uses and teaches children to use:

Flexible Thinking

Managed Emotions

Moderate Behaviors

Therefore, I suggest that you assertively seek assistance in assessing your situation and seek restrictions on specific bad behaviors. Ask the court or professionals to put protections in place – while not trying to eliminate the HCP parent from the children's lives. This shows that you are not engaging in all-or-nothing thinking and extreme solutions, while also showing the need for restrictions and protections. In high-conflict cases, the reasonable parent is often blamed for being a high-conflict parent, while the true HCP is more persuasive and charming, and often prevails. The assertive approach will help you deal more effectively with this problem, so that your proposals and responses are not likely to be viewed as those of a high-conflict person.

Using an assertive approach, you can demonstrate that you want an independent, neutral person to assess the situation and provide feedback about both parents' behavior. Then, each parent can make needed improvements in their own bad behavior. This way, you can demonstrate that you are also willing to look at your own behavior and make improvements.

With this assertive approach, you do not trigger as much defensiveness from the other parent and from professionals. At the same time, you do not give the HCP parent free rein to act negatively in your children's lives. The goal becomes identifying bad behavior and sincerely seeking the learning of new skills.

Once safety issues have been sufficiently assessed and addressed, then the actual parenting arrangement (such as having "primary custody") is less important than getting bad behaviors to be improved and getting the conflict to be reduced. Then, whatever parenting arrangement there is (including supervised access or limited time, when necessary), the children are protected from the worst behaviors while still having a relationship with both parents and learning what works with each of them.

Finding the Assertive Balance

Accomplishing this balance takes practice and flexible thinking. I know you may not like this approach, but I have seen the other approaches (too aggressive or too passive) generally fail while driving high-conflict cases – with the children as the victims of the ongoing conflict.

For example, here are three scenarios from my experience that don't work:

1. If your behavior is just as aggressive as the HCP parent, then the court may treat both of you as equally difficult, and the HCP parent may feel free to cause chaos and negativity in the child's life.

2. If you aggressively pursue all-or-nothing solutions and persuade the court to determine that the HCP parent is an "all-bad parent," then that parent usually becomes highly defensive and fights even harder – often in court or with out-of-court maneuvers.

3. If you are passive and the court accepts false or misleading allegations about you and wrongly determines that YOU are an "all-bad parent," then the HCP parent often becomes over-confident and escalates their negativity.

So the best approach seems to be the assertive, balanced approach, such as occurred with Jacob and Sarah.

Jacob and Sarah

Jacob was referred to me to be his attorney, because I was experienced with child sexual abuse cases (both true cases and false allegations). He was furious at being falsely accused of being a child molester two times at court, and still in the eyes of the other parents at his children's schools. He wanted me to obtain primary physical custody for him, with very limited – possibly supervised – contact with the mother. After all, she was having a highly negative influence on them and appeared unlikely to stop being who she was – an HCP. She seemed to have no awareness of the inappropriateness of her behavior, from making false allegations to manipulating her children's emotions while they were with their father.

Jacob was preparing to meet with the psychologist for the evaluation. I encouraged Jacob to take the assertive approach and to seek a balance in dealing with Sarah – and to tell the psychologist that was what he wanted.

Rather than try to almost eliminate her from the children's lives, I encouraged him to use flexible thinking in developing a parenting plan that would protect the children the most from further conflict while giving him the opportunity to teach them good skills himself.

He told the psychologist that he was seeking a shared parenting schedule, with half of the time with each parent. This was much less than he really wanted, but he had come to believe that this might work, if she was not allowed to upset the children at school or on the phone during his parenting time.

The psychologist had already determined that the allegations of child sexual abuse against Jacob had no basis, and that Sarah was unlikely to change her point of view – about anything! The psychologist was impressed that Jacob was willing to share parenting with her, despite the history of allegations. In the end, the psychologist recommended equal parenting time, using a "parallel parenting plan." This meant that when the children were with one parent there would be no contact with the other parent. It also meant that the parents would only communicate with each other by email, and only one email a day at most, and only about parenting issues.

Parallel parenting puts up an imaginary wall between the parents, without interfering with each parent's time with the children. The percentage of time with each parent is a separate issue. Parallel parenting plans can be 50-50 with each parent, 90% with one parent and 10% with the other, or any other percentage combination. The idea is to keep the parents from interfering with each other's parenting time and from being in frequent conflict over the children, by keeping them from having direct contact. This can be a very helpful approach in domestic violence cases and/or child alienation cases.

Sarah didn't like this recommendation, but she accepted it. Both parents' lawyers and the psychologist met with the parents to work out the details of this plan by agreement, without going back to court. Neither parent was identified as the "all-good" parent or the "all-bad" parent. In fact, neither parent was even identified as the better parent. I'm sure in Sarah's mind that she sees Jacob as an "all-bad" parent.

Jacob strongly believes that Sarah is an HCP, but recognizes that she has strengths and weaknesses. He has learned how to work with her, using flexible thinking, managed emotions, and moderate behaviors. He has also taught his children how to use these skills when problems arise anywhere in their lives – at school, with friends, with him and with their mother.

This case has remained fairly stable for several years. There have been bumps in the road, but all of the professionals involved have remained calm and helped the parents remain calm and focused on solving problems. They have stayed out of court and avoided many of the pitfalls that other more aggressive or more passive parents have fallen into.

Finding the Balance

Now I know that there will be parents and professionals who don't like the outcome in this case. Some will say: "Maybe he did sexually abuse the child and just wasn't caught. He should never have been allowed to have half of the parenting time, especially in a parallel parenting plan. It just exposes the children to a greater risk that he will abuse them and not get caught in the future."

Others might say: "She should have had supervised parenting time. How could you discourage him from protecting his children against such a manipulative and disordered parent? You should have sought sole legal and physical custody for him."

In fact, I have had cases where I pursued and won a no-contact order against a father who had committed child sexual abuse. I have had cases where I pursued and won a change of custody from a mother who was making false allegations. **But these cases did not end there with a clear,**

one-sided victory. In fact, these "victories" were just another small step in these high-conflict cases.

When I have won no-contact orders, the child has violated the order and/ or the court has eventually ended the order. In the absence of a criminal conviction, family courts are unlikely to keep an abusive parent from having contact with the child, although it may be supervised and the parent may be required to get treatment.

When I have won changes of custody because of false allegations or child alienation, the child has violated the order (run away to the favored parent's house) and/or the favored parent has run away with the child. These have been hollow victories.

These experiences have led me to encourage parents and professionals to use an assertive approach and to avoid eliminating one parent from the children's lives. This is not an absolute, every case approach. But I would encourage you to keep an open mind and consider the benefits to children of using this approach in almost every case.

Most states have laws giving primary custody to the parent who will most support the child's relationship with the other parent. *Any* reason to interfere with shared parenting may be viewed negatively by the court. Therefore, concerns about abuse, domestic violence, and alienation should not be tied to winning a custody victory, but rather should show a desire for the parent to get help while continuing in the child's life.

An assertive approach shows:

> **Flexible thinking**, such as making two or more proposals to solve a problem, and a willingness to allow objective professionals to assess parenting concerns.

> **Managed emotions**, such as not sharing one's intense anger, except in private talks with friends or professionals.

Moderate behaviors, such as requesting a parallel parenting plan to limit conflicts, while including both parents in the children's lives – and respecting objective professional judgments about whether a parent needs restricted contact, such as supervised access.

With Family and Friends

Try to avoid seeking "allies" against the other parent, no matter how bad you think he or she is. Instead, tell your family members and friends that you are trying to keep the other parent calm by making flexible proposals and avoiding intensely emotional interactions.

Don't ask family and friends to avoid talking to the other parent, if they have had their own relationship. Just ask them not to carry messages between you. Instead, tell them how the other parent should communicate with you directly, such as by email, if the other parent brings it up.

Tell your family and friends that there might be high-conflict behavior by the HCP parent, such as spreading rumors about you, so that friends and family know to check with you before making any assumptions.

Ask them for help, but without taking sides or even taking sides on an issue. "You know I want us all to treat the other parent with empathy and respect. Don't get aggressive or angry with her or him for my benefit. It will just make things worse and he/she will get aggressive and defensive back and just make my life harder. It's better to just let us work things out on our own, unless I ask for help."

The above example helps keep the other parent from over-reacting to your relatives and friends. HCPs get more defensive, not less, when they feel ganged up on. So don't let your family and friends "protect" you by being overly aggressive with her or him.

With Counselors

One of the biggest mistakes worried parents make is to take the child or children to a counselor without the other parent knowing about it. They usually eventually find out.

Along with that, avoid trying to get any counselor to take your side against the other parent. Many counselors naturally avoid taking sides, but some slip into it – they get "hooked." While it may feel good for a while to the parent whose "side" they get on, these counselors often lose respect and credibility in the eyes of their colleagues and the court when they do this.

Avoid telling your children what to say to the counselor. The issue of children being "coached" comes up a lot in family courts. Most of the time they haven't been purposely coached to say anything, but even your innocent conversations about the counseling could be interpreted as coaching.

For example, remember the case in Chapter 2 of the mother who "prepared" her daughter for seeing her father at a visitation center? She told her 4-year-old daughter: "Now remember, if you ever feel frightened of your father during the visit, make sure to tell the visitation lady [the professional visitation supervisor]." That set up the daughter to feel nervous around her father for no reason, and the mother was caught later in her deposition, as she tried to explain why their daughter was nervous on the second supervised visit but not the first (when she gave no instructions and didn't even tell the child where she was going).

Another example: "Make sure to tell the counselor the truth!" When a parent says that, the child no longer feels allowed to be talking about how he or she feels. Instead, he or she tries to figure out your view of "the truth." The child may feel like a soldier walking into battle hoping that they shoot straight. What a burden. Children given this instruction by a parent usually feel like they have to guess what that parent's version of the truth is, and then to parrot that to the counselor – so the counselor will tell the parent that he or she "told the truth." This is also often discovered.

For example, I've seen counselor's reports that say: "And the child walked in stiffly, quickly saying complaints about the other parent that sounded just like what I had read in the father's declaration. Then the child relaxed, as if he had completed an assignment given to him just before the session." This parent will be accused of coaching the child, even though the parent may not have intended to have that effect at all.

Also, avoid grilling them about what they said in the counseling session. "So, did you tell the counselor your concerns about your father?" It's better to just leave well enough alone. If the child wants to talk about the counseling session, you can be open and supportive, but otherwise, don't ask. And don't be directive about what should have been said or not said.

How you act about getting and using a counselor can be very alienating to your child. And, depending on the experience and ethics of the counselor you get, their own behavior may further the alienation. Counselors can have a powerful influence over children and vulnerable parents. Make sure you work with one who is very experienced at not getting emotionally "hooked" in high-conflict family court cases.

With Lawyers

The biggest mistake that parents make with lawyers is trying to find the "most aggressive" lawyer in town. While this may seem reassuring, it often backfires. I have opposed several of these most aggressive lawyers in town, and they look exciting and aggressive at the first hearing, but they often charge a lot and disappear from the case when the going gets rough.

In cases where I have gotten sanctions (a fine) against the other side, the aggressive lawyer who escalated the case with outrageous allegations and emotional arguments was long gone. By the time the parent was sanctioned, they had exhausted their funds on the high-conflict lawyer and represented themselves. Yet the damage that was done by the aggressive lawyer ended up falling on the parent. In California, it's usually just the client who gets sanctioned, even for misconduct that was contributed to by the lawyer.

For example, I had a case in which the mother made false allegations of child sexual abuse against my client and the daughter's cousin. The lawyer argued vehemently against my client and made several statements, not all of them true. In one statement, he argued that my client had agreed in a deposition that he had allowed a young cousin to molest his daughter while in his care.

This statement felt untrue to me, but I couldn't knowingly respond without re-reading the transcript of the deposition. After I read the deposition, it was clear that it was not true. My client never agreed that the young cousin had molested his daughter, and in fact insisted that nothing inappropriate had ever occurred. My client was eventually cleared of any wrongdoing, as was the cousin, and we were able to prove that the mother knowingly made false allegations.

At the hearing on our request for sanctions against the mother, I submitted a transcript of the deposition with the transcript of the attorney's statements at court. The judge sanctioned the mother $10,000 for making knowingly false allegations of child sexual abuse against my client. I believe that the attorney's false statements were part of that decision. Unfortunately for the mother, that attorney had removed himself from the case months earlier when she could no longer pay for his expensive services.

Sure he was aggressive – with her too! Don't let this happen to you.

You can bet that this filtered down to her daughter. Was the daughter alienated against the mother? No, because the father didn't share his frustrations with her. Had the daughter ever become alienated against this father, while she was in her mother's temporary custody while the allegations were investigated? No. She always had a good relationship with him and the amount of time with the mother was not enough to influence her negatively. Of course, another year or two might have made a difference.

However, the stress of the battle of her parents was very hard on her, especially after she was pressured to lie by her mother, which made her afraid to relax. But she had a reasonable father who was able to avoid "splitting" the parents. He spoke supportively of her mother – even while he was investigated for child sexual abuse – and was very careful not to share his upset moments with his daughter. He had had five years as the custodial parent before the mother's allegations. After the mother had eight months of temporary custody of the children, the children were returned to him and he was able to resume a strong relationship with them.

On the other hand, the mother ended up with supervised parenting time for an hour a week at first – a much worse result than if she had not hired her aggressive attorney, who escalated the case with no legal justification. You don't want an attorney who will simply agree with you and your fears. You want an attorney who will speak honestly with you, who will say "no" sometimes, and who has an good reputation in the legal community.

With the Court (the Judge)

Many people represent themselves in court these days. Whether you are "self-representing" or have a lawyer, it is very important to appear *flexible*, *managed*, and *moderate* in all of your court hearings.

As much as possible, appear *flexible* about your requests. When possible, suggest two options, in the event that the court does not grant one of your requests. In legal terms it's often presented as a request "in the alternative."

For example: "Your honor, I would like to request an equal sharing parenting plan. In the alternative, I would request that I have alternate weekends and every Wednesday overnight and Thursday evening for two hours." This shows that you are not an HCP, as HCPs often take a very rigid position and fight for it emotionally and blindly. If the judge disagrees with their position, then the person becomes argumentative, which usually makes things worse. Don't let this happen to you.

Avoid requests that suggest you want to eliminate the other parent from the children's lives. Instead, focus on the *behavior* that you are concerned about and seek court orders which will help the other parent improve their behavior as much as possible. When you appear to want to eliminate the other parent, you make yourself look like an HCP parent with *all-or-nothing thinking*. Then it looks like it's about you, rather than about the other parent's behavior. Don't let this happen to you.

Be careful to appear as managed as possible in court. Avoid emotional arguments or complaints about the other person. It makes it look as though you cannot contain yourself, even in a formal decision-making process such as a courtroom. The judge can just imagine what you are like at home with the children, if you can't contain yourself at court.

I have even had cases in which one of the parents ran out of the courtroom before the hearing was over, because they could not contain their emotions. If you prepare yourself to cope with being upset, then you are less likely to get as upset – especially since court is unpredictable. (For more detailed suggestions for dealing with a high-conflict parent in and out of court, see my book *Splitting: Protecting Yourself While Divorcing a Borderline or Narcissist.*)

It's better to practice being matter-of-fact in your presentation to the court. A reasonable person is much more persuasive, because they seem reasonable about important matters, so it will appear that they must be reasonable at home with the children. Practice what you are going to say at court with a friend or your attorney. Ask them to gently challenge you during your presentation, as judges will often interrupt with questions before you are done. Don't take it personally, that's just how they are.

However, if you have facts about the other parent's concerning behavior, make sure to present them to the court. Don't be too passive either. But present them in a matter-of-fact way, rather than with *unmanaged emotions*. Avoid labeling the HCP parent as an "HCP parent" or "personality-disordered parent." Leave that up to the professionals to decide. Just assertively provide a description of the behavior that concerns you.

Be *moderate* in all your behaviors, including parenting exchanges, telephone calls, emails, and so forth. It is amazing how many emails end up in court documents, to show how extreme the other person is. I've been at conferences where judges or lawyers have publically read examples of horrible emails. Since they are not confidential, they are subject to exposure in open court. I once had a client have his parenting time reduced, because his extreme language in his email correspondence made it appear that he was less responsible and not a good role-model for his children.

Remember, everything you do while you are going through a divorce can be potentially held against you in court. A shove or yelling incident can turn into the basis for a restraining order and limiting your parenting time with your child or children.

Children do much better when parents are able to talk and make agreements, without going to court.

And, of course, the best moderate behavior is to stay out of court all together and try to settle your case. Courts focus on past behavior and on negative behavior. On the other hand, mediation, collaborative divorce and negotiation are all better alternatives. They all focus on the future and building on the positive. Most of all, children generally do much better when their parents are able to talk and make agreements, without having to go to court. When parents can act resilient, their children usually do as well.

Communicating and Responding with an HCP Parent

Communications with an HCP parent can be very difficult. Email is strongly recommended for this situation, as it gives both parents time to think first and respond with *managed emotions* and *moderate behavior*. If you get a hostile email or other communication, you can use the following method, which I call the "B.I.F.F. Response":

A B.I.F.F. Response to Hostile Email

BRIEF

Keep your response brief. This will reduce the chances of a prolonged and angry back and forth. The more you write, the more material the other person has to criticize. Keeping it brief signals that you don't wish to get into a dialogue. Just make your response and end your letter. Don't take their statements personally and don't respond with a personal attack. Avoid focusing on comments about the person's character, such as saying he or she is rude, insensitive, or stupid. It just escalates the conflict and keeps it going. You don't have to defend yourself to someone you disagree with. If your friends still like you, you don't have to prove anything to those who don't.

INFORMATIVE

The main reason to respond to hostile mail is to correct inaccurate statements which might be seen by others. "Just the facts" is a good idea. Focus on the accurate statements you want to make, not on the inaccurate statements the other person made. For example: "Just to clear things up, I was out of town on February 12th, so I would not have been the person who was making loud noises that day."

Avoid negative comments. Avoid sarcasm. Avoid threats. Avoid personal remarks about the other's intelligence, ethics or moral behavior. If the other person has a "high-conflict personality," you will have no success in reducing the conflict with personal attacks. While most people can ignore personal attacks or might think harder about what you are saying, high-conflict people feel they have no choice but to respond in anger – and keep the conflict going. Personal attacks rarely lead to insight or positive change.

FRIENDLY

While you may be tempted to write in anger, you are more likely to achieve your goals by writing in a friendly manner. Consciously thinking about a friendly response will increase your chances of getting a friendly – or neutral – response in return. If your goal is to end the conflict, then being friendly has the greatest likelihood of success. Don't give the other person a reason to get defensive and keep responding.

This does not mean that you have to be overly friendly. Just make it sound a little relaxed and non-antagonistic. If appropriate, say you recognize their concerns. Brief comments that show your empathy and respect will generally calm the other person down, even if only for a short time.

FIRM

In a non-threatening way, clearly tell the other person your information or position on an issue. (For example: "That's all I'm going to say on this issue.") Be careful not to make comments that invite more discussion, unless you are negotiating an issue or want to keep a dialogue going back and forth. Avoid comments that leave an opening, such as: "I hope you will agree with me that …" This invites the other person to tell you "I don't agree."

Sound confident and don't ask for more information, if you want to end the back-and-forth. A confident-sounding person is less likely to be challenged with further emails. If you get further emails, you can ignore them, if you have already sufficiently addressed the inaccurate information. If you need to respond again, keep it even briefer and do not emotionally engage. In fact, it often helps to just repeat the key information using the same words.

Example

Joe's email: "Jane, I can't believe you are so stupid as to think that I'm going to let you take the children to your boss' birthday party during my parenting time. Have you no memory of the last six conflicts we've had about my parenting time? Or are you having an affair with him? I always knew you would do anything to get ahead! In fact, I remember coming to your office party witnessing you making a total fool of yourself – including flirting with everyone from the CEO down to the mailroom kid! Are you high on something? Haven't you gotten your finances together enough to support yourself yet, without flinging yourself at every Tom, Dick and Harry? …" [And on and on and on.]

Jane's Response: "Thank you for responding to my request to take the children to my office party. Just to clarify, the party will be from 3-5 on Friday at the office and there will be approximately 30 people there – including several other parents bringing school-age children. There will be no alcohol, as it is a family-oriented firm and there will be family-oriented activities. I think it will be a good experience for them to see me at my workplace. Since you do not agree, then of course I will respect that and withdraw my request, as I recognize it is your parenting time." [And that's the end of her email.]

Comment: Jane kept it brief, and did not engage in defending herself. Since this was just between them, she didn't need to respond. If he sent this email to friends, co-workers or family members (which high-conflict people often do), then she would need to respond to the larger group with more information, such as the following:

Jane's Group Response: "Dear friends and family: As you know, Joe and I had a difficult divorce. He has sent you a private email showing correspondence between us about a parenting schedule matter. I hope you will see this as a private matter and understand that you do not need to respond or get involved in any way. Almost everything he has said is in anger and not at all accurate. If you have any questions for me personally, please feel free to contact me and I will clarify anything I can. I appreciate your friendship and support."

And that's it: B.I.F.F.!

Whether you are at work, at home or elsewhere, a B.I.F.F. response can save you time and emotional anguish. The more people who handle hostile mail in such a manner, the less hostile mail there will be.

But What If There's Abuse?

Many cases with potential issues of alienation also have real issues of abuse. High-conflict parents often have difficulty restraining their own impulses because of their unmanaged emotions. They interpret events in all-or-nothing terms, which upsets them and they over-react. So they shove, grab, hit and sometimes hurt their loved ones, including the other parent and/or the children. As I described in Chapter 3, this is often "attachment behavior," but it can be very dangerous or even fatal when it comes from an adult.

So, safety first! Develop a safety plan and speak to a professional or go to a clinic where they deal with orders of protection. It is very important that you and the children are protected from this behavior. It's not something that usually goes away on its own, despite promises to change. Restraining orders that limit contact help in some cases, but get professional advice about whether it would help in yours. Restraining orders do not themselves prevent violence and some of the most violent people totally ignore them. Therefore, you need a safety plan as well, so that you have shelter if necessary.

HCPs generally don't change. What you see and get today is what you will see and get 1, 2, 5 years from now. Personalities generally don't change, except after years of intensive counseling – and most don't go to counseling. But some behavior change can occur, such as ending the physical abuse, with intensive batterer's treatment programs.

So it's better to seek court orders that focus on behavior change and safety, rather than focusing in court on custody battles. Studies have shown that abusive parents get custody at the same rate as non-abusive parents, and that many batterers get custody when they ask for it! This isn't necessarily how it should be, but it may be better to pursue or defend significant parenting time for both parents (70-30, 60-40, 50-50), rather than get bogged down in long-term, all-or-nothing custody battles – which the children will negatively absorb.

In many cases the courts determine that both parents should have significant parenting time, but that there should be limited or no direct contact between the parents themselves. All the exchanges occur at school or other places, without both parents present at the same time. This is the parallel parenting approach I described at the beginning of this chapter. This may be most successful when domestic violence or other abuse is hard to prove, so there aren't endless court hearings with lots of opinions and splitting, but little evidence.

Most parents in families with domestic violence believe that the children don't know about it. But they do! They will mirror their parent's behavior – both being violent and abusive, and being the victim of violence and abuse. It's very important that they see their parents working on their own behavior rather than fighting over who has custody.

Victims of domestic violence need counseling too, to help them become more realistic about the abuse and to see choices in their lives. Many feel trapped. Just blaming the "perpetrator" and requiring them to get counseling or group treatment doesn't solve the needs of victims. Both need help. In many cases, the victim also has attachment issues, which makes it especially hard to leave the relationship. They need a secure relationship, such as with a counselor, to build a Foundation of Resilience for themselves.

Child Sexual Abuse

In most family court cases of allegations of child sexual abuse, the perpetrator isn't in jail. From my experience, it's better to seek supervised contact immediately for the alleged perpetrator rather than no contact. If you are concerned about the safety of your child, he or she will be protected while in supervised parenting time. This is a *moderate solution*. The police or a psychologist can investigate the allegations while your child has safe contact.

If you are the alleged perpetrator, volunteering for supervised parenting time gives you an opportunity to be observed with your child. The observations of a professional supervisor have helped resolve more cases than any hearing with parents arguing about what "may have" happened weeks or months ago. While it could be tempting to be angry about being supervised, it's important to manage those emotions and recognize the long-term benefit. It's better to have a professional observation that shows a good relationship with your child, rather than having a cloud of unresolved suspicion over you while you argue that you're innocent.

I believe that investigators of child sexual abuse are better now than ever at evaluating what has gone on. I regularly receive notices about intensive training for investigators interviewing children in child sexual abuse cases, with the latest approaches. We have the knowledge to be much more accurate than in the past. Suggestive use of dolls and drawings in the past have been sharply criticized, so that police, social workers and psychologists are much more carefully trained now. But more resources are needed.

Parents should avoid trying to figure out themselves if their children have been sexually abused. Every discussion with the child about a possibly abusive event counts as an "interview" in many court cases, and too many interviews "taint" the child's statements. The courts are very skeptical of information obtained by parents from their children. In one case I had, there were 25 "interviews" the child went through before the case was resolved, as the parent repeatedly discussed the alleged events with the child and took the child to one doctor after another to determine if she had been abused. It's better to call the proper child abuse agency in your area or speak with a professional without your child present, so that the child's statements are not considered tainted.

If the allegations aren't resolved after an investigation by professionals, it's usually better to use *flexible thinking* in developing a shared parenting plan. That way you can keep an eye on how your child is doing, rather than fighting for extreme custody solutions that exclude one or the other parent – and spill over onto the child – and risk losing contact at all with your child.

False Allegations

What if the allegations of abuse are false? We know this happens some-times. Some cases are knowingly false and I have obtained sanctions (fines) against some parents when we were able to prove the allegations were know-ingly false. However, from my experience, most false allegations occur as a result of the unconscious splitting of HCPs, who view the other parent as an "all-bad" person who is capable of the most terrible behavior. Their fears start building until they believe that their own worst fears are true.

Research has shown that our left brains will make up facts that fit with overwhelming negative feelings in our right brains. For parents with "fear-ful attachments," it is not unusual that they confuse their internal inse-curities with external events. They jump to conclusions, then they fight with the life-or-death intensity that fits their fearful attachment, as though the imagined external events really threatened their lives or their children's lives.

For the target of false allegations, it can be tempting to seek to eliminate or severely restrict the other parent for their false allegations (knowingly false or honestly believed). However, this presents the same problem as in cases of abuse. It's hard to prove that the allegations were false or knowingly false, court decisions often swing back and forth as one side prevails and then the other, and the emotions of the endless court battle pass directly to the children.

In short, in domestic violence cases, child abuse cases, and false allegations cases, the same skills apply of being flexible, managed and moderate.

Conclusion

There are many HCPs in today's world, and they appear to be increasing. Many of them have a personality disorder, which means they are unlikely to be aware of their problems and unlikely to change their high-conflict behavior. Many of them are HCP parents, and many of them go through a divorce for one reason or another.

Therefore, the burden often falls on the reasonable parent to try to "contain" the HCP parent's behavior and influence on the children during the divorce process. By using *flexible thinking, managed emotions,* and *moderate behaviors* with everyone involved, you will make your life easier and help your children build their Foundations of Resilience for the rest of their lives – even while going through the divorce process. Think of this time as an opportunity for your children to learn positive skills – including that we all make mistakes and can learn from them.

The *skills* that children learn from a separation or divorce are more important than most of the decisions that will be made. Unfortunately, by focusing on decisions, parents and professionals can get stuck in long-term battles over the parenting schedule or trying to prove which parent is the all-good parent and which one is the all-bad parent at court.

When handling your divorce case, it is also surprisingly important to aim for *moderate behaviors* in the professionals you hire and to show *flexible thinking* in the requests you make of the court. You are the decision-maker about the people you work with and your proposals. You can show that you are not an HCP by the choices you make. The more that the people around you are also *flexible, managed and moderate*, the less stress there will be on you and on your child – and more bricks for your child's Foundation of Resilience.

Short Summary

Parents: When dealing with an HCP parent, most reasonable parents are tempted to take an aggressive approach (seeking to almost eliminate the other parent) or to take a passive approach (giving in on almost everything). An Assertive Approach is the best solution, as it allows the reasonable parent to look reasonable, while seeking restraints on specific behaviors of the HCP parent. This approach can include Parallel Parenting, to minimize contact with the HCP parent, and email communications that are B.I.F.F.: Brief, Informative, Friendly and Firm. This approach isn't easy, but it may protect the children from a high-conflict divorce.

Family and Friends: Your family member or friend will need a lot of support in using an Assertive Approach in dealing with an HCP parent – and other HCPs who may become involved in the case. You can help by brainstorming moderate solutions and requests. You can help by being a role model in how you communicate, such as using B.I.F.F. in your emails. If you have concerns about safety and care of the children by the HCP parent, help your loved one be assertive in explaining these concerns to professionals and seeking protection, without using unmanaged emotions or extreme behavior in presenting these concerns.

Professionals: Clients need a lot of help in using an Assertive Approach in dealing with an HCP parent. Encourage your clients to use: their flexible thinking by making two or more proposals for dealing with problems; their managed emotions by encouraging them to avoiding expressing intense anger except in private talks with friends, counselor or lawyer; and moderate behaviors by respecting objective professional judgments regarding abuse concerns, including the other parent in the children's lives and, when appropriate, requesting parallel parenting plans to limit conflicts. Use this approach in dealing with other professionals.

How Family and Friends Can Help

Laura Nelson's father accompanied her to the lawyer's office. "Is it all right if my father meets with us?" she asked. "He's very concerned about how my husband cares for my son."

After explaining that conversations with her father won't be legally confidential, the lawyer met with Laura and her father.

"That's right," Mr. Nelson said. "I really never liked him. I don't want him spending time with my grandson. I think he's a bad influence. He always seemed kind of rough and harsh with my grandson."

"Was he abusive?" Laura's lawyer asked.

"No, just verbally harsh. He'd say things like 'see what you've done now!' and 'I want my son to be tough, not a crying whiner.' Things like that. You have to go easy on a boy who's only 7 years old. Sometimes, when I ask, my grandson tells me he doesn't really want to see his father. I think he's a bad influence.

Can't you do something to keep him away from the boy? After all, he's my grandson!"

Grandparents, siblings, friends, neighbors, co-workers and new partners are often involved in high-conflict divorce cases. They really want to help, and they feel the intense pain of their loved one going through a high-conflict divorce – or any divorce.

I have had the above conversation several times with clients and their family members – often the grandparents of the child in the middle of a custody and visitation (or "access") dispute. From my experience, many custody battles are funded by the grandparents, either because the parents have exhausted their funds or because the grandparents never liked the other parent anyway.

I can certainly empathize with family members concerns, but I have to advise my clients that the family courts are required to provide significant time with both parents, except in cases of abuse. But even in cases of abuse, the courts very rarely exclude one parent from the child's life. Sometimes I have had this conversation with clients and family, like Laura and Mr. Nelson above:

Laura: "My ex is really a jerk. I'd rather that he have no contact with my son. Is there any way to accomplish this?"

Mr. Nelson: "I know you think Laura should settle her case with significant parenting time with each parent. But what would it cost to really go all out to keep the father out of my grandson's life? For Laura to have sole legal and physical custody?"

Lawyer: "Well, we'd need to gather declarations or affidavits from people who have observed his parenting behavior. Then, we could take depositions of those who have provided declarations/affidavits in support of him. Then, we could ask for a psychological evaluation, which would include him, Laura, your grandson, and possibly yourselves as grandparents. We should probably

retain our own psychologist for advice and interpretation of the informa-
tion we gather. Then, if we don't like the psychological evaluation report and
recommendations, we could have our psychologist critique the report and
recommendations. I would also need to research the latest developments in the
law regarding parenting plans, child abuse, parental alienation, false allega-
tions, domestic violence, and so forth. If any of those are present in this case,
it might help or make it harder, depending on who is accused of wrongdoing.
I'd say this custody battle might cost you about $20,000. Some are well over
$100,000."

Mr. Nelson: "Let me talk to Laura alone for a few minutes."

Lawyer: "Sure, go ahead."

A few minutes later.

Mr. Nelson: "Laura and I have decided to let the father spend time with
the boy. So we'll consider ways to settle the case. We'll just keep an eye on the
father, in case he does anything inappropriate in the future."

After observing so many people become involved in high-conflict cases, I
created two terms for the roles they seem to take – "Negative Advocate"
or "Positive Advocate." As you can probably tell, I think it's better to be a
positive advocate.

Negative Advocates

Negative Advocates are people who think they are helping, but really make
matters worse. They have gotten emotionally "hooked." They may not
know the full facts of the case, but they feel in their heart that they have to
protect their loved one or the children from the "all-bad" parent. They often become a stronger fighter for their loved one's position than their loved
one. They increase the "splitting" in the divorce, without even realizing it.

In the case example above, did you notice that Mr. Nelson and the boy had been discussing his father. *"Sometimes, when I ask, my grandson tells me he doesn't really want to see his father."* Why was grandpa asking the boy questions about his father? Does he think it will help the boy? Does he think it will help his daughter, Laura? Does he realize that he may be *suggesting* to the boy that he resist spending time with his father? Grandparents and other adults can be very influential when the parents themselves are emotional wrecks. Be careful what you suggest – to the child and to a parent.

Such conversations may seem totally innocent, but if the grandfather has his deposition taken some day, these conversations may come out as a negative influence on the boy's behavior – especially if he is resisting spending time with his father. And you would be amazed that some attorneys serve deposition notices on grandparents these days in high-conflict divorces.

Anyone can be a Negative Advocate – even professionals, such as lawyers, counselors, mediators and judges. But most commonly Negative Advocates are those close to the parents in a high-conflict divorce – their parents, siblings or other family members, or their friends, neighbors or co-workers. Here are seven characteristics to avoid, so you don't become a Negative Advocate or encourage someone else to become one:

General Characteristics of Negative Advocates

1. Negative Advocates are emotionally "hooked" by their loved one's anger, fear, charm, hurt, sadness, or other intense emotions.

2. Negative Advocates just want to help, but often inadvertently escalate the case.

3. Negative Advocates are usually uninformed about the details of the case and are often surprised when they find out later their loved one also made mistakes.

4. Negative Advocates are sometimes relatives or friends with high-conflict personalities, but more often are reasonable people who just got "hooked."

5. Negative Advocates often vanish or withdraw after hearing all the details of their loved one's behavior or hearing of the other sides' good behavior.

6. People with high-conflict personalities often put a lot of energy into recruiting Negative Advocates, and then they turn on them when they don't get what they want.

7. Negative Advocates usually engage in "splitting," voluntarily or under pressure. They see their loved one as "all-good" with nothing to improve on, and see the other person (other parent) as "all-bad" with no redeeming features. They encourage fighting to eliminate the "all-bad" parent as much as possible from the child's life, and they often pay for the custody battle or access dispute.

We have all been Negative Advocates in some way for someone. We often don't realize it until afterwards. As a lawyer, I know that I have to be careful not to fall into the trap of becoming a Negative Advocate. It has already happened several times. While it still happens occasionally, I have been able to catch myself much quicker than I used to. I always have to check myself for these following behaviors.

High-Conflict Behaviors of Negative Advocates

All-or-Nothing Thinking

Seeing one parent as "all-bad" with no redeeming value

Seeing favored parent as "all-good" with nothing to change or improve

Advocating for no contact between the children and the "all-bad" parent

Or demanding 50-50, with no flexibility

Having only one solution to each problem

Automatically believing the worst things said about the "all-bad" parent

Unmanaged Emotions

Angry lectures at "all-bad" parent, at children, slamming down phone, making threats

Sudden outbursts of anger when discussing problems and solutions with professionals

Intense blaming of one parent/professional, to children, friends, family and professionals

Intense or prolonged complaining to own family, friends and professionals about case

Trying to make parents, children, and/or professionals feel anxious/guilty if disagree

Extreme Behaviors

Encouraging or demanding or paying parent to seek no contact orders with the other parent

Encouraging, demanding, or paying parent to seek radical changes of custody/access

Allowing interferences with "all-bad" parent's time; making excuses for the favored parent

Hiding important negative information about a parent, such as plans to move or surprise attacks

Threatening to eliminate the "all-bad" parent from the children's lives through the court

Publicly labeling the "all-bad" parent as "The Alienator" or "The Abuser"

Writing declarations/affidavits against the "all-bad" parent and filing them with the court

Treating the other parent as "all-bad" despite a positive relationship before the divorce

Positive Advocates

Positive Advocates support the parents and the children with encouragement, caring, information and ideas, rather than taking sides, blaming and demanding aggressive action from their loved one. They don't even speak in terms of "sides" in the case. They encourage realistic options and may help gather information. But they are careful not to do more work than their loved one on the case, and try not to direct the case.

In the second scenario above, Mr. Nelson used his influence to encourage Laura to avoid fighting a custody battle. He also, apparently, decided that he did not want to be the one funding such an expensive custody battle. Perhaps he became a Positive Advocate.

From my experience, Negative Advocates are often emotionally hooked and uninformed. Their passion to help their loved one comes from the emotions that they have absorbed, consciously and unconsciously. If they can become informed, then they often become Positive Advocates – helping their loved one be flexible, managed and moderate.

General Characteristics of Positive Advocates

1. Avoid making assumptions
2. Investigate problems
3. Provide support and information
4. Avoid taking too much responsibility for others' behavior or problems
5. Avoid doing more work than the people involved in the disputes
6. Avoid getting in the way of others' feedback and natural consequences
7. Avoid taking "sides"

Reasonable Behaviors of Positive Advocates

<u>Flexible Thinking</u>

Seeing other parent as having a mix of good and bad qualities and behaviors

Reminding others that both parents have good and bad qualities

Supporting best relationship possible with the child and other parent, even if limited

Proposing shared parenting, with flexibility

Proposing several solutions to any problem

<u>Managed Emotions</u>

Containing his or her angry emotions around children at exchanges and at home

Taking a break when discussions of problems get heated; avoiding bad times to talk

Regularly making positive statements about other parent to child, family, and professionals

Containing his or her own sad emotions around children; getting counseling to help, if needed

Telling children about positive benefits of spending time with both parents

Moderate Behaviors

Supporting parenting schedule, even when it's inconvenient, until parents make new schedule

Not supporting competing events, activities

Gathering information and discussing options, without working harder than the parents

Actively supporting both parents' relationship with the children, even if limited

Taking breaks when upset

Practicing respectful communication at all times

Young Parents

Tommy was about one year old when his parents (both around 20) really split up. They had never been married and both lived at her mother's house for a few months, but it didn't work out. They came for mediation of their parenting plan and child support. They just bickered like 3-year-olds themselves and after two hours had made no progress.

The mediator suggested that they might make more progress if they each invited someone to the next mediation session to help them — someone who knew

them well and often helped them make decisions. Of course, they would have to agree to have these Advocates present in the mediation, since they themselves were the decision-makers.

They really liked that idea, and they each agreed that they would bring their mothers.

At the next mediation session, the young parents and their mothers reached a complete agreement about Tommy's parenting schedule and child support.

Mom's Mother: "Oh, I know my daughter can sometimes get overwhelmed if she has Tommy for too long without a break. So it will be great for his father to spend at least an hour with him every day. I can help out too, but I also have a life I'm trying to live. So you can really be a help that way."

Dad's Mother: "And it's really important for my son to be able to keep his job and work full-time. So for now, I think it's better if he only has an overnight on the weekend with Tommy. He often has a hard time getting up in the morning and I have to remind him several times, now that he's staying with me again. But I think the hour-a-day schedule is a really great idea, then 24 hours at our house all day Saturday until Sunday morning."

Sometimes Positive Advocates are the solution to a potentially high-conflict divorce. These young parents were good at arguing, but not good at decision-making – at least not yet. By seeing the respectful way that their mothers helped them make decisions, they can use these skills in the future – and Tommy won't absorb as many negative emotions from them and will be much less likely to become alienated as he grows up.

New Partners

New boyfriends, girlfriends, husbands or wives can also be Positive Advocates or Negative Advocates. Sometimes they get reluctantly get drawn into a high-conflict divorce and other times they may drive the high-conflict custody dispute.

When Ivan married Lynn, he told her she should get primary custody of her 8-year-old daughter, Jerilynn. Lynn had about 40% of the parenting time and the father, Jerry, had about 60% of the parenting time. Jerry had afternoons off and was available when Jerilynn got home from school. On a camping trip with Jerilynn, Ivan and Lynn demanded to know every detail of life at Jerry's house.

Ivan directly asked her: "Don't you want to live with your mother? It's just not right that you only see her 40% of the time. A daughter should live with her mother."

Unfortunately, this camping trip led to allegations of child abuse against Jerry and the appearance of alienation of Jerilynn from her father. However, these were eventually determined to be unfounded. Almost a year later, Jerilynn's parents spent a combined $50,000 on lawyer's fees, psychological evaluator's fees, an attorney for the child, and visitation supervisor fees for several months.

After several months, Jerry was allowed to have unsupervised parenting time. At his request, there was a court order allowing for the recording of phone conversations between Jerilynn and her mother while Jerilynn was at his house. Her mother knew about this court order, but she still made extreme statements about Jerry and was blatantly trying to manipulate Jerilynn to say things against him during these recorded phone calls.

In the calls, Jerilynn could be heard trying to get her mother to stop talking about her father. Instead, Jerilynn just wanted to talk about her pets. At court, the judge considered her behavior potentially alienating, although Jerilynn had not become alienated yet.

Lynn ended up with much less parenting time than she had before with her daughter. Would she have pursued a request to change custody and to pressure her daughter, if Ivan hadn't pressured her? Did Ivan just think he was just doing what Lynn wanted?

It's often hard to know which came first: Was the new partner a Negative Advocate for a high-conflict parent; or did the new partner become a Negative Advocate for the HCP parent? In either case, an HCP seems to have been involved and they routinely gather Negative Advocates around them.

Heidi and Franco

Two years after their divorce, both Heidi and Franco had married new partners. After their divorce, their daughter, Joanie, had lived primarily with Heidi. Franco's income was higher and he paid her child support. After Franco lost his job, a dispute arose about child support, the parenting schedule, and other issues. They all agreed to meet with a mediator. Franco and his new wife were very demanding.

"Joanie wants to live with us full time now," said Franco. "So you should pay me child support, Heidi."

Heidi was furious. "How dare you even suggest such a thing! You shouldn't even be talking to her about where she lives. That's totally inappropriate. You always were a bully."

"Wait a second," Heidi's new husband interrupted, turning to Heidi, then to Franco and his wife. "Let's talk about all our options. That's one idea. And we have other ideas too."

The mediator decided not to interrupt.

"No!" Franco's new wife chimed in. "There are no other options. She's going to live with us full-time. She doesn't want to live with you anymore."

"Well," Heidi's new husband said calmly, "She hasn't said that to us. She seems to be doing fine. However, Heidi and I discussed increasing her time with you on the weekends, so that you can pick her up at school Friday and take her back to school Monday mornings, instead of coming back and forth to our house. Also, we are willing to have you pay no child support for three months, to give you time to get another job. Then, based on your new income, we can re-calculate support with the mediator here. What do you think of those ideas?"

After about two hours, they all reached an agreement — mostly along the lines of what Heidi's new husband had proposed. He was a Positive Advocate and didn't get hooked into the anger and more extreme proposals of Franco and his new wife. As you can see, Franco's new wife was a bit of a Negative Advocate, with intense emotions and all-or-nothing proposals. ("There are no other options," she said.) In reality, there are many options for handling any particular problem.

Did Joanie become alienated? No. At least not at age 8. However, I would have some concerns if Franco and his new wife were to keep using all-or-nothing thinking and unmanaged emotions around her. This increases the risks that Joanie will absorb their emotions and mirror their behaviors over time. However, with Heidi's new husband showing flexible thinking and managed emotions, Heidi and Joanie may be able to stay mostly reasonable and resilient themselves.

Most people, even HCPs, can manage their issues and make decisions if there are enough reasonable people around them.

Modifications

As a mediator, I always let the parties decide if anyone else may be present during a mediation session. I have had several cases in which one or both parents wanted to modify the parenting plan or child support, and one party had remarried and the other didn't. Sometimes the new spouse wants to attend. You can imagine that this might be a difficult situation.

The decision is always up to the parents, since they are the legal decision-makers for the child. I usually encourage them both to agree to have the new spouse present, because he or she is already in the background and can easily undermine any new agreements. In most cases, the parents agree to have the new spouse present. Surprisingly, in several cases the new spouse was almost like another mediator.

For example, I have had several cases where the new wife got along with the first wife better than the ex-husband and the first wife. The new wife would make proposals for scheduling or support payments, and the first wife found them reasonable. Then the ex-husband would get upset about something, and the new wife would calm him down and make another reasonable proposal.

The first case I had like this was quite surprising. Since then it has happened several times and I have been very encouraged. I am convinced that most people, even HCPs, can manage their issues and make decisions if there are enough reasonable people around them.

Conclusion

It's especially useful to see how a Positive Advocate among family and friends can be really helpful in resolving potentially high-conflict divorce cases. If you are a family member or friend, you can be really helpful, so long as you are aware of avoiding the pitfalls of becoming a Negative Advocate.

Grandparents, new spouses or partners, friends and others should always be aware that you may be pressured to become a Negative Advocate in a high-conflict divorce. Almost everyone is around someone with a high-conflict divorce at some time in their lives. You may be caught by surprise, and the amygdala in your brain may get emotionally "hooked" before you consciously realize it.

However, you can always be a Positive Advocate instead of a Negative Advocate. And you can always get "unhooked." The best way to make sure you are a Positive Advocate is to talk to someone else neutral and ask if they think you are being a Negative Advocate or a Positive Advocate.

Some family and friends even talk to a counselor for themselves, to try to understand the HCP and how to be involved – or not. This can help you keep perspective, so you can help your loved one and help the parties keep perspective. Remember, positive behavior and emotions are contagious too. With your positive role, you can help the parents and children keep perspective, and add bricks to their Foundation of Resilience.

Short Summary

Parents: Family members and friends can be very helpful to you in many ways while avoiding a high-conflict divorce. However, you have to be careful to discourage them from being Negative Advocates for you. This means avoiding asking them to always agree with you about the other parent. Instead, ask them to be a Positive Advocate, by providing encouragement, information and ideas for you, without taking over or hating the other parent. When dealing with an HCP parent's Negative Advocates, avoid getting angry at them and instead provide them with accurate information, using a method such as the B.I.F.F. response in Chapter 8.

Family and Friends: Grandparents, new spouses or partners, friends, neighbors, co-workers and others should always be aware that you may be pressured to become a Negative Advocate in a high-conflict divorce. Divorce is such a stressful time, that it's easy for the parties to seek advocates who totally agree with them. This sometimes gets them in trouble, as described in this chapter. It's best to be a Positive Advocate, by providing encouragement, information and ideas for them, without taking over or hating the other parent. Be careful not to be too directive about what your family member or friend should do. Sometimes just listen.

Professionals: In high-conflict cases, family members and friends often become much more involved than in regular cases. Professionals must be particularly careful to deal with these advocates, whether negative or positive, with empathy and with clear boundaries. Issues of confidentiality, splitting professionals and staff, and who pays the fees will often arise. It often helps to give helpful tasks to family member and friends, to help them be Positive Advocates. Often they may have useful information that you would not otherwise get.

Be careful not to become too close to your client(s), so that you don't become a Negative Advocate yourself.

How Lawyers Can Help

In his book, A Promise to Ourselves, *Alec Baldwin (2008) describes his frustrations with lawyers. After he left a particularly angry voicemail for his 11-year-old daughter, which was leaked by someone to the media in April 2007, he was back in family court:*

> *During the proceeding in June, [my ex-wife's lawyer] Hersh brandished a letter of apology that I had sent to my daughter and plopped it in front of me in the witness box. The letter had been torn in half, presumably by my daughter. In order to put his signature touch on this, Hersh bent over to arrange the severed pieces to form a recognizable whole. Right to the end, Hersh, one of the most malicious human beings I have ever encountered, never missed an opportunity to 'advocate' on behalf of the truly angry litigant. Their goal was to show that my daughter did not want to see me again. More than $3 million in joint legal fees had been spent. In my mind, all of it was a buildup to this; so that Hersh and his client could have the pleasure of sticking that letter in my face. (p. 185)*

Lawyers can be Negative Advocates, as Baldwin describes. Regardless of how the parents behave, lawyers can choose to be Positive Advocates. It's easy to imagine how this lawyer's negative behavior and the emotions associated with it is passed to his client (the mother), to Mr. Baldwin, and assuredly passed to the child by both parents.

This isn't to excuse the father's negative behavior either. The point is that lawyers' behavior can be part of the family court Culture of Blame. Perhaps for this reason, one or both parties does not have an attorney in approximately 75% of divorce cases in many family court systems today.

From my 17-years' experience as a family lawyer, I believe that 80-90% of family lawyers sincerely want to help their clients resolve their divorces in a fair manner that does not hurt the child's relationship with either parent. Of course, they don't make the headlines. Therefore, I encourage parents to at least consult with a lawyer before deciding not to use one. The vast majority of divorces are resolved by agreement, often with lawyers helping the parties negotiate, with lawyers serving as mediators, or with lawyers using the Collaborative Divorce approach.

The Reasonable Lawyer's Dilemma

Lawyers are often the ones who determine whether a divorce will be high-conflict or low-conflict. Parents usually do not know what the legal options are and are easily influenced by their lawyers. In alienation and abuse cases, lawyers are faced with the dilemma of encouraging peaceful settlements out-of-court or protecting children and parents – which often requires court intervention. Resolving this dilemma requires close cooperation, ideally between a reasonable client and a reasonable lawyer.

In child alienation cases, lawyers and clients must watch out for HCP behavior, as there are HCP lawyers and HCP clients. In the first part of this chapter, I describe some of these behaviors, so that you can avoid them, whether you are a lawyer or potential client. Unfortunately, these behaviors are usually not obvious at first. However, sometimes you can see signs of *all-or-nothing thinking, unmanaged emotions* and *extreme behaviors* if you look for them in what a lawyer or client says from the start.

In the second part of this chapter, I will describe how to use *flexible thinking* and *moderate legal requests* in dealing with child alienation issues, assuming that both the lawyer and the client are reasonable and are trying to find the best balance of peaceful settlements and court intervention. The second part of this chapter is also helpful in considering approaches for a parent representing himself or herself.

In this book I don't address finding a lawyer and working with a lawyer in general, or specific strategies for dealing with a high-conflict opposing party, all of which I address in depth in my book *Splitting: Protecting Yourself While Divorcing a Borderline or Narcissist*.

For Lawyers: Resisting the High-Conflict Client's Demands

Under the law and ethical rules, lawyers are not supposed to be "hired guns." Many clients and some lawyers don't yet understand this. Many clients seek "the most aggressive attorney in town." But the Courts of Appeal are starting to send a different message:

> An attorney in a civil case is not a hired gun required to carry out every direction given by the client. As a professional, counsel has a professional responsibility not to pursue an appeal that is frivolous or taken for the purpose of delay, just because the client instructs him or her to do so. Under such circumstances, the high ethical and professional standards of a member of the bar and an officer of the court require the attorney to inform the client that the attorney's professional responsibility precludes him or her from pursuing such an appeal, and to withdraw from the representation of the client.

In re Marriage of Gong and Kwong (2008) 163 Cal. App. 4th 510, 521.

This case was unusual, in that the court sanctioned the lawyers directly. Usually in family law, at least in California, when a lawyer or client is sanctioned for misconduct, it is the client who must pay the sanction. In the cases where I have sought and won a sanction against the other party, it is the party who pays – not their attorney, even though the attorney may have been a driving force. Now, if you are a lawyer representing a client who insists in pursuing an unreasonable position, be aware that you may pay the fine for fulfilling your client's every demand.

Lawyers are constantly put in the position of being asked to pursue a frivolous approach. Most say "No." Unfortunately, many child alienation cases are significantly driven by a high-conflict parent and an attorney who can't say "No." That's either because of their own high-conflict personality, or because they get emotionally "hooked" by their client and inadvertently become a Negative Advocate. This is avoidable and usually comes back to haunt the client and the attorney, as the above case explains.

The more aware that lawyers become about the dynamics and demands of high-conflict personalities, the less likely they are to get "hooked." So if you're a parent, don't hire a lawyer who seems like a Negative Advocate, and don't ask a lawyer to take an all-or-nothing, unmanaged and extreme approach. And if you're a lawyer, be consciously aware of taking a flexible, managed and moderate approach – even when your client demands more extreme behavior.

For example, when I first became a lawyer, I had the advantage of knowing about personality disorders. I remember one of my first clients who wanted a high-conflict divorce.

Mr. Wall was getting divorced, after finishing a couple years in prison for bank fraud. His wife didn't have an attorney, so I called her up and discussed my client's proposals in a long phone call. It seemed to go well.

The next day, I received a call from my client. "Bill, my wife says that she felt very comfortable negotiating with you and that she doesn't plan on hiring an attorney. She said you seem fair enough and explained things in a friendly manner."

"Good," I said. "I advised her that it's always good to at least consult with an attorney. But I think your case will settle fairly easily. She seemed pretty agreeable to most of your proposals. I think I can keep it pretty cooperative."

"Bill," Mr. Wall said sharply. "I can't have that! Before this is all over, I want her crying and pleading and begging! You're being too friendly in these negotiations, and I can't have that!"

"Well," I said. "What you're suggesting is really not my style. I don't work that way. Perhaps you should find a lawyer who does. "

"Actually, I think I have," he replied. And that was that.

But that client didn't have children, thank goodness. Fortunately, he's a rare example from the approximately 400 clients I have represented as a family lawyer, and about 1000 cases I have handled as a divorce mediator.

For Parents: Avoiding High-Conflict Lawyers

Unfortunately, there are some high-conflict lawyers who like high-conflict divorces.

At one of my first family court trials, the opposing lawyer came up to me right before we started and said, "Here, sign this. It's the agreements we made yesterday over the phone."

I looked it over. With the local court rules, we were required to "meet and confer" by the day before the trial to try to see what agreements we could resolve, to narrow the issues and to limit the amount of actual time we needed from the judge for the trial.

"This isn't what we agreed," I said irritably. I was stressed out enough about having one of my first trials. "I can't deal with this now."

His reply has stuck in my head for 17 years.

"Well, if you were a REAL lawyer, you could deal with it," he smirked.

What the heck did that mean? I thought. Maybe because I was a counselor for 12 years before becoming a lawyer, he thinks that I'm not a real lawyer like he has been for years and years. Then, I suddenly realized that he was simply trying to distract me and upset me right before the trial began. No way I was going to let that happen. I decided not to get emotionally hooked.

In fact, the above experience motivated me to be highly assertive throughout the trial. While we each won on some issues and lost on others, I developed a zero tolerance approach to his many manipulations over two days. I responded assertively to his aggressive behavior in court, by providing the court necessary information, but without the emotional dramatics the other attorney provided. In retrospect, he energized me and taught me a lot about high-conflict behavior – so that I learned how to respond to it without getting hooked into high-conflict behavior myself.

Several years later, I was at court and overheard this same attorney talking to a young new attorney. She was clearly irritated with him: "This is ridiculous!" she said, looking at a paper he was pushing on her. "I never agreed to that!" It was trial day, and he was at it again!

High-Conflict Lawyers Affect on Children

The above lawyer didn't just try to make new attorneys miserable. One day, I was at court for a short hearing. Most parenting decisions are made at short hearings of 10-20 minutes.

It was just before the court session began. This lawyer, who I'll call Mr. Sensitive, was standing over his client as she was sitting and reading the Family Court Services report and recommendations for her parenting plan. The recommendations come after a 1 ½ hour meeting with both parents and a court mediator, who is trained as a mental health professional. If the parents don't reach an agreement, then the court mediator writes a recommendation, which the judge usually adopts as the court's temporary orders at the short hearing. (Private mediators usually don't write recommendations, as private mediation is supposed to be totally neutral and confidential.)

There are no attorneys present during these court mediation sessions, but they often advise their clients on what to say or not say. Obviously, Mr. Sensitive had advised her on what to say or do. Now, his client was in tears, holding her head and really sobbing, as she held her report. Mr. Sensitive was leaning over her, saying: "You blew it! You blew it!"

Imagine her next interaction with her child. Will it be intense sadness and tears, at the mother's loss of her hoped-for parenting plan with the child? Will it be anger at the child, as the mother blames him or her, the way her lawyer blamed her that morning? In either case, you can imagine that it will be very hard for her to contain the emotions of "losing" in her parenting mediation, and then losing her own attorney's support. Children know how to read their parents emotions – especially fear and anger. There's no reason to think that her child will not absorb this lawyer's emotional attack on her mother.

Fortunately, I have run into very few family lawyers who are like that. Unfortunately, those few get a lot of business, so I've had to deal with them over and over again during my 17 years. They have taught me a lot. I use their examples to help motivate my clients to stay out of court as much as possible. They have probably done more for the private mediation business than any advertisement could ever do.

But they have also contributed significantly, I believe, to child alienation.

Working Together With an Assertive Approach

Let's suppose you are a reasonable lawyer or you are a client who has found a reasonable lawyer – a Positive Advocate. What should you do and what should you expect, so that you do not add some bricks to the Wall of Alienation? Use an Assertive Approach, as described in Chapter 8.

First of all, use flexible thinking. Avoid all-or-nothing solutions. Lawyers' advice to rejected parents in alienation cases is often extreme: from encouraging the parent to give up, to seeking radical change of custody orders. I recommend against either of these approaches, at least until all other alternatives have been sufficiently tried.

Should I Just Let Go?

The father is the rejected parent. He asks his lawyer: "What should I do? My son says he doesn't want to see me anymore. In fact, he is begging me to stop bothering him and his mother. I'm thinking of just stopping all contact and leaving the state. There's nothing here for me anymore. It's too painful to keep being exposed to this rejection."

"I suggest that you do that," Lawyer A says. "Just write your son a goodbye letter and tell him you hope he will get together with you after he's 18. It's a sad situation, but I respect your willingness to keep him out of the conflict."

Lawyer B says: "I can understand how you feel. However, that would give your son the message that all-or-nothing solutions are appropriate. That would not be a good lesson for your son to learn for his future relationships. On the other hand, you don't seem to have many good options right now – but you still have options.

"You could write him a letter and say: 'I understand your request, but you are a child and you need both of your parents. You need to learn the lessons of life from more than one parent. This is not a decision that you can make or should try to make. I will do what I think is best, with advice from expe-

rienced and reasonable people. I love you and always will. I will not accept ending our relationship as a reasonable solution to today's problems. While I'm not sure what to do right now, I will keep looking for answers and ways to let you know that you have my love and support in your life.'

"Or you could ask the judge for reconciliation counseling, where you meet with your son to discuss ways of improving your relationship.

"Or you could ask the judge to order New Ways for Families which involves short-term counseling for each parent, followed by parent-child counseling with each parent and the child.

"Or you could ask for a change of custody to you, but that raises a different set of problems which we will discuss.

"These are just a few of the ideas you can consider. You need to know you have options, but each option has consequences."

The question of giving up almost always comes up for "rejected" parents. It is a tragic situation with no simple answer. I always empathize with my clients when they raise this idea, but they rarely act on it. I have always disagreed with those who recommend the "goodbye letter" as an appropriate solution to alienation, such as Lawyer A did above. It is the wrong message to send, even if a parent gives up for a while. Lawyers should give the message that this is not a "reasonable" solution.

Abusive parents are rarely asked to give up their relationships with their kids. Instead, they are asked (or ordered) to stop their abusive behavior. And their kids rarely ask them to get out of their lives. Quite the opposite, from my experience: Most abused kids want their parents to stop the abuse, but keep their relationships.

So this request is unique to alienation cases and the answer should be a flexible response, not an all-or-nothing, extreme solution.

It is important to know that recent research shows that many alienated children as adults say they wished their rejected parent had not given up. They secretly wanted to keep their relationship going with that parent. Here's what some of them told research psychologist Amy Baker (2007) in interviews as adults:

Melinda

Melinda was 3 years old when her parents separated and her father subsequently kidnapped her. She and her siblings had no contact with their mother for several years. Eventually, Melinda's mother won back her rights to have visitation with her daughter and they spent every other weekend together. In response, Melinda's father and stepmother began a campaign of alienation primarily through denigration of the mother. Melinda was not allowed to talk about her mother in her father's home and not allowed to bring home any presents given to her by her mother. Melinda absorbed these negative messages about her mother, believing her to be lazy and irresponsible, just as her father had portrayed her to be. "She and I didn't get along... we had a lot of problems." When Melinda was 13 years old, her mother discovered that Melinda had been sexually abused by her father; and custody reverted back to the mother. When asked what her mother did to protect the relationship in the face of the alienation campaign, Melinda offered that her mother fought for custody in the courts and she won the right for visitation. She recalled her mother never giving up on the relationship. (pp. 204-205)

Iris

...When [Iris] was 14 years old her mother packed up the children and drove several hundred miles away.... Iris had no contact with her father for several years and came to believe that he did not care for her. "Right after we left, my aunt and grandmother told me he was trying to get in touch with me and my brother but Mom had us so convinced that he wasn't, and being our mother of course we believed her. Oh, I was heartbroken. I was so totally distraught that he didn't love me anymore." During the period in which there was no contact, her father sent gifts by way of an aunt, but Iris did not find out until later that they were actually from her father. As a teenager she ran away to her father's house for a short period of time and her father at that point had an opportunity to defend himself....

Despite the newfound closeness she had with her father, Iris decided to return to her mother's home. She recalled her father saying to her, "You need to make the decision that is right for you and I will respect whatever decision you will make." However, during the interview she expressed the wish that he had been more persistent in trying to convince her to not return to her mother who was emotionally rejecting and physically abusive. "I think at the time if he had told me the truth about her I wouldn't have gone." Iris wished that he had told her, "Look your mom is really not normal and what she is doing to you is really not ok and I really don't want you to go back there." She believed that if he had said those words to her, she would have remained with him. (p. 209)

Amy Baker summarized her findings from forty interviews:

The adult children felt hurt and angry when the targeted parent finally gave up trying to have a relationship. No matter how adamant they had been that they wanted nothing to do with the targeted parent, they were still shocked when the parent respected that choice and walked away. It was usually experienced as rejection...

...The adult children did not feel that the targeted parent should have believed or responded to the child's rejection. Regardless of how adamant they had been that they wanted nothing to do with the targeted parent, they still did not want the targeted parent to accept that at face value....In essence, they were asking the targeted parents to act as if there were two children: the alienating child going through the motions of the alienation and the child who loved the targeted parent and never wanted to lose that relationship....

Thus, many of the adult children felt that the targeted parents should have tried harder and should not have given up. But they did not believe that in the end the targeted parent would have been effective at mitigating or preventing the alienation. A few went so far as to say that if the targeted parent had tried harder, the alienating parent might have behaved even worse.

Many of the adult children found out after the fact that the targeted parent had tried harder than they had known. Some found out about court cases fought, that there had been letters and gifts that had been returned to the targeted parent unopened. In most cases learning about these attempts had meaning. Even many years later they were grateful to learn that the targeted parent did more than they had known. (pp. 212-214)

These interviews are a powerful indicator that children want to have a relationship with both parents. While this is understandably very hard for the rejected parent, it does suggest the importance of not giving up. It also makes clear that anger at the child for the rejecting behavior is really not appropriate, because the child may feel obligated to go "through the motions of alienation." Lastly, the average duration of the child's alienation in her study was 20 years. This goes against the unsupported theory that children will always come around after they are 18 years old. That is no longer generally believed to be true.

The following example doesn't happen very often, but it reinforces the message that giving up based on what a child says should not be taken at face value. It's also a message to legal professionals that children's "expressed wishes" are not always what they seem, and may change.

Martin

Martin was 12 when his mother, Emma, slit her wrists and was taken to the hospital. She had been depressed for a while and Martin's father, Fred, had just said that he wanted a divorce. Emma survived, but Fred said she couldn't come home and that he was getting a divorce and would keep Martin – even though Emma had always been the primary caregiver. By the time the parents got to a court hearing to fight over custody of Martin, Emma was doing much better. She had become stable on medications and was doing well in her therapy. She asked to resume custody of Martin.

But before the court hearing, the parents met with a court mediator, who also met with Martin. Martin told the mediator that even though he had mostly been raised by his mother, he wanted nothing to do with her anymore. He described several concerning things about her. When Emma was told about this rejection, she was devastated. But she decided to fight back and not allow herself to become depressed.

At court the judge made an order for her to have two short visits a week with Martin. But he refused to see her. She believed that Fred was telling him things about her that weren't true. She focused on getting stronger, moved to another community and started a part-time job. She prepared herself to move on in her life, accepting the divorce from Fred. He had become a stranger to her. But she didn't want to give up on Martin, and sent him letters explaining her love for him and wanting to understand his rejection.

Then, a surprising turn of events took place. As Fred learned that she was getting stronger, he changed his mind about the divorce and told her he wanted to work on reconciling. Emma wasn't sure, but agreed to couples counseling. Over several weeks, their relationship improved. Fred admitted that he had exaggerated about her to Martin, because he was so angry and frustrated with her.

Now Martin was angry at Fred and wanted to talk to his mother. "I'm sorry I said lots of bad things about you. Dad didn't make me do it. I just thought that's what I had to do. I was afraid to upset him and I couldn't count on you anymore. I don't know what to do."

It took several weeks of family counseling, but eventually Emma reconciled with Martin and she moved back into the house. All of them became much more honest and open. Emma just remembers how close she came to ending it all and she's so glad she never gave up on Martin.

Should I Seek a Change of Custody?

This is one of the most common all-or-nothing responses to child alien-ation that lawyers often consider, threaten or request at court. I have tried this, won changes of custody, and seen it fail. Many parents and lawyers threaten this, and just threatening this escalates the case into extreme be-havior. This should only be considered as a last resort.

When an HCP custodial parent hears that you are seeking a change in custody, he or she is likely to become extremely agitated and this is passed directly onto the child. The HCP then also hires the most aggressive Nega-tive Advocate lawyer available and your life may become miserable for the next several months or years. The child's life also becomes miserable, living with the HCP custodial parent in this chronic state of agitation, for which you are blamed verbally or non-verbally. It doesn't really matter. I have seen such cases in which the alienation really began after this request was made and the all-or-nothing battle was started.

I am familiar with several cases in which the court did order a change of custody, after one parent engaged in extreme behaviors to block a relationship with the other parent. In some of those cases, the parent losing custody skipped the court hearing and disappeared. In one of those cases, the disappearing parent phoned the courtroom clerk right after the hearing took place in her absence. I begged the clerk not to tell the outcome, but the clerk did anyway. To my knowledge, my client never again has seen his son or the other parent in over a decade.

In other "disappearing" cases, the parent was found, the children were taken away from the disappearing parent, given to the parent who "won" custody, and the battle continued to rage on in family court.

In another change-of-custody case, the parent losing custody was at court. My client (the father) had virtually no relationship with his daughter before the change of custody, which was the basis for the change. The mother had engaged in a repeated pattern of alienation against him for years. Once the change of custody was ordered, the mother took a job out of state. An all-or-nothing response to an all-or-nothing decision. The child continually ran away from the father to a family friend's house, until she was old enough to emancipate herself.

In another recent change-of-custody case, the mother was told she was not allowed to see her children for six months while the father was being given an opportunity to establish a good relationship. On her way riding home from court, she was reportedly very quiet, then she jumped out of the car at full speed on the freeway and died after being hit by several cars.

In other change-of-custody cases, some authors report children becoming suicidal.

I know that this change-of-custody approach is popular for parents who have been the rejected noncustodial parent. It has been the recommended solution by Dr. Gardner for "severe alienation" cases. The problem is that it is an all-or-nothing, extreme solution to this problem. While I can certainly empathize with parents who have been the target of extremely alienating behaviors, I believe that this approach has several defects:

1. It teaches the child that all-or-nothing solutions for parent-child relationships are reasonable and appropriate, and that some of the most powerful people in our society (judges, therapists, lawyers) endorse these all-or-nothing solutions.

2. It tears apart whatever attachment the child has had with the favored parent. In the cases that I have observed, the child's attachment with the favored parent is a preoccupied, dismissive or fearful attachment, and the child has been working very hard at holding on to whatever attachment existed. The change of custody and concurrent elimination of contact with the favored parent (usually intended to be temporary by the courts), represents the total failure of the child's life-long attachment behavior with that parent. A much more serious loss than most lawyers or other professionals realize. It is not a corrective experience, but rather a failure of many years of attempted coping. Just because it clears the way to beginning a meaningful relationship with the rejected parent does not mean it is an overall healthy experience. One does not have to exclude the other parent.

3. It so frequently escalates the defensive behavior of the favored parent, usually an HCP, that it is very difficult to manage a smooth transfer to a healthy relationship. In one recent Canadian case, the whole family ended up opposing the court-ordered solution with one of their own (which the court then adopted, of course). Why go through such ex-

treme and public all-or-nothing solutions? As the 18-year-old son said in that case, the professionals were part of the problem.

4. It so frequently escalates the defensive behavior of professionals and child abuse advocates, that it generates such an emotional and extreme public outcry that it distracts from all of the other work of the court and lawyers. It feeds the public perception that lawyers and judges are giving children to "The Abusers" in divorce cases, which detracts from overall respect for the court and the positive efforts and work of family law professionals. It also adds to the culture of blame and fear that gets absorbed by children in our society, so that they believe one of their parents could be a monster. This anxiety, I believe, in turn feeds alienation rather than reducing it.

5. It is enthusiastically embraced as a fitting punishment for the favored parent. However, it also punishes the child. If the favored parent is an HCP, then he or she will not "get it" by being punished in this manner, and will continue to put significant energy into sabotaging the judge's order with his or her own all-or-nothing behavior.

With that said, there may be extreme cases where such an order may be appropriate, but it must include both parents in an educational and counseling process that teaches skills for the children and both parents, so that there can be a future of more secure relationships with both parents, whenever possible.

In general, my concern is that "rejected" parents and lawyers immediately seek a change of custody at any early sign of alienation or potential alienation. That contributes to the all-or-nothing culture of the family court case, which usually escalates it rather than teaching skills and reducing the conflict while strengthening both parents and their relationships with the children. Reasonable counseling and education alternatives exist for less-than-severe cases, which I will address in Chapter Eleven: How Counselors Can Help.

Should I Fight for 50-50?

This is a very common request in family courts and one of the common responses to child alienation. There is a lot of logic to this request, as it gives the children lots of time with each parent, it puts them on an exact equal basis as parents, and it gives a chance to clear up negative information coming from just one parent about the other. I have many cases with a 50-50 parenting plan in my mediation cases, where the parents request it jointly or agree to it after discussion with one parent requesting it.

However, a rigid imposition of 50-50 is quite different from a plan decided by the parents themselves. Jennifer McIntosh, a psychologist in Australia, indicates that there is a near presumption for "shared care" of the children there now. Her studies show that a "rigid shared care" parenting plan is the worst of four options, according to the reports of children.

A. Children were most satisfied when one parent had primary care

B. Children were next most satisfied when they had no contact with one parent, as it protected them from high-conflict disputes

C. Children were next most satisfied with "flexible shared care"

D. Children were least satisfied with "rigid shared care"

Her results showed that the quality of attachment was more important than the amount of time the child spent with a parent. The children were more enthusiastic about spending time with a parent when the arrangements were more flexible. Under the rigid shared care, children had more internal symptoms (stomach problems, self-blame) and more difficulty with their self-regulatory mechanisms (managed emotions, moderate behaviors). What was most important was the predictable, stable and responsive care, whereas the structure of the relationship was less important.

I have had the same experience with imposed 50-50 arrangements by the courts, when they forced uncooperative parents to work together. These plans were very unstable and often one parent or the other would return to court to request primary physical custody. Such imposed plans seemed to increase the level of conflict, rather than decrease it. Of course, such plans are common in voluntary mediation – by agreement.

Should I request a Parallel Parenting Plan?

On the other hand, the concept of parallel parenting has become a very useful mechanism to help keep parents away from each other while each still had contact with the children. A successful case with this arrangement was described in Chapter 8.

For example, research shows that in domestic violence cases the courts traditionally have given substantial time to the perpetrator of the violence, regardless of the violence. It is not clear why this is, except that the courts may either not believe in the allegations of violence or they believe that they are true but not serious enough to restrict contact for that parent with the children. This is one of those highly controversial areas of family law and a huge amount of time is spent arguing about it.

Instead, parallel parenting is a solution for the victim parent, so that there is no forced contact with the perpetrator of the violence. Under a parallel parenting plan, each parent's time with the children is to be uninterrupted by contact with the other parent (no phone calls, no joint decisions to be made, and so forth).

A parallel parenting plan could be any amount of time for each parent. While it may not be a 50-50 schedule, I have still seen many parallel parenting cases with substantial parenting time for both parents (60-40, 70-30). Since the courts often struggle with sorting out the type and severity of domestic violence allegations, parallel parenting may be a moderate approach that can last throughout childhood without constant returns to court.

Rather than requesting a rigid 50-50, it may be appropriate in some domestic violence cases and alienation cases to request substantial time with each parent in a parallel plan (which could be 70-30 or 60-40), so long as the children are protected from risk of ongoing abuse. In some types of domestic violence cases, there is little risk of violence after the parents have separated. In others, the risk remains high, especially when the perpetrator has a violent "power and control" type of high-conflict personality which may become focused on the child.

Under a parallel parenting plan,
each parent's time with the children
is to be uninterrupted by contact
with the other parent.

In some cases with parallel parenting, the courts do not allow flexibility within the plan, so that changes are not constantly being made. For this reason, it may be the most stable plan in cases with allegations of domestic violence, child abuse or child alienation. Otherwise, families with these allegations are subject to a lot of manipulation by an HCP parent seeking constant change and control, whether a perpetrator of domestic violence, child abuse or child alienation.

In my mind, this inflexible schedule is not all-or-nothing thinking, but rather a way to manage emotions and keep behaviors moderate by reducing the opportunities for conflict. It is a way to set limits on the HCP's often extremely manipulative and demanding behavior. This also helps the child develop a sense of stability, which will increase the chances of having a more secure attachment with each of the parents.

Seeking Orders for Counseling

Most researchers into child alienation say that counseling is really what is needed, and I agree. In reality, from my experience, it matters less which parent has "custody" than that the parents get help in changing the parenting behavior of one or both parents. Counseling and improved parenting will contribute much more toward building a child's Foundation of Resilience in the long run, than fighting over time (as long as both have significant time, such as at least 30%). There are several possible types of counseling orders which lawyers can and should pursue. These will be the focus of the next chapter about how counselors can help.

A Lawyer for the Child

In some states, including California, the judge can appoint a lawyer for the child. This lawyer (known as a Guardian ad Litem or Minor's Counsel) is supposed to represent the child's expressed interests or best interests or both, depending on the state's laws. As many people know, "expressed interests" by a child and the child's "best interests" can be two very different things in alienation cases.

Alienated children usually show all-or-nothing thinking to their lawyer about the rejected parent. They usually ask their lawyer to use their legal influence to eliminate the rejected parent from their lives. They are seeking a Negative Advocate, just as their favored parent has sought Negative Advocates, including the child. Since this is all contagious, it can also spread to the lawyer for the child. Therefore, Guardians ad Litem (GALs) and Minor's Counsel must be careful to manage this relationship with their eyes wide open about what the child says.

In general, this lawyer should also take a resilient approach, demonstrating flexible thinking, managed emotions and moderate behaviors. This means that the lawyer must connect with the child and redirect the child to learning and strengthening healthy skills.

Finding this balance with an angry or fearful child is not for the faint of heart. Yet many do this extremely well. They help the child and the parents reach realistic resolutions which often help them stay out of court and avoid getting stuck in high-conflict behavior. The biggest problem is that one skilled lawyer cannot fix alienation or abuse alone. There needs to be a team approach to help the child and parents learn skills for resilience, rather than the alienating behaviors they have learned prior to the lawyer's appointment.

This often leads back to establishing a counseling process. Often Minor's Counsel or the GAL can convince the parents and child to have an individual child therapist. As you already know, I will address this in the next chapter. I believe that the issue of counseling must be addressed before the child's lawyer can make recommendations to the court or encourage agreements between the parents regarding living arrangements. In high-conflict cases, it matters less where the child resides primarily, so long as both parents have significant parenting. What they really need is to change their behavior enough to support the child in developing a Foundation of Resilience.

Conclusion

Whether a parent has a lawyer or represents himself or herself, you are encouraged to use flexible thinking and moderate behavior in the orders that you seek. Don't give up and just accept the child's apparent rejection. That teaches the child all-or-nothing thinking is normal and acceptable. This may become how they handle future relationships with their own spouses, children, co-workers and neighbors.

I have represented parents who were alienated from their own parents. They have had more difficulty maintaining a balanced and secure relationship with their own children – some of whom become alienated against them. This problem is contagious and can be passed from children to their children, unless there is some form of positive intervention.

On the other hand, avoid extreme solutions that include complete changes in the child's life, such as a radical change of custody before trying less severe measures. Likewise, a rigid 50-50 custody arrangement will often fail without the full support of both parents. Since alienation seems to be the result of many factors, simply having a 50-50 schedule will not change the emotions and negative behavior that spills over to the child. Even parents who have primary physical custody sometimes become the rejected parent. These emotions and behaviors need to be addressed in counseling, as I will discuss in the next chapter.

Lawyers can have a huge impact on a family at the time of a divorce. They can have a negative impact by escalating high-conflict behavior in the family court Culture of Blame (adding bricks to the Wall of Alienation), or they can have a positive impact in helping families by being flexible, managed and moderate in the solutions they seek (bricks for the Foundation of Resilience).

Since HCP parents tend to seek HCP lawyers (highly aggressive lawyers give them a false sense of security), it is usually up to the reasonable parent to find and work closely with a reasonable lawyer to successfully address these issues. You can add bricks to your child's Foundation based on your own behavior, regardless of the other parent.

I strongly recommend against self-representation when dealing with any abuse or alienation problems, unless you have consulted with a lawyer and he or she has said that you don't need one. Child abuse, domestic violence and child alienation are all very difficult issues. Judges tend to respect parents more who respect knowledge of the law and who seek professional help in matters as serious as raising their children.

Short Summary

Parents: Dealing with lawyers can be one of the most worrisome aspects of the divorce process, especially if the other parent is an HCP and you have children. However, the vast majority of family lawyers sincerely want to be helpful and they resolve the vast majority of their cases to the satisfaction of their clients. It helps to interview several lawyers to find the best one for you. Pay attention to see if they are the flexible, managed and moderate type – who will help add to your resilience and your child's Foundation of Resilience in their approach to your case. Representing yourself in a potentially high-conflict case can be risky and you are encouraged to at least consult with a lawyer for an hour or two. Resist the urge to seek a highly aggressive lawyer or one who pressures you to settle without explaining all your options.

Family and Friends: Resist the urge to tell your family member or friend to hire the most aggressive lawyer in town. This often plunges a divorce into a high-conflict court case, which increases the risk of alienation as the child absorbs the battle. You can help your family member or friend by encouraging them to seek a lawyer with an Assertive Approach, who is not too aggressive (unnecessarily escalating the case) or too passive (pressuring to settle at all costs). You can help research lawyers and possibly help with costs, but remember all the prior chapters and avoid playing too strong a role, including becoming a Negative Advocate.

Professionals: Lawyers can make a huge difference in keeping an alienation case calm so that it does not escalate and drive the child further away from a parent. Create a cooperative relationship with your client, as having an HCP parent on the other side can be very confusing and filled with rumors and accusations, which may or may not be true. Take abuse concerns seriously and encourage your client to respond with moderate behaviors and as much information as possible, rather than unmanaged emotions. Resist the urge to make extreme requests in court, such as changes of custody or strict 50-50, unless all other efforts have failed. Avoid giving in to a bad settlement if you have real concerns about abuse or alienation.

How Counselors Can Help

It was a high-conflict case, in and out of family court. By agreement of the parents, a psychologist was appointed to evaluate the family and make recommendations. He recommended that a lawyer be appointed for the children, two girls ages 7 and 9, and that a child therapist be appointed. The case moved slowly.

First, the lawyer for the children interviewed the girls (her clients) and eventually recommended that the parents have a 50-50 parenting schedule, rather than about 8 hours a week with the father under their current plan. There were no allegations of abuse, but the mother was concerned that the father, an addict in recovery, might abuse them someday. The children's lawyer said that the children's relationship was weakening with their father since the court case began, because he had so little parenting time.

Several months after the children's lawyer made her recommendation, the children's therapist was appointed, to help improve the girls' relationship with their father. After the first phone call between the children's lawyer and the children's therapist, the following letters were exchanged:

The children's lawyer: "Since my last visit with my clients, it is reported to me that they are having increased anxiety and negative responses to parenting time with their father. It is not clear to me what the source for those behaviors is, but I view this 'decompensation' as alarming and, at the same time, in need of modification. You stated in our conversation that you told the girls that you will try to persuade the parties not to 'force them to spend more time with their Father.' Whether that encouraged them to become more negative with their Father, I'm not sure. On the other hand, prior to your involvement, they were subjected to the stress of their parents and it appears to be continuing."

The children's therapist replied: "It is clear from your letter to me that you do not accurately recall much of what I said to you in our earlier conversation. I do not know whether you simply misunderstood or chose to misrepresent my comments, nor do I see the necessity for your employing a hostile and non-collegial tone in your writing. It is also of concern to me that you appear to be practicing beyond the scope of your license in rendering psychological diagnoses and prescribing treatment plans. These children are not decompensating. It is neither accurate nor appropriate for you to be using this term."

Sense a little tension here? The above "split" between professionals is not unusual in child alienation cases, as the all-or-nothing thinking of HCP parents is contagious and many professionals get emotionally "hooked" – especially in today's Culture of Blame.

This split also highlights several key issues or dilemmas in the alienation debate when it comes to counseling, which I will address in this chapter. I will make several recommendations to resolve these dilemmas with flexible thinking and moderate solutions – and I hope to manage my emotions in the process.

I have written this chapter primarily for counselors and other profession-als, as counseling has become the focus of resolving child alienation cases. However, parents, family and friends are encouraged to read this chapter to understand the issues and options available for addressing alienation. There are many very knowledgeable and helpful counselors who can assist with alienation and/or abuse issues.

On the other hand, the majority of counselors today are unfamiliar with alienation issues, personality disorders (and HCPs), and family court cases, so they can potentially make things worse. By understanding the issues contained in this chapter, you can interview counselors and determine their experience and orientation. Ideally, you will find a counselor who has experience with alienation issues and who can work collaboratively with other professionals to address this problem without splitting. Here are the current issues or dilemmas:

1. What's the goal of the counseling?

   Should it be reconciliation with the rejected parent, or just help-ing the children cope with the stress of their parents and the present arrangement?

2. Should children be "forced?"

   Should the children be forced to go to counseling with one of their parents, or should they move at their own pace, regardless of how slow or unmotivated?

3. Who should be involved in counseling?

   Should the child and the rejected parent each have their own in-dividual counselors? Should they ever meet together? Should the favored parent be involved in any counseling? Should the favored parent meet with the child? With the other parent?

4. Should the child counselor be involved in deciding the parenting schedule?

Should the counselor help the children to accept a 50-50 parenting plan, or should the counselor help the rejected parent accept the status quo of minimal or no contact?

5. Should counseling and court work together?

Should the court order a specific type of counseling with deadlines, specific goals and follow-up, or should the court leave these specifics up a therapist, Guardian ad litem or a Parenting Coordinator?

6. Should there be different approaches for mild, moderate and severe alienation? If so, what should they be?

7. How can we prevent professional splitting?

Should one of these professionals be put in charge of the other, should one get off the case, or is there another solution? Can they support each other?

Goals of Therapy

The goal of alienation counseling should be: ***To teach and practice skills for resilience and conflict resolution.*** The *way* that the issue of child alienation is addressed is more important than most of the decisions. Counselors must teach the parents specific skills that will help them make more reasonable decisions on a daily basis and must help parents teach their children these skills for their close relationships for a lifetime.

For much of the past 30 years, there have been two models with different goals of counseling for parenting conflicts in divorce, neither of which fits most alienation cases:

A. The "Getting Over It" model: In this approach, counselors provide supportive individual counseling to help parents and children get over the divorce and move on. The issue has been the divorce and getting over it and back to "normal." However, these counseling methods don't work well with the influx of high-conflict people into today's family courts, who often have personality disorders and have never had "normal" close relationship skills. They remain stuck in anger and/or grief for years after the separation. They need to start at a much more basic level of learning skills.

B. The Abuse model: In cases of physical abuse, sexual abuse or neglect, children have been powerless and victimized and need to very gradually resume contact with the abusive parent. Such children should be able to go at their own pace for this readjustment period, and feel safe before having substantial contact. However, in most alienation cases, the rejected parent has not been abusive. The problem is the all-or-nothing thinking and contagious emotions and behavior of the favored parent and others in the child's environment or Culture of Blame. This model is inappropriate for most alienation cases, because there is nothing for the rejected parent and child to "work through."

Instead, the whole family needs to learn and strengthen basic skills for future conflict resolution and close relationships. Such a goal focuses on the future, which everyone can influence, rather than the past – which just gets HCP parents stuck in blaming and defending. It takes the "split" out of counseling in high-conflict divorce cases. Learning skills is a positive goal that can help everyone, without having to have a winner and a loser, or having counseling as a punishment. This also provides all parents with a healthy role to play – namely teaching their children positive skills for a lifetime.

In the past, the emphasis in counseling in alienation cases has been on persuading children and parents to act reasonably. But they already think they are acting reasonably (because of their insecure attachments and all-or-nothing thinking) and such pressure to change just builds their resistance to change – it hasn't reduced it, no matter how skilled the counselor is. The structure of the counseling process has defeated its goals.

For example, in the case above, after two years of child counseling, things got worse instead of better. Joint sessions also failed between the father and each daughter. The mother was not involved in any of the counseling sessions and refused to participate when invited. The judge wanted to follow the counselor's advice on when the father's time would increase. But in two years, the counselor never recommended an increase in the father's time, as the counselor believed the children weren't ready for it – they remained too "uncomfortable" with him. The older daughter, age 14 by then, stopped seeing her father. The younger child continued to have about 8 hours per week of visitation and seemed to enjoy her relationship with her father. But she resisted any increase in parenting time, apparently for fear of rocking the boat with her mother.

Should Children be Forced?

The question of having a significant relationship with both parents should not be a counseling issue or goal. It must be a given – a non-negotiable subject. Since one of the parents and the alienated child are adamantly opposed to increasing the other parent's time with the child, such child counseling is like waiting for a child to improve her relationship with the dentist before going to his office to have needed dental surgery.

It helps to reframe this issue into one of expectations. Parents "expect" their children to go to school, to the dentist, to the grandparents, and expect their children not to use drugs, have sex, and have their bodies pierced. You usually don't think about the word "force" with these issues, because they are such basic assumptions. The issue of how to make this a non-negotiable issue will be addressed in the next chapter regarding the court's orders and involvement in these cases.

In cases where the rejected parent has been determined to have been abusive, then the child should have some influence over the pace of contact, just as in any case of abuse. However, from my experience, even abused children will have a relationship in their minds with both of their parents and its best to have this be a realistic relationship in real life – so long as contact with an abusive parent is supervised as needed.

Who Should Be Involved in Counseling?

This has been an area of great controversy. Most commonly, courts have ordered individual child counseling and individual therapists for one or both parents. Most therapists have tried to fix alienation this way. Few have been successful, as the problem exists at a "family systems" or family Culture of Blame level.

Instead, we need to recognize that families operate as a system or culture, which children absorb non-verbally and unconsciously. The whole culture surrounding the family – each parent, counselors, lawyers, family and friends – must support the learning of the three skills for resilience in order for the child to learn them. (Of course, it would certainly be easier if our society's larger culture supported these skills as well, rather than being the Culture of Blame it is today.)

By shifting the focus onto parents and children learning skills for resilience, rather than focusing on specific decisions, it reduces the resistance to counseling that will lead to positive changes. The whole family needs to be involved.

Individual Child Therapy Has Failed. Just doing individual therapy with an alienated child has consistently failed time and time again. It's like putting an alcoholic in individual therapy to stop drinking, while they still live in a Culture of Alcohol. Years ago, alcoholics and medical professionals learned that alcoholics must have a group program, learn small recovery skills in small steps, and be surrounded by other recovering alcoholics. With children, being in individual therapy really doesn't work, if the most powerful people in their lives (parents, grandparents, professionals) are not attempting to change any behavior – especially if they are still living in a family Culture of Blame.

When I give seminars to therapists, lawyers and judges, I often ask them if they know of any alienation case that has been resolved by an individual child counselor who didn't work with the family. No one out of hundreds of participants has said yes.

Parent-Child Interaction Therapy (PCIT) is a highly successful program for young children and their abusive parents (physical child abuse or neglect). It focuses on interactions between the parent and child, rather than putting them each in individual therapy. It's based on research that shows that counselors must work with the parent-child *relationship* for either of them to change their behavior. This program focuses on very specific skills, rather than discussions of past behavior and feelings about their relationship. These principles seem very applicable to alienation cases, which are a parent-child relationship problem with both parents and child in need of skills.

Individual Parent Therapy Doesn't Work Alone. As described in the Introduction to this book, individual therapists for each parent get quickly emotionally "hooked" into supporting their clients as is. Therapists have to form a "therapeutic alliance" with their clients, which makes it nearly impossible to disagree and redirect a client's attention to making important changes. However, individual therapy may work in conjunction with parent-child counseling, if there is enough structure as explained below.

If parents and children should be involved in counseling together, who should be involved? The rejected parent and child? The favored parent and child?

Traditionally, courts have assumed that alienation indicates that something is wrong between the rejected parent and the child. However, I rarely see that, except in cases of confirmed abuse. In most cases of child resistance I have had or read about, the rejected parent did not "cause" the alienation, although he or she may have reinforced it unintentionally. On the other hand, it makes sense to have the rejected parent and child meet together with a counselor, especially to clear up the child's distortions about that parent and his or her beliefs, as one part of the counseling – but not as the only counseling.

Joint rejected parent and child therapy helps. I have had several cases in which a child has been surprised to learn about the rejected parent's flexible opinions of the favored parent. The children usually believe that the rejected parent hates and blames the favored parent. Rejected parents with flexible thinking and managed emotions can clear up some of those misconceptions.

Joint favored parent and child therapy is essential. However, it also is essential that the favored parent participate in counseling with the child. Alienated children often get the message – mostly non-verbally and un-consciously – from their favored parents that they are not allowed to have a normal relationship with the other parent. Having a counselor work on this issue between favored parent and child may be a helpful step.

Structure is needed. The therapy needs to be very structured and focused on learning and practicing skills. Otherwise, in alienation cases, the ther-apy quickly deteriorates into one or both parents complaining about the other. Consequently, neither parent works on his or her own skills. HCP parents constantly avoid responsibility and want counselors to take their side in order to have a false sense of security. Non-HCP parents need skills for dealing with the HCP parents, rather than being allowed to just vent about them.

It takes a very strong and secure therapist to manage this work, and most programs dealing with personality disordered clients (such as Dialectical Behavior Therapy and Schema Therapy mentioned above) use writing ex-ercises and short lessons to give their work structure. Individual therapy can be part of this, if there are writing exercises to structure the learning of skills. However, such individual therapists should be part of a consultation group or other support system, as this work can be very stressful and it's easy to slip into feeling anger and frustration, especially with high-conflict clients.

I agree with Janet Johnston, who has been studying high-conflict families for over 20 years and who apparently coined the phrase "high-conflict families" over 20 years ago. She advocates for strong intervention including all family members. Johnston and co-authors (2009) say:

> We eschew a simplistic focus on single or primary causes of an alienated child and an adversarial stance that polarizes the family around faultfinding, assigning blame, and metering punishment (Bancroft & Silverman, 2002; Gardner, 1998, 1999)...
>
> Alienated children need a *family-focused intervention* that includes all parties, the child, siblings, both the aligned and rejected parents, as well as other family members (e.g. stepparents or grandparents) determined to be contributing to the dynamics. The goal is to coordinate co-parental functioning and to support each parent in providing the child with warmth, nurturance, and containment. In addition, the goal is to shift the child's (and parent's) distorted, rigidly held, polarized, and defensively split views of one parent as "all bad" and the other as "all good" into more realistic and measured ones, rooted in the child's actual experience of both parents. (p. 373)

Should Counselors Decide the Parenting Plan?

For the past 30 years, in California and several other states, counselors have been tapped by the courts to make parenting plan recommendations when parents have not been able to make these plans themselves. This makes sense, as counselors have more mental health training than judges, who usually just have legal training and experience as lawyers. If the parents cannot reach an agreement with a court counselor (also called a court mediator), then the counselor writes a recommendation. While the judge makes the final decision, he or she usually follows the counselor's recommendations, completely or with some modifications.

As a mediator at heart, I was initially uncomfortable with court counselors/ mediators writing recommendations. I prefer "pure" mediation, in which the parents make their own decisions and it's all confidential. However, as I worked more with cases with HCP parents, I realized that these recommendations are very helpful in helping HCPs become more realistic. Once the HCP parent recognizes what is likely to happen at court (sharing the children), they often avoid gearing up for a big battle to eliminate or severely restrict the other parent. If a parent has been abusive, then the reality of some restriction is more likely to be accepted in this private meeting with a counselor/mediator than in open court.

However, what I have just described is having a counselor serve in the role of a mediator or recommender, and not in the role of a true counselor doing counseling. So long as these roles are performed by different people, this can work fine. A counselor doing true counseling should not be recommending or deciding the parenting schedule. With HCP parents, a counselor who also makes decisions will be pressured to make favorable decisions, whether it's the HCP's own counselor or the child's counselor. This destroys the goal of the counseling – to assist with learning skills and developing more effective behaviors.

Unfortunately, many parents and judges ask counselors – especially individual child counselors – for their recommendations, and many counselors gladly provide them. In general, counseling for HCP parents should emphasize helping them learn skills to make decisions, rather than making the decisions for them. HCPs often want professionals to make their decisions for them, then blame them for making the wrong decisions. Counselors for HCPs and their children need to focus more on teaching skills and less on being experts who make wise decisions for them.

Ultimately, the parents should be assisted to make their own good decisions. If they are not able to, then the judge should make these decisions for them. Once decisions have been made, then counselors can help parents and children learn skills to implement the decision. If a court has ordered restricted parenting time, then counselors should assist parents and children in discussing their feelings and developing strategies for coping with this. If a court has ordered fairly equal shared parenting, then counselors should assist parents and children in discussing their feelings and developing strategies for coping with this.

Should Counseling and Court Work Together?

Counseling in high-conflict cases needs to be closely coordinated with the court. Currently, this rarely occurs. In most alienation cases, HCP parents are ordered into counseling at or near the end of a court case, with no specific goals after the big decisions have been made. HCP parents rarely follow through. Then at the next hearing, in a year or two, the judge expresses frustration, but there are no consequences.

In the most severe alienation cases, this pattern of non-compliance has become ingrained for years. Therefore, counseling should really have accountability with a subsequent court hearing or reporting to some authority figure, such as a Minor's Counsel or Parenting Coordinator. (See more about Parenting Coordinators in Chapter 12.)

Ideally, courts need to order counseling with specific goals to work on and specific deadlines for completing these goals or completing a certain number of counseling sessions or program sessions. In a sense, family courts need to adopt some of the procedures of Drug Courts or Mental Health Courts, where there are strict requirements which must be met upon return to court. When they are met, people are praised and when they are not met there can be severe penalties (fines or going to jail).

Family courts today have strict expectations for child support enforcement, with monthly requirements to fulfill. If HCP parents were held equally accountable for attending counseling and strengthening positive skills, I believe there would be a lot fewer cases of child alienation – and possibly child abuse.

Parents are most motivated at the beginning of the case. Ideally, with a focus on skills, counseling should be ordered as early as possible – *before* big decisions are made. Then, parents should return to court and explain their progress. Not only will this hold them accountable to attend counseling and work on skills, but judges will be better able to determine their ability to change and improve their parenting. In many cases, one parent works hard at improving their skills and the other parent makes minimal or no effort. This information is more useful to the court than hours of "he said, she said" hearings about what each parent did in the past.

Should there be different approaches based on severity of alienation?

The answer is Yes! However, all of the principles explained above still apply to all cases. There are four levels of alienation to consider. I won't try to define them, but rather suggest methods of handling them:

1. **Prevention:** There are many cases in which signs of alienating behavior are present and obvious early on, well before a child is resisting contact with either parent. When a parent requests restrictions on the other parent's contact with the child (such as no contact, supervised or limited time), there is a risk of alienation developing over time. There may or may not be domestic violence, child abuse, substance abuse or other harmful or risky behaviors, but the battle over these issues often triggers splitting by one or both parents. Rather than waiting to evaluate the case, the parents could be immediately required to participate in a short-term, skills-focused counseling process to "immunize" them against becoming a high-conflict case.

A new program that takes this approach is New Ways for Families™ which I developed for High Conflict Institute. This is currently being tried in the San Diego family courts. Each parent has six individual counseling sessions using a structured workbook with writing exercises focused on the three skills of *flexible thinking, managed emotions,* and *moderate behaviors.* Then, each parent has three parent-child counseling sessions to teach their children the same three skills. The parents never have to be together during this process, so that it can be ordered immediately at the start of a case, even in cases of domestic violence. Then, after these counseling sessions, the parents can return to court and be quizzed on what they learned. It puts the burden on the parents to learn and demonstrate skills before the case becomes a really high-conflict case.

Other approaches are to immediately assign parents to attend a parenting class, a co-parenting class or a parallel parenting class. Usually, each parent would attend a different class at a different time. Unfortunately, classes are often much less effective with HCP parents, as they need an individual counselor for more of an "attachment" to build skills upon. That's why I developed New Ways for Families as a counseling-based method, rather than as a parenting class.

The point with prevention is to do this at the *front-end* of potentially high-conflict cases, rather than waiting for the case to escalate and child alienation to take hold. It is much harder to reverse than to prevent by teaching skills for resilience at the start of a divorce. In a sense, the parents are being taught and encouraged to create a Culture of Learning Skills as they head into the divorce, rather than a Culture of Blame.

2. **Mild Alienation:** In these cases, children may have started resisting contact with a rejected parent, but are still continuing to spend time with that parent. The same approaches can be used as mentioned under Prevention above.

Parenting classes that specifically focus on high-conflict divorce can be particularly helpful here. There are many, often with names such as High-Conflict Intervention or High-Conflict Diversion. Classes for children can also help, with names such as Kids' Turn.

3. **Moderate Alienation:** Family Restructuring Therapy is a method used for several years specifically with high-conflict families by Stephen Carter and other psychologists in Edmonton, Alberta, Canada, who have trained others around the United States and Canada. It involves both parents and the child in concrete steps to resume regular contact with both parents. It is a very directive approach, Carter (2010) explains:

> Family Restructuring Therapy has two main branches. First is working with the parents to have them address parenting issues in a future focused approach where we strictly control the sessions and teach proper communication skills. The second branch is parent-child reunification therapy. In this approach we meet with the parents individually and the child(ren) individually to discuss the process and to ensure their cooperation. When we have the child and alienated parent together we help the child address concerns from their perspective. The "alienated" parent acknowledges that those issues are real from the child's perspective. Then we work towards the future to address how such things could not happen again and to build a plan for how things will be different. If needed, we have a parent-child session with the "alienating" parent who often pays lip service to wanting the child to reunite with the other parent where we have them tell the child we expect them to reconnect with the other parent. The process either works or at least provides excellent anecdotal information for the Court to use in making further decisions.

It is essential that the parent respond appropriately to the child and if they do not do so, the session is immediately terminated and the parent returns to working with their individual psychologist to learn how to behave constructively in the process. It is also expected that as progress is made, increased contact takes place between the parent and child, closely monitored by the psychologist.

For over a decade, Janet Johnston and her associates in the San Francisco Bay area have been using a family counseling intervention model that includes both parents and the child. Johnston (2010) and her colleagues describe their approach as follows:

> Our multiple goals of treatment, therefore, include remedying the child's developmental deficits, transforming the child's distorted "good/bad" views and polarized feelings towards both parents into more realistic ones; restoring appropriate co-parental, parenting roles in the family; and establishing the kind of parent-child contact that benefits the child and matches the parent's capabilities to provide.
>
> ....
>
> Our observations of visitation resistant children in therapy indicate that a range of outcomes for parent-child relationships can be anticipated through the late teen and young adult years. Generally, it is prudent to have modest expectations for change with about ½ achieving positive outcomes in terms of multiple goals of intervention (as listed above). Highly successful outcomes are achievable with a minority of families and are more likely with early intervention and preventive measures, before the child's stance and family dynamics becomes immutable and bogged down in litigation. Also, the prognosis is good when the aligned parent is appropriately

protective, the rejected parent is calm and patient in forming a bond with the child, and both actively encourage the child to separate/individuate from one parent and reunify with the other. (pp. 112-114)

4. **Severe Alienation:** This is the most controversial area. The key questions are: How much coercion should be used to protect a child from a highly disturbed favored parent (a severe HCP)? Should there be a change in custody? Should the HCP parent have no contact or very limited contact? Should the HCP parent be involved in the therapy that reconciles the child with the rejected parent? With the mixed success of counseling methods, even by very experienced therapists, more extreme measures are being tried for more severe cases. But are they extreme, if they help alienated children learn to be flexible, managed and moderate?

Family Bridges ("A Workshop for Troubled and Alienated Parent-Child Relationships™") is an intensive 4-day education and activity program for alienated children to reconnect with the rejected parent. It's designed to help children and parents adjust to a court order that places children with the rejected parent and restricts the favored parent's contact for a period of time to allow the child and the rejected parent to consolidate a better relationship. After the custody order is made, the rejected parent may use his or her authority to enroll the child in the program at various locations throughout the U.S. and Canada. Warshak (2010) describes what happens next:

> In more than one-third of the cases (9 children in 4 families), in which the workshop did not begin in the immediate aftermath of a custody trial, the children attended the workshop without strong resistance and without need for any special safeguards. In the 8 cases in which the workshop took place immediately following a custody trial, the court ordered that the children be brought to the courthouse and the judge

personally and authoritatively informed the children of the decision and affirmed that it was nonnegotiable. It is not uncommon for children to react by screaming, refusing to go, threatening to run away, sobbing hysterically, and, in one case, hyperventilating...

To minimize the risk of dangerous acting out, some judges have uniformed police officers and bailiffs in plain sight to emphasize the court's authority. Some judges make it clear to the children that the court expects them to work on repairing their damaged relationship with the rejected parent, that failure is not an option, that refusal to cooperate will not result in a custody award to the favored parent, and that the sooner the children heal their damaged relationship with the rejected parent, the sooner they will have contact with their favored parent....Repeatedly we have seen children (even those who had been out of contact with a parent for several years) back down from their threats and within 24 hours appear relieved, relaxed, communicative, and sometimes affectionate with the rejected parent. A case worker who observed the workshop said she would not have believed her client could change so rapidly if she had not seen it herself. (p. 61)

. . . .

In none of these seven cases did the transport professionals or the off-duty officer use any physical force or physical restraint nor has any child complained of mistreatment. The children reveal, usually the second or third day of the workshop, that when they learned of the court orders, they thought of running away, but the presence of the transport professionals helped them resist this impulse and they are glad they did. (p. 62)

By the conclusion of the workshop, 22 of 23 children, all of whom were severely alienated at the outset, and had prior failed experiences with counseling, had restored a positive relationship with the rejected parent as evidenced by the children's own statements, by the observations of the parent and workshop leaders, and by the observations of the aftercare specialist. (p. 67)

The families described above involved reunification with 7 rejected mothers and 5 rejected fathers. It appears to involve creating a culture of non-blame and learning, with a focus on the future not the past – rather than "deprogramming" as some press reports have stated.

Apparently, only four of the 22 children regressed to rejecting behavior after being with their favored parent again. They attributed this to having contact too early with that parent. One of my concerns was that this program did not take the favored parent into account. However, Richard Warshak indicates that he also had that concern and they now offer a parallel program for favored parents.

Joan Kelly (2010), who wrote about "child alienation" with Janet Johnston, as I mentioned in Chapter 3, has generally positive comments about the program:

Despite initial skepticism regarding aspects of the Family Bridges workshop, a careful reading of the detailed description provided by Warshak led this author to an overall favorable impression of the program.... [T]he daily structure and manner of presentation of the Family Bridges workshop were guided by well-established evidence-based instruction principles and incorporated multimedia learning, a positive learning environment, focused lessons addressing relevant concepts, and learning materials providing assistance with integration of materials.

....

....These materials focused on (a) how distortions in memory, perception, and thinking occur, the role of suggestibility and negative stereotype formation, and the ease with which this happens; (b) influences of authoritarian and authority figures on thinking and relationships; (c) the development of better critical thinking skills; (d) research on divorce and children, including how high-conflict in particular impacts children and the beneficial effects of the continued involvement of two parents for the majority of children; (e) materials and exercises organized around applications of the learning to their own situation; and (f) acquiring and practicing communication and conflict resolution skills.

...[T]he child learns that the goal is to "facilitate, repair, and strengthen" the ability to have a balanced and healthy relationship with *both* parents. (p. 83)

Peter Jaffe is a researcher who has worked extensively with mothers who are victims of domestic violence. His concern about the Family Bridges program is that it is too new to know the long-term results, while not rejecting its potential for some families.

Renewed debate on alienation has been sparked by recent innovations in court-ordered (or 'judicially suggested') short-term residential programs for alienated children and their parents. Warshak's (2010) article on the Family Bridges workshop has helped to demystify that intervention and clarify the purpose and nature of such psycho-educational programs, which may have promise for some families.

Given the recent cases and media attention, we are concerned that there may be an increase in the diagnosis of alienation and the promotion of intrusive interventions in cases where they are not warranted.

> There is the potential danger of a misdiagnosis leading to a change of custody, and the children placed at risk if the rejected parent is abusive or neglectful, inadequate, or a virtual stranger to the child. There is also a risk that important attachment relationships with the favored parent are disrupted or severed, resulting in traumatic separations and loss. (p. 138)

Jaffe expresses the overall consensus when he says: "We have to recognize that, the formal authority of the court should be used very early in the process to hold parents accountable for their behavior and prevent ingrained conflict patterns." (p. 139)

What surprises me is that there is not more disagreement about taking such a strong approach to severe alienation. It seems clear that most professionals now agree that alienation is a problem and that there are few solutions when it becomes severe.

Overcoming Barriers Family Camp ("A Program for High-Conflict Divorced Families Where a Child is Resisting Contact with a Parent") is another program which has addressed severe alienation. This program has been held once a year (a 3-day and a 5-day program) for the past two years. Ten families have been served so far, including referrals by court order. They involve both parents and the children, with a program that covers subject matter similar to the Family Bridges program. Some aspects of the program are described by Sullivan and colleagues (2010):

> ...The two psychologists met with the parents in highly structured meetings (sometimes modeling more child-focused, functional interactions for the parents), to agree to and carefully choreograph connections between the rejected parent and the child and attempt to address their polarized perspec-

tives about the child's response to their high-conflict in a more functional manner.

Sadly, many of the co-parents had not met in a supportive format such as these meetings for months or years. The only time they saw each other was when they both appeared in court. The work had varying degrees of success – some families were able to agree to a parenting plan (with parenting time for both parents) while others moved back into the court system for more litigation about their custody issues. (p. 124)

....

OBFC holds promise for helping those families on the continuum of alienation and/or estrangement, where questions of safety, poor parenting, and enmeshment exist, but where severe mental illness, acute and ongoing domestic violence, or substance abuse is not a factor. The camp provides a "holding environment" where both parents (the rejected parent who sought a court order) and the favored parent who resisted a court order) on exit interviews and follow-up view the camp as an overwhelmingly positive experience. (p. 130)

Both the Family Bridges and the Overcoming Barriers Family Camp programs hold promise for reuniting rejected parents while preserving a relationship with the favored parent. However, the over-riding and consistent message from all writers in the above journal articles is that early intervention is necessary.

Early intervention is why I developed the New Ways for Families program as a minimally intrusive parallel counseling approach for both parents as soon as one requests restricted parenting – which is usually when the defensiveness and related alienation begin. If this or other early intervention methods were used (as described under Prevention and Mild Alienation), severe alienation may become less prevalent and there may be less need for programs such as Family Bridges.

What's blocking early intervention in these cases? Could it be professionals arguing over abuse versus alienation – in a highly emotional context, which results in professional splitting?

How Can We Prevent Professional Splitting?

What gives me hope in studying the alienation issue is that so many professionals are moving in the same direction: Alienation is real. Abuse is real. We need to investigate quickly, then move into prevention of alienation – and further abuse. If all professionals can get on to the same page about alienation, we can move much more quickly to save families from high-conflict divorce and save children from losing one of their parents – while still protecting them from abuse and improving parent behavior.

Reasonable parents and professionals need to hold professionals account-able for splitting, such as occurred in the beginning of this chapter. Professionals need to become informed. One of the reasons I wrote this book for professionals, as well as parents, is that many professionals are not up to date on this issue and spend a lot of time arguing with each other – with intense personal hostility in some cases. It's time for that to stop. We know more now and we know that we can be part of the problem. Counselors know about counter-transference and how to avoid getting emotionally "hooked" – and how to get unhooked once we realize it.

Counselors have to realize that they cannot fix alienation on their own, and can educate lawyers and judges about family systems and the need to include the whole family in counseling, rather than looking for blame. When I became a lawyer, I realized that lawyers and judges really need the useful knowledge of counselors, and that counselors should speak up more about the damage that can be done by joining in the adversarial process.

It can be flattering to therapists to be the experts and make recommendations to the court. But counselors need to resist that role and speak up more for children and the harm that can come to them from the adversarial approach. I believe that lawyers and judges are more willing to listen than ever before. Counselors should be given the opportunity to do more counseling and less evaluating of parents – even HCP parents. Today's parents and children will be helped more by counselors using their training and experience to teach skills for resilience, to deal with resistance to positive change, and to show everyone empathy, respect and compassion in resolving these difficult issues.

Conclusion

Counseling is the key to confronting, reducing and preventing child alienation. It must include everyone in the child's family "system," including each parent and working on the child's relationship with each parent. Counseling should not be a place to negotiate whether a child has a relationship with one parent – that should be a given.

Counseling must start at the beginning of a potentially high-conflict case, because that's when splitting by the HCP parent or efforts to protect by the reasonable parent really escalate into a public fight. When there are sufficient concerns, there should be an assessment for domestic violence, child abuse, substance abuse or false allegations. However, skills-focused counseling can proceed even while an assessment is taking place. We already know what three basic skills HCP parents need and reasonable parents can benefit from using these same skills to help cope with the other parent.

With the right kind of counseling, which focuses on skills, the parents may be able to resolve the case themselves and avoid a high-conflict case all together. That is what will prevent or reduce alienation more than any repair work years later. Before a Wall of Alienation really begins to be built, counselors can help turn those bricks into a Foundation of Resilience instead.

Short Summary

Parents: This section was written primarily for counselors and other professionals. Parents may find it interesting or overwhelming. What is important to know is that a wide range of counseling methods are being developed and tried for addressing child alienation. They include: Prevention (parenting classes, children's classes, and parallel short-term counseling); Mild Alienation (similar methods); Moderate Alienation (more directive counseling involving both parents and children); and Severe Alienation (highly structured programs involving the child with one or both parents). All programs and researchers recommend early assessment if abuse issues are alleged and early counseling methods before alienation grows.

Family and Friends: Family and friends can encourage immediate counseling if a child resists contact with one of the parents. This is no longer a problem that can be ignored as a passing phase. If a parent is dealing with some degree of alienation already, then it is best to help that parent become informed about current options. There has been a lot of conflict among professionals in the past about how to deal with alienation, but now most professionals agree that abuse concerns should be investigated and that alienation issues should be addressed with both parents involved.

Professionals: It is very encouraging to see professionals moving in similar directions. Abuse concerns and alienation concerns do not have to be in conflict. There is general agreement that abuse concerns should be investigated immediately when raised, and that alienation issues should be addressed immediately when raised. It has become clear that separate counselors for parents and children don't work to resolve alienation issues. Instead, counselors or programs that involve the whole family are needed. Rejected parents and favored parents need to meet with the child in order to support each other and promote relationships with both. We know more than ever about what doesn't work and there are new options available in treating alienation. Counselors who work with abuse and alienation issues should be informed and experienced.

The Future of Family Courts

A judge in Canada decided that both parents had "overused" the family court system, so he barred them both from having any further hearings without court permission. The Globe and Mail reporter, Paul Waldie (2008), quoted the judge as saying:

> *"The parties have gorged on court resources as if the legal system were their private banquet table. It must not happen again.... Both sides have shown an inability to abide by court orders such that their access to this court should be restricted.... Some day, a wise person in a position of authority will realize that a court of law is not the best forum for deciding custody and access disputes, where principles of common sense masquerade as principles of law."*

The reporter further described the case:

The couple [was] married for one year and have an eight-year-old daughter. Under their divorce, the mother won custody and the father received extensive access. Their legal battle has centred mainly on terms of the access and it has dragged on for seven years, involving 12 different judges, a dozen lawyers, 25 court orders, 2,000 pages of court filings, three contempt motions and one suspended sentence.

At one point the mother, 32, was so paranoid about the father she pulled the girl out of a good school just because the father attended a meet-the-teacher day, according to court records. She also took the child to dozens of medical appointments in the hope of finding a doctor who would support her allegations of emotional abuse by her ex-spouse, court records show.

Last year, Judge Quinn convicted the mother of contempt for violating a court order at least 19 times. He said she showed "not a hint of remorse, only a redoubled intention to prove her conduct correct."

The judge said the father, 38, withheld child support and failed to make contributions to an education fund for the child, but still spent more than $200,000 fighting the case with a "scorched-earth" mentality. The father was so "hot-headed, stubborn and suspicious" that when Judge Quinn was considering punishment for the mother's contempt, the father pushed for a 30-day sentence.

"Had the father taken a more noble and forgiving approach, had he, for example, asked the court not to send the mother of his daughter to jail, I believe that his request would have shrunk the rift between both sides from a chasm to a crack, making possible a tolerable peace," said the judge, who issued a suspended sentence. "That day, all chance was squandered for the child ever to com-

fortably breathe the name of one of her parents in the presence of the other...." (p. A12)

The Judge's Dilemma

I have written this chapter primarily for judges and other court professionals. However, parents, family and friends can also benefit from knowing the issues and dilemmas judges face in today's family courts.

Most family court judges know about the above types of high-conflict cases and they are frustrated by them. For the past six years I have provided seminars and training to judges on dealing with HCPs. They are eager for tips about how to handle the above emotional issues with respect and efficiency, while doing their official job of making legal decisions. They have huge case loads and often a thankless job. Yet I have never met a group of more sincere and wise people, who care deeply about children and families.

This presents a dilemma to judges: How do you efficiently resolve issues for people, when *"the issue's not the issue?"* Up to now, many judges have used anger, shame, lectures, threats, setting strict limits, and so forth. On the other hand, many use patient listening, friendly comments, humor and words of encouragement. Most judges I have observed use some combination of both.

Some judges crack down hard on the apparently offending party:

For example, remember the judge in Chapter 5. He felt helpless to reconcile the 15-year-old daughter with her father, so he focused his anger on the mother:

"She is alienating the child against her father. She is behind this decision and if there was any way I could punish her for it, I would. But I have no legal authority to do so, so I am just going to leave her with my message – that I believe she is ruining her child's life."

Other judges try to appear balanced in their frustration, like the judge in Chapter 4:

"All I see before me are two pig-headed parents who don't care about their sons."

Unfortunately, none of this is effective in dealing with an HCP. In fact, such statements usually escalate the HCP parent. In the *"ruining her child's life"* comment, the mother was already extremely anxious. By criticizing her publically, her anxiety increased, which increased her fear and anger toward the father, which of course spilled over emotionally to her daughter, which may have strengthened her daughter's resolve to avoid the conflict – by avoiding her father.

In the *"pig-headed parents"* case, the father had a history of domestic violence against the mother and an intense drive to control their sons. The mother was a quiet woman who was very careful to do everything the court told her to do, including not discussing the case with her sons and not expressing frustration about the father in their presence. So when they were both criticized at court, it escalated the father – who became more demanding and controlling – and discouraged her. From her point of view, the judge had joined her abusive husband in criticizing her, once again.

Both approaches of reprimanding a parent are "wall" bricks, which can add to alienation. There is a high likelihood that the emotional absorption and reaction to them will be passed on the children by one or both parents, which will make their children more anxious, and more likely to split their parents into all-good and all-bad to resolve the conflict.

The judge in the opening example above was right. What are custody and access (visitation) disputes doing in court anyway? Court is an adversarial process and by its structure it promotes a Culture of Blame. While lawyers, judges and most ordinary citizens in the past were able to cope with this adversarial process, today's increasing population of high-conflict people cannot handle it. They lack the ability to contain their upset emotions and to restrain their extreme impulses during the process of litigation. In this chapter I will address a different role for the court with high-conflict families.

High-Conflict Cases are Different

Many judges agree that there needs to be a different role for the court in high-conflict cases. In arguing for more case management with high-conflict cases, the Honorable Justice Donna J. Martinson (2010) has stated:

> While professionals may not agree on the exact nature of alienation or on what the best responses should be, it is crystal clear that in alienation and other high-conflict cases the stakes for children are high. They can be seriously damaged. The longer the problem continues, the more harmful the situation can become and the more difficult it will be to resolve. Not only is harm caused by the alienating behavior and the conflict associated with it, but the court process itself may exacerbate the conflict, placing the children in the middle and affecting their lives on a daily basis in highly destructive ways. There are also long-term adverse consequences for children including but not limited to difficulty forming and maintaining healthy relationships, depression, suicide, substance abuse, antisocial behavior, enmeshment, and low self-esteem. (pp. 180-181)
>
> ....
>
> In alienation and other high-conflict cases, it is exceedingly difficult to achieve the goal of a just, timely and affordable decision on the merits. These cases involve a disproportionate number of people with personality disorders (which can involve lack of insight into the parent's own behavior, blaming the other parent, seeing oneself as victim, and a disregard for authority and the law), mental health issues, substance abuse

problems, and patterns of controlling behavior. These traits manifest themselves in the court process, in a number of concerning ways, at the instance of one or both parents, and at all three stages of the process [pre-resolution stage, resolution stage (trial) and enforcement stage]. (pp. 181-182)

....

"As a result, one or both of the parents is financially and emotionally drained. Not infrequently the more disturbed parent exhausts or frightens the other parent into a settlement that fails to meet the needs of the children. The children may be irreparably harmed by the litigation process or settlement. (p. 182)

....

Alienation cases are almost always high-conflict matrimonial cases. We need a system where we can stream out the high-conflict cases and deal with them immediately. (p. 185)

[Quoting *Epstein's and Madsen's This Week in Family Law*]

....

Case management by the same judge can be critically important in dealing with high-conflict cases. Mental illness or personality disorders are commonly a component of high-conflict cases. The illness or disorder is often not immediately apparent. Familiarity with the 'problem' litigant promotes an understanding (sometimes even a more sympathetic understanding!) of that litigant. (187)

[Quoting Justice David Aston of Ontario Superior Court of Justice.]

We need a system where we can stream out the high-conflict cases and deal with them immediately.

One Judge Per Case

To effectively help families help themselves, there needs to be one judge throughout the case who can truly manage the case and set limits on inappropriate behavior. When I started practicing law in 1993, one of my earliest cases involved allegations of child sexual abuse. Over the course of the case, we had nine hearings with seven different judges before it was resolved. A few years later, our court system went to an "independent calendar" system, in which a case was permanently assigned to one judge who ran his or her own calendar. It is hard now to imagine what it must be like without such a system.

More Structure and Accountability

The theme of this book has been that high-conflict parents often raise high-conflict children who learn to become alienated in their present and future close relationships. The way to avoid this tragic outcome is to have the children learn and practice three basic skills for resilience, rather than learning or reinforcing the skills of splitting – seeing people as all-good or all-bad. Family courts can help parents, children and society by focusing more on these skills and less on making parenting decisions for parents.

The role of the family court must be to provide more structure – placing more responsibility on parents for reasonable settlement (while protecting from abuse) – and requiring more accountability. It's much like raising a teenager. This requires a shift in how judges think about and relate to high-conflict parents, rather than any substantive change in laws or procedures – although some may be necessary in some jurisdictions.

It is important for judicial officers to restrain themselves from the urge to make all of the decisions for high-conflict families, in an effort to reduce the conflict. Without involving the parents in learning skills and increasing their ability to make some decisions, however minor they may be, making decisions for them will not reduce the conflict and will be a waste of time. Instead, judicial officers should take charge of such families by taking charge of the structure and accountability – not making most of their decisions. In this chapter, I describe how this may be done.

Structure for Learning Skills

How should high-conflict cases be handled differently by the judge? It's important to recognize that their problem is a lack of conflict-reducing skills – a lack of *flexible thinking, managed emotions,* and *moderate behaviors.* For whatever reason, high-conflict parents cannot stop themselves from self-harm and from harming their children. One or both parents is truly "out of control" – they can't control their all-or-nothing thinking, their unmanaged emotions and their extreme behavior. Alienation is just one symptom of their high-conflict personalities. More than having decisions made for them, they need to be required to learn and use these basic skills. The courts actually have the opportunity to help them get started, while still supervising them.

First, courts need to provide a structure for high-conflict parents. Right from the start of a potentially high-conflict case, judges should order parenting classes or short-term counseling that teaches them to work on these three basic conflict-reducing skills.

How does the judge know that it is a potentially high-conflict case? When one or both parents seek to restrict the other's parenting time. (That is how the author's New Ways for Families method is designed to begin.) This triggers a "parenting contest" which rapidly escalates both parents' defensiveness — which is passed on to the child.

Courts don't need to wait for an evaluation of abuse or even allegations of alienation to know that high-conflict behavior and alienation may be just around the corner. When the parenting contest begins is when alienation will begin to grow, as HCP parents engage in more and more splitting to "win" the parenting contest — whether the HCP parent is the initiator of the court's involvement or defending against allegations, or both — and the child begins to absorb one or both parent's high anxiety, stress and anger.

A request for restricted parenting means something is seriously wrong in the family. This should trigger three theories of the case in the judge's mind:

1. The "restricted" parent is an HCP and needs restrictions because of out-of-control behavior, such as domestic violence, child abuse or substance abuse

2. The parent requesting restrictions is an HCP with a personality disorder or traits and is distorting the other parent's reasonable behavior or

3. Both parents may be HCPs with serious problems

   In *all* of these cases, putting both parents into a parenting class or short-term counseling will benefit both of them and their children, and help head off a high-conflict case. We already know what skills they need.

Of course, the court should concurrently make temporary orders, such as temporary protective orders, temporary child support and temporary parenting plan. By making orders for boosting their conflict reducing skills, the court shifts the focus onto *both* parents to work on themselves, rather than just focusing on the accused. This helps avoid splitting, lowers HCP expectations of vindication or revenge, and sends the message that court is really not where they belong with their parenting issues.

Second, courts need to follow up with accountability at all future hearings. When the parents return to court, the judge should first quiz them on what they have learned in their parenting class or counseling, before considering any motions before the court. HCP parents won't use these skills, except by repetition and being constantly reminded by professionals. The court should make clear that it is their responsibility to be solving their parenting problems reasonably, and will only make decisions for them after all other reasonable methods have been exhausted. The court should be a very reluctant decision-maker in the area of parenting for high-conflict parents. Here's why:

Why Not Just Make the Decisions?

Most judges like making decisions and are very good at it. However, with high-conflict people, **the issue's not the issue!** As the case at the start of this chapter demonstrates, with HCPs the issue is their personality-based lack of conflict resolution skills and insecure relationships. They bring one issue after another to court for the judge to decide. Ironically, the better you are at making decisions for them, the more likely they are to depend on you for more in the future.

Yet the court never satisfies them – and cannot satisfy them. What they are really looking for is:

- **Vindication** – that he or she is the "good parent" and that the other parent is the "bad parent," for everyone to see, once and for all. Court is where vindication is officially bestowed in our society. (Particularly characteristic of Borderlines.)

- **Respect** – to make up for all the disrespect the person has received in his or her life. Court is where one can prove that he or she is a superior person and that the other parent is grossly inferior in every way. Being granted custody is the ultimate award. (Particularly characteristic of Narcissists.)

- **Revenge** – for abandoning the relationship, which may have been the most secure relationship the person ever had. Humiliation in the public process of Court is the most powerful weapon in today's society that is accessible to anyone. (Characteristic of Borderline, Narcissistic, and Antisocial HCPs.)

- **Protection from internal fears** – to help insecure people feel safe from their frequent and extreme fears. Court has the power to lock people up, keep them away, and teach them a lesson so they will stay away forever. In today's frightening world, the courts will protect you. (Characteristic of Paranoid HCPs.)

- **Dominance** – to put the other person in their place and dominate them again. Court is where one can regain control of someone who is beginning to act too independent. He or she can draw the person back into their life by serving papers requiring attendance at hearings, by serving subpoenas, by taking depositions, by delivering documents requiring responses, by demanding hundreds of personal documents, by seeing each other at court for hearing after hearing.(Characteristic of Antisocial and Borderline HCPs.)

- **Attention** – to finally be able to tell one's story to the person with all the power. To have one's "day in court." Court is where one is allowed to freely use all of the drama one can muster, including tears, anger, charm, vulnerability, witnesses and evidence on one's behalf to exclusively focus on blaming an "all bad" person. (Particularly characteristic of Histrionic HCPs, but all of the above.)

It is for these reasons that you don't want to create a dependency on you for making their decisions. You cannot get it right, because you are missing the point. The decisions they want are based on feelings – such as feeling vindicated, protected, dominating of the other party. Since legal decisions cannot meet such personality-based feelings, they will never be satisfied in court.

Strongly Promoting Settlement

Hopefully by now it is clear why I am promoting settlement efforts in cases of HCP parents – who lack settlement skills. This is a huge opportunity for family courts to help children by requiring their parents to learn conflict resolution skills and to practice them in their parenting and at court. This may only be at a very minimal level, but this must become an expectation of the court. When judges and other professionals make brilliant decisions for parents, it removes the motivation for them to learn to make any decisions themselves for their family. Therefore, judges should repeatedly quiz parents on what they have learned and how they have practiced their skills.

The more that judges send the message that settlement is the standard expectation, the more that parents will try to fulfill that expectation. Praising them for their successes means a lot to HCP parents, who are constantly looking for validation from the court. It's better to give validation for small successes in reaching agreement *with* the other parent, than for big "wins" *against* the other parent.

Treatments for personality disorders have been showing us that many HCP parents may be able to change, with sufficient structure, learning small skills in small steps, and enough encouragement. Therefore, courts should shift the burden to parents to acquire and practice their skills in making decisions about their children. Judges should resist the urge to just make the decision for them, as much as possible.

I remember one day when I was in court and heard the judge addressing an attorney, his client and a self-representing party. The judge told them to go into the hallway and try to settle their issue of the day.

10-15 minutes later, they came back into the courtroom without an agreement. The judge said that it was unlikely he would have time to address their matter after all that morning. They would have to come back in the afternoon. However, he suggested that they try one more time to settle their issue by negotiating in the hallway. It was obvious that the lawyer was really upset about this, as he apparently needed to be in another court that afternoon.

10-15 minutes later, they came back into the courtroom. When the judge had a moment during another lengthy hearing, the attorney announced to the judge that they had reached an agreement. The judge immediately stopped his present hearing and invited the lawyer and the parties to come forward and recite their agreement for the court record – to make it a binding agreement and court order.

The message of the morning in that courtroom was that serious negotiations will be expected of everyone, and that settlements will always take precedence over arguments in the judge's schedule. It was an ideal example of shifting the burden to the parties to resolve their dispute.

Resist the Urge to Fix It

Judges are great at making decisions. They are wise, well-educated, sincere, and like solving problems. Therefore, it's hard to get them to hold back and put the burden back on the parents to make decisions to the best of their ability. However, it is far better for the parents to struggle with using their flexible thinking in making proposals, to struggle with learning to use managed emotions, and to reflect openly on their extreme behaviors.

They may not be perfect and may make less sophisticated decisions than a judge. However, it will be better for peace in the family and better for the long-term impact on the children. Their parents should struggle with these responsibilities and develop their skills, rather than running to court to get a brilliant decision from the judge each time a problem arises.

When the judge decides – or a court mediator or other professional – HCP parents interpret it to their children something like this:

Mom: *"Well, the judge decided that your father cannot pick you up Friday until 6pm. The judge is concerned about how much time you have with him."*

Dad: *"The judge is keeping me from picking you up at school. He doesn't understand how unfair that is, so I am meeting with my lawyer to try to change that. Hopefully, pretty soon I can pick you up at your school."*

However, if the parents have to resolve that issue:

Mom: *"Well, your father and I agreed today that he can pick you up at 5pm at my house. It's not what I prefer, but it's what we agreed."*

Dad: *"Your mother and I agreed that I will pick you up at 5pm. She didn't want me to pick you up until 6pm, but we reached an agreement. So make sure you're ready to just come out of the house. I don't want us to argue around you."*

This is a small step. With time, each parent may become more able to drop the additional comments after their first sentence above. This may seem like such a minor issue, but high-conflict parents have difficulty making any agreements. Yet most of them can make decisions if professionals restrain themselves from doing it for them and require them to learn and practice skills for making decisions. If one parent is not an HCP, that parent can be a role model of making proposals and focusing on the future, not the past, in making decisions. It's important not to assume both are HCP parents.

Of course, decisions regarding protection may need to be made by the court. But as many decisions as possible should be made by the parents – much more than occurs today with high-conflict families. The "fight or flight" response of many courts and other professionals is to get angry and make the decisions for them. We have to resist that urge, so that the parents can practice skills that will benefit their children.

Having the parents make these decisions at the courthouse, with a mediator, or with a Parenting Coordinator (described below) may be necessary. And once the decisions are made, the court may require that the parents cannot keep changing them, so that one HCP parent is not constantly manipulating the other. The place to start is to require them to learn the skills and practice them in small steps – then hold them accountable.

What About Domestic Violence and Abuse?

In cases of domestic violence or child abuse, the same skills of flexible thinking, managed emotions and moderate behaviors apply. By requiring the parents to practice these conflict-reducing skills, you may help them reduce abusive behavior as well. We all know that most perpetrators of domestic violence or child abuse are going to have a future relationship with their children, so it will help to give them some tools to make it better – with restraining orders and other orders as needed.

Having the parents learn and practice these three skills will help the court in making its future decisions. When the parents come back to court, the judge should ask them what they have learned from their class or counseling. Their answers should help the judge see who is motivated to change and who is not. Then, the judge should ask them how they would deal with a hypothetical parenting problem in the future. This will help the court see how they are applying their skills – or not. The court can always wait and see if the parents are able to make improvements, then order assessments for those who appear unable to do so.

What About Child Statements and Behavior?

High-conflict cases usually include allegations of child abuse, domestic violence, substance abuse, false allegations and child alienation. While judicial officers are encouraged to order skills training, they will still need to address the allegations. It is important to acknowledge that a parent "might be right" when he or she says that the child has been abused. There must be no presumption that there isn't abuse. It must be investigated somehow.

On the other hand, there should be no presumption that there is abuse, either. It's important for parents to know that their concerns are taken seriously, but that many aspects of children's behavior are not automatic signs of abuse or intentional alienation, such as statements or behavior.

Children can be accurate reporters of events that happen to them. But, as a therapist, I also learned that children can be influenced by their parents, especially in families with abuse or alienation. Children say what helps them survive.

A recent tragic case when a child's statements should not have been believed was Charlenni Ferreira. She died in 2009, after allegedly receiving numerous blows to her head by her father or stepmother. Apparently she suffered numerous severe injuries and broken bones over several years that were not discovered until she died.

A school nurse lodged a child abuse report in 2006 and she was seen several times by various professionals. She walked with a limp, but Charlenni convinced them that she was treated by her parents "like a princess." Her case was closed in 2007. She regularly attended school until her death.

In divorce cases, many courts seriously consider the child's expressed wishes regarding where they live. In general, courts do not want to have children exposed to this type of decision-making. Yet when a child insists he or she does not what to live with a parent, it bears investigation. The following example shows a child's responses to questions by a judge. This is rare, as most courts do not interview children, but may have a counselor or lawyer do this.

Q: Tell me what you think about if you stayed at your dad's more than at your mom's to, kind of, even out that you used to stay with your mom more?"

A: Well, I think that my mom might get mad instead of my dad because then my mom would never – I would get to see him more, and I won't get to see my mom – I mean, I will get to see my mom less, and I really want to see my mom more than I want to see my dad.

Q: Okay. Have you told anybody that before? Did you tell Dr. Wilson that you wanted to see your mom more than you wanted to see your dad?

A: No, sir.

Q: Okay. When did you decide that?

A: I decided it when I was talking to the counselor, but I never did tell him that.

Q: Okay. All right. Now, if I said that your mom wouldn't get mad if you spent more time at your dad's, how would you feel about it?

A: I think that would be kind of okay.

Q: Okay. So I don't want to – I don't want to tell you what to say. But what I'm trying to find out is: Your concern about living with your dad is you wouldn't be happy or you're afraid your mom would be less happy?

A: My mom would be less happy.

In this case, the judge made the unusual decision to give custody of the totally alienated older daughter to the mother and custody of the partially alienated daughter to the father.

> As a general rule, this court disapproves of custody determinations in which siblings are separated. If the trial court identifies a compelling reason for the separation, however, then such a decision may be justified.

> In the present case, the trial court's finding that the present alienation between the father and the older daughter was irremediable at this time was well supported by the record. There was also evidence to support the trial court's finding that the mother had attempted to negatively influence the younger daughter's relationship with the father. It is clear from the record that the parents are incapable of cooperating in a joint-custody situation. The trial court's finding and the record demonstrate that the trial court believed that the positive good that would result from a change of custody of the younger daughter would offset any disruptive effect that might be caused by the change in custody. The trial court had a compelling reason for separating the daughters because of the older daughter's current inability to get along with the father and the mother's negative influence on the younger daughter in regard to the father.

M.W.W. v. B.W. (2004) Ct of Civ App of Alabama, 900 So. 2d 1230, 1235-1236.

Likewise, children's behavior is not always an accurate indicator of abuse or alienation. There should be no presumptions. For example, if a child runs away from a parent to the other parent, it may be a sign of abuse but it may be a sign of alienation. I have personally seen that type of behavior more often in alienation cases than in abuse cases.

The court can take a moderate approach to the family, while ordering some form of investigation. Most cases do not need extreme changes in each parent's contact with the children at the start of the case while investigations proceed, such as significantly reducing one parent's time or requiring no contact. Taking this moderate approach can be especially appropriate in cases where there has been no input from the child's school or other parts of his or her life indicating serious problems.

It's often these extreme temporary custody orders that tip the family into a parenting contest that seriously escalates defensiveness and ultimately alienation. One option is to order short-term parent-child counseling with each parent, to have the counselor observe the relationship of the child with each parent – the alleged abuser and the alleged protector.

For example, our New Ways for Families program includes the option of having the parent-child counselor testify in court about his or her observations of both parents as soon as six or eight weeks into a case. Since the counselor does not serve as an expert, there is no evaluation or recommendation. This reduces the likelihood of heating up the case as much. The counselor can indicate to the court if there is an apparent need for further evaluation – or not. At the same time, this counselor can be assisting the parents in working with their children. Of course, either parent could block this counselor from testifying by refusing to sign a release of the counselor's confidentiality. However, this in itself would be revealing to the court for making future decisions.

Eliminating the Parent Contest

The key to managing high-conflict cases is to eliminate the parent contest, in which each parent attacks the other and defends himself or herself, and gets stuck in all-or-nothing thinking. If there are parenting behavior concerns, then they should be addressed as *problems to solve*, rather than *competitions to win*. The point is to avoid making it a contest between the parents – to avoid the dangers of splitting and the children absorbing a battle, which will affect their future relationships.

Instead, the court should expect each parent to compete with himself or herself. If a parent has engaged in abusive behavior, then the court can say:

> *"While you are working on your issues, the other parent is going to have most of the parenting time. But this will be temporary, if you can demonstrate improvement to the court. For now, the other parent will fill in for* **your parenting time**. *This is not a contest with the other parent. It's an expectation by the court that you will succeed and that I will be able to have you spend* **your parenting time** *with your child yourself in the future. I hope that is the case at our next hearing."*

Such an approach eliminates the contest and any sense of victory for one parent. Instead, it is more like a helping hand while one parent works on himself or herself. It's important to give high-conflict people hope.

With such an approach, the court and professionals can keep the focus on future behavior, while ordering the appropriate treatment. *"Yes, there was an abusive incident. Now, let's see if you can learn to manage your own emotions better so that your behavior never reaches that point again."*

Ironically, many HCP parents don't want the other parent to change and improve their behavior and their relationship with the children. They just want to eliminate the other parent – a splitting approach. This may become obvious as courts and professionals emphasize learning skills over making extreme decisions.

3 Key Questions

The court can reinforce this accountability at any time by asking each parent to tell the judge:

- Three positive traits or skills of the other parent
  (to avoid all-or-nothing thinking)

- Three ways that the parent is protecting their children from their upset emotions during the divorce (to avoid contagious unmanaged emotions)

- Three behaviors they are using to avoid conflict with the other parent (so they are consciously avoiding extreme behaviors, rather than being impulsive)

Such questions of the parents provide a pro-active way of preventing bad behavior, rather than trying to correct it afterwards. Most HCP parents want to succeed, but have a hard time controlling themselves. These questions substantially shift the focus to future behavior, rather than past disputed behavior. This may reduce defensiveness, which is a barrier to positive behavior change, and should help protect the children from the conflict.

If you are going to ask the parents the above questions, it helps for them to know about it in advance and to think about it and prepare their answers. This preparation reinforces the importance of being accountable in this fashion.

One possibility is to give all parents notice that these three questions will be asked at their first court hearing. If the parents know these questions are coming, it will put their other requests into perspective and their answers may help the court know a little about their thinking. The more reasonable their answers, the less likely they are to be high-conflict parents. Of course, this should not be the only factor to consider, as some HCPs can be very smooth and convincing at the start.

Equal Empathy, Attention and Respect

Parents and professionals are used to court being a place for shame and blame. Lawyers shame and blame parents, and judges shame and blame parents (and sometimes lawyers). HCPs need the reverse. They are much more responsive to validation and empathy.

At one court hearing, the court denied my client's motion for a reduction in child support. Then the judge said: "I can understand that it must feel like you are the only one hitched up to the plow and pulling." When we left the courtroom, I asked how he felt about that decision (with which I disagreed). He didn't like the decision, but he said: "The judge understands what it feels like to be in my shoes. I don't need to fight his decision." And that was the end of it. Over the years, we settled whatever issues arose and never went back to court.

High-conflict parents are looking for empathy, attention and respect from the court and legal professionals, because they aren't getting these from the people around them — because of their own self-defeating behavior. The average person just seeks legal decisions and usually can settle their case once they know the law. HCPs want more, and they don't even realize this.

This empathy, attention and respect must be provided very equally. HCP parents are very sensitive to being compared and losing. Since their issues are really personality-based, the importance of being interpersonally equal must not be lost in decision-making. The most effective judicial officers I have seen remain calm and are very equal in their eye contact, tone of voice, and comments to each parent, even while making decisions that strongly favor one side or the other. For example:

Ma'am, you might be right that the father has been abusive with the children and that is why I am giving you this temporary protective order. Sir, you might be right that the mother is misrepresenting events or that they are totally not true. I will need more information at the next hearing to help me understand what is really going on.

However, you should both know that when you ask me, a stranger, to make your decisions for you, one or both of you may be disappointed. Therefore, I encourage you to reach your own agreements as much as possible. I am also going to order you to participate in a short conflict resolution skills program before our next hearing. I am ordering you both to take this without any assumptions about either one of you, as you both will need to use these skills in the future regardless of what has happened in the past.

You will benefit in learning new ways to deal with the other parent. If the other parent is a difficult person, that is all the more reason to learn and practice these skills. Your children will benefit from both of you taking this program.

Controlling the High-Conflict Emotions of Court

Regardless of the issues, judges may consider imposing the following seven steps at hearings to reduce the emotional intensity and risk of adding bricks to the Wall of Alienation for a child.

1. That all presentations must include positive information about the other parent, if negative information is going to be presented. (To avoid all-or-nothing thinking.)

2. That all presentations must include more than one proposal or solution to the problem. (To focus on the future and avoid all-or-nothing thinking.)

3. That each parent must explain their efforts to solve the problem before using the court process. (To avoid reinforcing using the court to solve parenting problems.)

4. Inform the parties that statements should not emotionally compare one parent to the other as a better person. (To reduce splitting.)

5. That no physical gestures, such as finger-pointing, raised voices, puffed up anger, and dramatic accusations will be allowed. (To avoid emotional contagion.)

6. All presentations must be matter-of-fact, with information presented in as neutral terms as possible when describing concerning behavior, including abuse. (To avoid emotional contagion.)

7. Before the court hears evidence about the other parent's negative behavior, the court should require that each parent must describe examples of their own parenting behavior problems and efforts to change. Or each parent should be quizzed on hypothetical parenting examples in which they can describe how they will use *flexible thinking, managed emotions,* and *moderate behaviors.*

All of this puts the burden on the parents to focus on improving their own behavior more than focusing on the other party. HCP parents seek to avoid responsibility and place it on the court's shoulders – then complain or appeal when the judge doesn't "get it right."

It is unfortunate that such civil behavior must be spelled out, but we are all learning that high-conflict parents – and some high-conflict professionals – lack the ability to stop themselves. Therefore, it will take the court and reasonable professionals to stop them from their destructive behavior. It will take more than a reprimand or angry feedback from the bench.

The problem is that HCPs lack self-awareness and lack behavior change. Trying to "make them see" the inappropriateness of their own behavior will fail. Instead, they need much more structure for how they speak in court and much more intervention from the court when they misbehave. We have learned, the hard way, that HCPs need lots of structure – to keep them out of trouble. Matter-of-factly stopping inappropriate behavior and requiring positive behavior, like that described above, may be more constructive.

HCPs also respond better to positive feedback and encouragement, than to criticism and efforts to shame them into good behavior. In a sense, the court holds the power to provide elements of a "secure relationship," by being consistent, being predictable, not over-reacting to their upset emotions, focusing them on the next task and encouraging them on their way.

Hearing Children's Input

Over the past decade there has been an increase in interest in having children's input in the divorce process. I agree that children should have some way to participate in the process, but I strongly disagree that professionals should put children in any type of decision-making role. For all the reasons explained above, the parents should be in that role instead.

For example, the research by Jennifer McIntosh in Australia shows that Child-Inclusive Mediation is more successful than Child-Focused Mediation in high-conflict parenting disputes. The difference is that the Child-Inclusive approach has a professional meet with the children and then meet with the parents to share the children's concerns about the divorce. Then the parents use that information in making longer-lasting and more satisfying decisions.

It may be tempting to have the judge meet with the children, as a short cut. However, this reduces the expectation that parents must work hard at making the good decisions and considering their children's concerns. Giving the children direct access to the judge, while the parents do not have comparable access, turns the potential power structure of the family upside down.

It must be further understood that children in high-conflict families are like prisoners in a war zone. They will say and do whatever they think is necessary to survive. Children say everything is fine, when it really isn't. And they say everything is awful with a parent who they feel secure with, in order to placate a parent with whom they feel insecure. If professionals don't realize this, they will make matters much worse, rather than better.

The best approach is to help the parents hear their children's concerns, then to help them work on ways to make reasonable decisions based on those concerns. The judge should make those decisions only as a very last resort.

Parenting Coordinators

One of the ultimate solutions to removing high-conflict families from the family court Culture of Blame, is to mostly remove the case from family court after the big decisions are made. Since high-conflict parents often return to court many times after the divorce is over, Parenting Coordinators are a valuable alternative for parents who still cannot make their own decisions. By ordering or encouraging the parents to stipulate to a Parenting Coordinator, they will have someone they can go to with petty complaints without incurring the cost of court and without the court having to deal with such petty matters.

Parenting Coordinators are usually trained mental health professionals or lawyers who have some degree of authority to resolve minor disputes between the parents. They can hear the parents on short notice and make decisions for them on short notice with little expense. Depending on the jurisdiction, Parenting Coordinators' decisions are enforceable or are considered recommendations which the parents can challenge at court if they feel strongly enough about the decision.

Parenting Coordinators can also recommend or order further counseling, parenting classes and/or skills-building programs, to help them strengthen their own conflict resolution skills and parenting skills. Remember, with high-conflict parents, "the issue's not the issue." If they are primarily seeking validation, revenge, dominance, and so forth, they should do it outside of court as much as possible.

Information about Parenting Coordinators can be found at the website of the Association of Family and Conciliation Courts at www.afccnet.org.

Ideally, someday, parenting decisions will be made entirely out of court. The only parenting issue to be decided in the courts will be criminal behavior related to parenting, which should be decided in criminal courts. The remainder of the issues in family courts should be about property, support and related issues. Most of those decisions don't require seven years of hearings for a one-year marriage, like the case at the start of this chapter.

Reducing Stress on Children

In Chapter 6, I explained some of the recent brain research on the effects of stress on children's brain development. Scientists have learned that prolonged stress can trigger the release of excessive cortisol in the brain and body. This can cause damage to children's brain development over time, especially the corpus callosum which helps their right and left brains work smoothly together to manage problem-solving, even while being upset. We also know that prolonged stress often occurs in high-conflict divorce cases, especially those that spend a lot of time in the family court Culture of Blame. In other words, prolonged conflict between a child's parents may be as serious as child abuse.

Martin Teicher (2002), the brain researcher, suggests that this can have long-term effects on the future of our culture, as follows:

> Society reaps what it sows in the way it nurtures its children. Stress sculpts the brain to exhibit various antisocial, though adaptive, behaviors. Whether it comes in the form of physical, emotional or sexual trauma or through exposure to warfare, famine or pestilence, stress can set off a ripple of hormonal changes that permanently wire a child's brain to cope with a malevolent world. Through this chain of events, violence and abuse pass from generation to generation as well as from one society to the next. Our stark conclusion is that we see the need to do much more to ensure that child abuse does not happen in the first place, because once these key brain alternations occur, there may be no going back. (p. 75)

Unfortunately, we live in a society that is increasingly becoming focused on blaming individuals for complex problems. The adversarial court process of deciding who to blame for a child's behavior is harmful – not only because it's often inaccurate, but because pitting parents against each other harms children in the long run. The goal of determining who is the better parent has become the problem.

We also have to recognize the harmful exposure of children to our larger Culture of Blame. Children today witness more acts of violence on television and in video games than most children in true war zones. We have to realize that the sights and sounds of people committing violence, yelling at each other, and making disdainful remarks can all trigger stress in children. These images and sounds will also be mirrored in children's brains and some will be acted out sooner or later.

Conclusion

To every extent possible, we need to reduce the stress on parents and children in our courts and our society. We need to admit that child abuse is real and that child alienation is real, and that we need to work together at addressing these issues. We need to admit that our family courts often have a Culture of Blame, which can be just as abusive to parents as they are to their children.

The court (the judge) is in a good position to prevent child alienation from the start or to reduce it by mandating efforts for positive change – from ordering parenting programs and classes, to setting limits on emotional attacks during the hearing process. However, if the court does not set standards and impose limits, high-conflict parents will continue to escalate their inappropriate behavior and to impose their inappropriate needs on the children – which leads to alienation.

The judge sets the tone in the case from the very first court hearing – often an emergency hearing in potentially high-conflict cases. Judges who apply the principles described above should feel a much better sense of control over their courtrooms and less stress, as their clients are doing more of the work.

Raising resilient children – while avoiding high-conflict divorce – takes a team effort, including the actions of reasonable parents and all reasonable professionals. By learning and practicing the same three basic skills, parents can be supportive of each other and can be supportive of their children's skill development for a happy and productive future.

If you are a parent facing a divorce, the choice to build a Wall of Alienation or a Foundation of Resilience for your child is yours. The choice to build a Culture of Blame or a Culture of Learning Skills is all of ours.

Best wishes!

Short Summary

Parents: Family court should be the last place for parenting decisions. The adversarial structure of family court creates a "parenting contest" that no one truly "wins." And judges do not have the ability to see what actually occurred in a family's home. Therefore, if parents are unable to agree on making parenting decisions, it is much better to get assistance from professionals (mediators, lawyers, counselors) and training in conflict-reducing skills, than to bring these matters to court. Reasonable parents will want the other parent to get help in improving their skills. A court decision alone rarely changes an HCP's behavior. Even orders for protection usually expire someday, so that any skills learned may help in the future. Courts of the future will expect parents to work harder at settling their parenting issues. Criminal abuse will be the main exception.

Family and Friends: Family and friends can make a big difference in whether a loved one goes to court or makes serious efforts to settle their case out of court. Reasonable parents are often disappointed by the experience of family court, because it is not a truly reasonable process – it often is a very emotional process. The adversarial process of court and the right to seek modification of parenting orders creates an endless opportunity for attack and defend hearings, which spill over onto the children. Encourage your loved one to choose his or her battles and to use out-of-court resources as much as possible. Help your loved one separate emotional issues from legal issues. Consultation with experienced professionals will help determine whether or not to go to court.

Professionals: High-conflict parents are different from most parents in the past in family court – and they appear to be increasing. Some families have one HCP parent and others have two. HCPs have personality-based problems of all-or-nothing thinking, unmanaged emotions, and extreme behaviors. For this reason they are unable to make healthy parenting decisions and often have behavior problems, such as domestic violence, child abuse, substance abuse, false allegations and alienation of their children. They come to court seeking judges to resolve their personal/emotional problems, to which they are blind. Unfortunately, family courts try to solve these problems as though they were legal issues — and therefore fail, because the issue's not the issue. Their lack of conflict-reducing skills is the issue. Therefore, courts should emphasize providing a structure and accountability for learning the skills of flexible thinking, managed emotions, and moderate behavior, instead of making the decisions for them. While some court decisions will still have to be made to provide protection, this shift in emphasis should guide the future — so that both parents will become the best parents they can be and they can focus on helping their children build a Foundation of Resilience — rather than being endlessly engaged in an all-or-nothing parenting battle that will never end.

Before You Go To Family Court

MAKE SURE YOU HAVE REALISTIC EXPECTATIONS: In Family Court, the judge will never really know what is going on in your case. The family court's job is to decide narrow legal issues based on limited permissible evidence. Hearings are mostly short and to the point. In real life, Family Court is not like most court cases on television or the movies – or even the news. Trials are rare, as most cases are resolved by hearings and/or settlement by agreement of the parties – often with the help of knowledgeable attorneys.

DO NOT EXPECT VALIDATION OR VINDICATION: The judge does not decide your character as a person – or who has been "all good" or "all bad." In Family Court, it is assumed that both parties have contributed to the breakup of the family and that it is not a matter of "fault," but of "irreconcilable differences." Finding fault is against the principles of Family Court. Instead, family courts focus on problem-solving. If the court finds that someone has acted improperly, then the focus is on What Should Be Done Now – such as modifying parenting time, support, property division, issuing restraining orders, and in rare cases sanctions may be ordered. Rather than punishment and blame, the court prefers to order drug treatment, domestic violence programs, individual counseling, and parenting classes.

AVOID EMOTIONAL REASONING: When people are upset, our perceptions can be distorted temporarily or permanently. Our emotions may cause us to jump to conclusions, view things as "all or nothing," take innocent things personally, fill in "facts" that are not really true, unknowingly project our own behavior onto others, and unconsciously "split" people into absolute enemies and unrealistic allies. This happens at times to everyone, so check out your perceptions with others to make sure they have not been distorted by the emotional trauma of the divorce and related events. Many cases get stuck in court for years fighting over who was lying, when instead it was emotional reasoning which could have been avoided from the start.

PROVIDE THE COURT WITH USEFUL INFORMATION: The judge does not know your family or your issues, except for the information that is properly submitted to the court. Make sure to provide important information, even if it is embarrassing. The court cannot sense the behavior of each party. If you have an abusive spouse, the court needs sufficient information to make helpful decisions. If you hold back on important information, it may appear that abusive incidents never occurred and that you are exaggerating or making knowingly false statements. If you are accused of actions you did not take, the court will not know this information is inaccurate or false unless you sufficiently inform the court.

BE CAREFUL ABOUT UNVERIFIABLE INFORMATION: The accuracy of the information you provide to the court is very important. Based solely on what you say in declarations or testimony in court, the judge may make very serious orders regarding the other party, yourself, your children, and your finances. If it later turns out that you made false or reckless statements -- even if you were well-intentioned -- there may be negative consequences, such as sanctions (financial penalties), loss of parenting time or restricted contact with your children.

TRY TO SETTLE YOUR CASE OUT OF COURT: Today there are many alternatives to going to court which can be used at any time in your case, including Divorce Mediation, Collaborative Divorce, negotiated agreements with attorneys, and settlement conferences assisted by a temporary settlement judge. The expense for each of these is much less than for court hearings and prolonged disputes. You have nothing to lose, and you can still go to court afterwards if you do not reach a full agreement. By trying an out-of-court settlement, you can limit animosity and protect yourself and children from the tension of court battles for months or years.

Yes, No or I'll Think About It

Whether in a divorce, a workplace dispute, or a conflict with a neighbor, it's easy to get caught up in defending our own behavior and point of view. This is especially true when we are dealing with a high-conflict person (HCP). They quickly "push our buttons," and it's easy to react before we know it. They often seem driven to engage in negative conversations rather than trying to solve problems. The focus quickly becomes personal attacks and counter-attacks.

But you don't have to join in. Instead, you can use two simple steps that seem to help, no matter what setting you are in. If you think you are going to be dealing with an HCP, avoid getting hooked and feeding the conflict by reminding yourself of these two steps before you start talking. And if you are in the middle of an argument, you can always shift to this approach.

First, let's look at a couple of typical high-conflict arguments in divorce and workplace disputes:

DIVORCE:

Joe [responding to negative feedback]: "So what! Sometimes I have to work late on Fridays, so I'll be late for picking up the kids. You'll just have to live with it if you want me to keep my job. You don't give a s—t about how hard I work to pay you child support!"

Mary: "You are so insulting. I have half a mind to go back to court and just end your visitation. Wait 'til the judge sees all these rude emails you keep sending to me!"

WORKPLACE:

Steve: "You always talk loud in your cubicle next to mine. You are a rude and insensitive person. I don't know why you had to pick this cubicle. It was really pleasant in this office before you moved in!"

Sharon: "You know, you're an a—hole. I have to make a lot more calls than you do. How can you say such B.S. You know you're the busybody here. Nobody likes you. They've all told me, behind your back!"

Instead of getting caught up in these defensive and personal disputes, just focus on two steps:

1. At any point in the dispute, you can say "What do you propose?" Or you can just make a proposal.

2. In response to a proposal, you can simply say: "Yes" "No" or "I'll think about it." (If you can both agree to use this approach, you probably are not dealing with an HCP.)

1) First Person: MAKE A PROPOSAL

Whatever has happened before is less important than what to do now. Avoid trying to emphasize how bad the problem is. With a high-conflict person, this just triggers more defensiveness. Plus, people never agree on what happened in the past anyway. Picture a solution and propose it.

For example, in the DIVORCE dispute: "If you're going to be late to pick up the kids on Fridays, then I propose we just change the pickup time to a more realistic time. Instead of 5pm, let's make it 6:30pm."

Or in the WORKPLACE dispute: "I propose that we talk to our manager about finding a better cubicle for you, since you have so many phone calls that need to be made."

2) Second Person: YES, NO, or I'LL THINK ABOUT IT

All you have to do to respond to such a proposal is say: Yes, No, or I'll think about it. You always have the right to say: Yes, No, or I'll think about it. Of course, there are consequences to each choice, but you always have these three choices at least. Here's some examples of each:

YES: "Yes, I agree. Let's do that." And then stop! No need to save face, evaluate the other person's proposal, or give the other person some negative feedback. Just let it go. After all, hostile attacks are not about you. They are about the person making the hostile attack. You are better off to ignore everything else.

NO: "No, I don't want to change the pickup time. I'll try to make other arrangements to get there on time. Let's keep it as is." Just keep it simple. Avoid the urge to defend your decision or criticize the other person's idea. You said no. You're done. Let it drop.

I'LL THINK ABOUT IT: "I don't know about your proposal, but I'll think about it. I'll get back to you tomorrow about your idea. Right now I have to get back to work. Thanks for making a proposal." Once again, just stop the discussion there. Avoid the temptation to discuss it at length, or question the validity of the other person's point of view. It is what it is.

When you say "I'll think about it," you are respecting the other person. It calms people down to know you are taking them seriously enough to think about what they said. This doesn't mean you will agree. It just means you'll think about it.

MAKE A NEW PROPOSAL: After you think about it, you can always make a new proposal. Perhaps you'll think of a new approach that neither of you thought of before. Try it out. You can always propose anything. (But remember there are consequences to each proposal.) And you can always respond: Yes, no, or I'll think about it. (And there are consequences to each of those choices, too.)

AVOID MAKING IT PERSONAL: In the heat of the conflict, it's easy to react and criticize the other person's proposals—or even to criticize the other person personally, such as saying that he or she is arrogant, ignorant, crazy or evil. It's easy and natural to want to say: "You're so stupid it makes me sick." Or: "What are you, crazy?" "Your proposal is the worst idea I have ever heard." But if you want to end the dispute and move on, just ask for a proposal and respond "Yes" "No" or "I'll think about it."

Is Your Child Alienated?

IS YOUR CHILD REJECTING ONE PARENT? In divorce or separation, 10% - 15% of children express strong resistance to spending time with one of their parents – and this may be increasing in our society. It may be the father or mother. It may be the parent the child "visits," or the parent where the child lives. Is this the result of abuse by the "rejected" parent? Or is this the result of alienation by the "favored" parent? The idea that one parent can alienate a child against the other has been a big controversy in family courts over the past 20 years, with the conclusion that there are many possible causes for this resistance. Most courts take reports of alienation very seriously and want to know if this is the result of abuse or alienating behavior. Resistance to spending time with a parent is always a serious problem. This needs to be investigated, fully understood, and treated with counseling in many cases. Otherwise, the child's future relationships may be much more difficult.

IS THIS THE RESULT OF ABUSE? The first concern of the courts is protecting the children. If there are reports of child abuse as the cause of the child's alienated behavior, the judge may make a protective order restraining contact with the "rejected" parent, such as a temporary order for supervised visitation. If you are the "rejected" parent you may feel that supervised visitation is unnecessary or insulting. Yet this may be your biggest help, as someone neutral can observe the child's behavior and your relationship. Often the judge will say that he or she will not make any assumptions and wants more information before understanding the cause.

IS THIS THE RESULT OF "PARENTAL ALIENATION SYNDROME?" It is important to know that the courts across the country have not adopted the idea that there is such a syndrome. A syndrome requires a generally accepted cause and effect, and there are many possible causes of children's alienated behavior (abuse by a parent, alienating behavior by a parent, lack of emotional boundaries by a "rejected" parent, lack of emotional boundaries by a "favored" parent, developmental stage, outside influences, etc.). Also, despite alienating behavior by some parents, many children are not resistant to spending time with the other parent. So it is not accepted as a syndrome. However, the courts generally recognize that some children are alienated – they just don't know the reason automatically and often want more information.

WHAT ARE THE SIGNS OF AN ALIENATED CHILD? Children who are not abused, but are alienated have emotionally intense feelings but vague or minor reasons for them. A child might say: "I won't go to see my father!" Yet she might struggle to find a reason: "He doesn't help me with my homework." Or: "He dresses sloppy." Or: "He just makes me angry all the time." Another child might say: "I hate my mother!" Yet again the reasons are vague or superficial: "She's too controlling." "She doesn't understand me like my dad." These children complain that they are afraid of the other parent, yet their behavior shows just the opposite – they feel confident in blaming or rejecting that parent without any fear or remorse. Some of them speak negatively of the "rejected" parent to others, then relax when they are with the "rejected" parent. Others run away, rather than spend time with the rejected parent. All of these behaviors are generally different from those of truly abused children, who are often extra careful not to offend an abusive parent, are often hesitant to disclose abuse and often recant even though it's true.

WHY DO ALIENATED CHILDREN FEEL SO STRONGLY? Alienated children generally show intensely negative emotions and an absence of ambivalence. New research on the brain suggests that this may be the result of the unconscious and nonverbal transfer of negative emotions from parent to child. The parent's intense angry outbursts (even if they are rare), intense sadness, and intensely negative statements about the other parent may be absorbed unconsciously by the child's brain, without the child even realizing it. The child then develops intensely negative emotions toward the other parent (or anyone the upset parent dislikes), but doesn't consciously know why. This may explain the vague or minor reasons given by alienated children for intensely rejecting a good parent. This spilling over of negative emotions from upset parent to child may have begun years before the divorce, so that the child is very tuned in to the upset parent, and automatically and instantly absorbs their emotions and point of view.

DOES CUSTODY MAKE A DIFFERENCE? If one parent has almost all of the parenting time, then the child will not have his or her own experiences with the other parent to know that he or she is not bad. Most states expect children to have substantial time with both parents – except in cases of abuse. Ironically, the amount of time is generally not the biggest factor. The biggest factor is if one parent is constantly spilling over intensely negative emotions to the child about the other parent, while the other parent is following court orders and not addressing these issues at all. For this reason, children can become alienated against either a non-custodial parent or a custodial parent. This can be either the father or the mother. It's like a bad political campaign, with one side campaigning hard and the other side not campaigning at all.

HOW CAN YOU PREVENT ALIENATION? You might be alienating your child against the other parent or against yourself, without even being conscious of it - especially during a divorce. Here are seven suggestions:

1. POSITIVE COMMENTS: Regularly point out positive qualities of the other parent to your child.

2. REPAIRING COMMENTS: All parents make negative comments about the other parent at times. If you realize you made such a comment, follow up with a "repairing comment": "I just spoke negatively about your father [or mother]. I don't really mean to be so negative. He has many positive qualities and I really value your relationship with him. I'm just upset and my feelings are my responsibility, not his and not yours."

3. AVOID REINFORCING NEGATIVE COMMENTS: Healthy children say all kinds of things, positive and negative, about their parents – even about abusive parents. If there is abuse, have it investigated by professionals. If not, be careful that you are not paying undue attention to their negative comments and ignoring their positive comments.

4. TEACH PROBLEM-SOLVING STRATEGIES: If your child complains about the other parent's behavior, unless it is abusive, suggest strategies for coping: "Honey, tell your father something nice before you ask for something difficult." "Show your mother the project you did again, she might have been busy the first time." "If he/she is upset, maybe you can just go to your room and try not to listen and draw a picture instead."

5. AVOID EXCESSIVE INTIMACY: Children naturally become more independent and self-aware as they grow up. Be careful not to be excessively intimate with your child for the child's age, as this may create an unhealthy dependency on you. Examples include having the child regularly sleep with you in your bed beyond infancy; sharing adult information and decisions (such as about the divorce); and excessive

sadness at exchanges or how you miss the child when he or she is at the other parent's house.

6. AVOID EXCESSIVE COMPARISONS: When you emphasize a skill or characteristic that you have, don't place it in comparison to weaknesses of the other parent. You each have different skills and qualities that are important to your child. By comparing yourself positively and the other parent negatively (even if this feels innocent), you can inadvertently influence your child. Remember that your child is a combination of both of you, and thinking negatively of one parent means the child may think negatively about half of himself or herself.

7. GET SUPPORT OR COUNSELING FOR YOURSELF: It is impossible to go through a divorce without getting upset some of the time. Protect your child from as much as possible by sharing your upset feelings with adult friends and family, away from your child. Get counseling to cope with the stress you are under.

WILL THE COURT ADDRESS THIS ISSUE? Routinely, in a divorce or separation, the court will order that neither parent shall make disparaging remarks about the other parent within hearing of the child. Some courts may ask you for 3 positive comments about the other parent or 3 steps you are taking to protect the child from absorbing your negative emotions toward the other parent. Think about this seriously, so that you are prepared to answer this question if it is raised. Most of all, practice the suggestions described above.

Don't Use "Force"

"I won't force the children to go with the other parent," is one of the statements I hear sometimes from parents going through a separation or divorce. This statement has become so common (three times in one day recently), that a short article on this subject may be helpful.

Expectations

Parents have a lot of expectations for their children, for their own benefit. You expect them to go to school. You expect them to do their homework. You expect them to come home at night. You expect them to brush their teeth. You expect them to do their chores. You expect them not to swear in public. You expect them not to have sex. You expect them not to use drugs, etc., etc.

We use all of our resources to "force" them to do (or not do) these things. But we don't use the word "force" with these activities. We use the word "expect" – a positive word for their long-term benefit, rather than a negative word. And your children get the message. So try not to use the word "force," with all its negativity. Instead, use the positive word "expect." "I expect you to go with your mother/father – we both expect that."

It's Not an Option

Of course, children will resist doing a negative option. They don't want to see the dentist. They don't want to go to school on some days. Even parents don't want to go to work on some days. But most of us go to work anyway, because we need to get paid. It's not an option to stay home.

Somehow, children get the message that going to the other parent's house after a separation or divorce is optional. If you give them a choice and imply it will be a negative experience, any healthy child is going to want to avoid it. Since children have so few options in their lives, if you give them an option to avoid something negative, they will avoid it.

Children Don't Like Moving

Most of the time, children like being where they are. When given a choice, many children who live in two households would rather stay where they are at the moment. It doesn't mean that they don't want to see their Mom or Dad, it just means that they don't want to stop what they're doing, get up, pack up, and go somewhere else. Once they get to the other house, they act just the same way. Don't take it personally: most of the time children just prefer where they are and what they're doing. They live in the present.

Use Positive and Negative Consequences

If children don't do the things that we expect, we usually use consequences with them rather than physically picking them up and taking them. This is especially true with teenagers. Instead, we take away privileges or give them new opportunities when they succeed.

Take school, for example. If your child refuses to go to school, do you: Take them out for ice cream? Spend more personal time and attention with them? Take them shopping or to the movies? Allow them to watch TV all day? Surf the internet? If you do, do you think they would increasingly stay away from school? Of course. I have worked with families where this occurred. Instead, if a child resists spending time with the other parent without a very good reason, use the same consequences you would use if they refused to go to school. And don't blame it on the other parent – just be matter-of-fact. In a separation or divorce, attitude is everything.

Avoid Assumptions

In a separation or divorce, it's easy to misinterpret a child's resistance to spending time with one of the parents. It may be about something very minor and the child will change his or her mood soon, unless you give this mood excessive attention or power.

It is easy for a parent to jump to the conclusion that the child has the exact same thoughts about the other parent, such as complicated anger about adult issues that the child may not know about or understand. Or you may be concerned that your child's sadness or anger toward the other parent may mean he or she has been abused or treated badly. While these things could be true, be careful to check them out without making assumptions.

Emotions are Contagious

On the other hand, children do absorb their parent's emotions. It's an important part of how they learn about life, and how they stay connected to their parents. Recent brain research explains how "mirror neurons" cause children to mirror their parents' emotions, as well as behavior. So your child may have picked up your intense emotions about the separation or divorce, and show the exact same fear, sadness, or anger – yet have no logical explanation for it. While it may seem like the child has the same feelings and thoughts that you do, your child may actually just have the same feelings – your feelings.

So be careful not to let your child see or hear your upset feelings about the other parent. Arguments or physical confrontations between parents that are observed by a child can be particularly distressing for a child and may increase their resistance to one parent. Children need to be protected from their parents' behavior sometimes.

Get Family Counseling

If a child develops a resistance to spending time with one parent, it is potentially a serious problem which needs to be treated sooner rather than later. If there is a child abuse issue, it needs to be addressed and stopped. If there has been domestic violence (an incident or a pattern), then this is an important problem to be treated, rather than ignored. Children may be the first to show a problem which needs family attention. And if it is a child absorbing a parent's negative emotions about the separation or divorce, this also needs to get addressed and resolved. Often the best approach is for a counselor to meet with each parent and the child or children before resistance turns into refusal. And if a child is refusing to see a parent, then it is even more important to take this approach as soon as possible. By meeting with both parents at separate times with the child or children, parents can help and support each other in helping their child. Getting an individual counselor for the child is less effective.

Conclusion

Maybe you can't "force" a child to spend time today with one parent. But you can have consequences, investigate the situation, and get the help of a family counselor. In the long run, it will be better for all of you.

Evaluating Sexual Abuse Reports
in Family Court

One of the most difficult issues which can confront parents, counselors, attorneys and judges is the concern that a child has been sexually abused. Evaluating an allegation against a parent is especially difficult in the context of separation or divorce. The child's statements and behavior may be responses to the stress of the divorce and wrongly interpreted as sexual abuse. Or true sexual abuse reports may be wrongly discounted as a weapon in the divorce conflict.

I have handled several cases with sexual abuse reports as a family law attorney and as a superior court mediator. In one family court case, over a 12-month period there were nine hearings involving seven different judges, a psychological evaluation, professionally supervised visitation and no finding of sexual abuse. In another case, there was an extensive evaluation by a university department, considering many theories and a finding of sexual abuse. Unfortunately, many cases reach less clear results, and drag on for years.

With training, these cases can be more quickly and clearly resolved. To this end, I have provided seminars for CPS workers and in 1997 I co-wrote a 60-page Proposed Family Court Protocol with my colleague, William Benjamin, CFLS. The following is a summary of my on-going review of the research and recommendations.

No Assumptions

Reports of child sexual abuse (CSA) are made in only a small percentage of divorce cases, according to the most extensive study of this issue in 1989 by Thoennes and Tjaden. They found that half of the reports in divorce cases were confirmed to be true, a third were confirmed to be untrue, and the rest were unclear. With lying increasing in society, half may be untrue now. Therefore, one cannot safely assume a report is probably true or probably not true. An assessment of several factors and theories must occur.

One cannot assume a report is true
or not true. An assessment of several
factors and theories must occur.

Until the 1980's, it was generally assumed that CSA allegations were not true. Children's testimony was considered unreliable. During the 1980's and early 1990's, children's advocates properly persuaded the public and law-makers that child sexual abuse is a real and serious problem. However, the pendulum swung too far. Most reports were assumed true and children's statements assumed accurate.

By the mid-1990's, research confirmed that children are suggestible and may wrongly confirm the investigator's theory of a case. After a landmark 1994 New Jersey Supreme Court case, several convictions were overturned because of this confirmatory bias by investigators. Now interviewers must be careful to avoid tainting the child's statements.

Five Theories of CSA Reports

There are at least five possible explanations or theories to be considered when there is a child sexual abuse report in a divorce case. An investigator must keep an open mind in gathering evidence, and explore all theories.

Pre-existing Abuse: In some families there has been on-going sexual abuse. Its discovery may be the reason for the divorce. It is also possible that it was not discovered until the divorce process began, because the child may not have felt safe to disclose it until the parents were separated.

Divorce-Related Abuse: Sexual abuse may occur for the first time after the separation of the parents. The abusing parent may turn to the child for emotional/physical needs, or suppressed sexual urges may no longer be controlled by the presence of the other parent.

Sincere-But-False Allegations: Researchers indicate that the majority of false allegations are sincere. A parent may misunderstand or overreact to vague distress or ambiguous statements by a child. The stress of going from one tense parent to another at the beginning or end of visitation may be misinterpreted as abuse.

Intentionally-False Allegations: Some parents falsely report abuse in order to obtain an advantage in court, such as a change of custody or a significant reduction in the other parent's contact with the child. They may knowingly represent the child's anxious behaviors as signs of sexual abuse.

Sexual Abuse by Someone Else: There may be sexual abuse actually occurring, but by some other adult -- or even another child (often with an abuse history of their own). A young child may be frightened or confused and indicate that it is their own parent instead of the actual abuser.

Many Factors to Consider

There is no single factor that is conclusive for the presence or absence of child sexual abuse by a parent. Researchers have found that several child behaviors are common symptoms of emotional distress, which may simply be a response to a difficult divorce. Examples are: bed-wetting, nightmares, clinging, constipation and even redness in the genital area (often related to normal bathing issues).

On the other hand, researchers have found that only about 30% of confirmed true cases of child sexual abuse have medical evidence. Therefore, the absence of injury or medical evidence cannot be used as proof there is no abuse.

Gathering Evidence

Since there is no single factor which is conclusive, anyone investigating a report should look at the context and totality of the evidence available.

Many Sources: Any investigation of child sexual abuse should include information from several sources. This would include others who know the child and/or the parents, and their patterns of functioning and behavior. Mental health professionals doing custody and visitation evaluations are required to obtain information from more than one source.

Interviews With the Child: This has been an area of great controversy and much research in the past few years. There is now growing agreement among researchers that the way a child is interviewed can significantly influence their answers. Therefore, most professionals now know what leading questions are and that they should be avoided. Leading questions suggest a specific answer, or highly limited choices. Until recently, these were commonly used.

Use of Anatomical Dolls: Professionals remain split over the use of anatomical dolls. Some say that they are necessary to elicit information from very young children, while others say they are still too suggestive. When they are used, more careful procedures have been developed in recent years.

Drawings are also used. The key point is that these tools are used to confirm or elaborate, and not used as the initial or primary basis of an evaluation.

Parents Should Avoid Questioning Child: A child's answers can be influenced by the way their parent (or any other adult) asks them questions, and these answers can become part of their memory. This can permanently taint the child's report, resulting in a true report being thrown out or a false report being prosecuted. If a parent has concerns that their child has been sexually abused, they should immediately contact a professional -- ideally one trained in identifying the presence or absence of sexual abuse: their therapist, attorney, or CPS.

Relationship with Child: Interviewing the child with each parent reveals a great deal about the report of abuse in a divorce case. Is the child comfortable or uncomfortable being with the accused parent? Is the child comfortable or uncomfortable being with the accusing parent? Does the child show anxiety during visitation exchanges, but relax with one or the other parent alone? Is the child over-involved with either parent's emotional needs? Does either parent have age-inappropriate expectations for the child?

Timing of the Report: Does the report coincide with a benefit or disturbing event for the reporting parent? If so, it increases the likelihood it is false -- if not, it may be true. In a divorce case, it is easy to determine if there is a hearing pending, a custody battle, or a major financial decision to be made. Sometimes, a former spouse's re-marriage or new baby may trigger a report. If there is no related event and the report embarrasses or harms the accuser, it may be true.

Family Court Decision-Making

Courts are faced with two conflicting concerns: Immediate protection of the child and obtaining an objective evaluation. At times, professionals have prematurely reached incorrect conclusions in their efforts to make quick decisions. The following is based on our Proposed Protocol:

Protection of the Child: To be initially safe, a court should order supervised visitation -- without forming any judgment about the underlying report. No Contact orders are to be avoided, because supervised visitation is usually sufficient for the child's safety and the accused parent should be observed with the child as soon as possible.

Gathering Evidence: Investigators (CPS workers, police, therapists) should gather as much information as possible without forming conclusions. This information should be readily accessible to attorneys for the parties.

Evaluating Evidence: A well-trained psychological evaluator should evaluate the family, and examine the information gathered from all sources. Only then should a recommendation be made to the parties and to the court.

Making a Finding: The court should reach as clear a conclusion as possible. It is recommended that the court make a finding about the likelihood that abuse occurred or that a false allegation occurred. By avoiding a conclusion, families have often remained in long-term chaos and continually return to court. A case should be examined until the pattern of evidence is clear enough to make a judgment.

Orders and Treatment: Regardless of whether there is evidence of sexual abuse or false allegations, the family is seriously in need of help. Long-term orders should be made to address the dysfunction in the family, including counseling for the child and the parents. Consequences are also important. If there is likely abuse, then there should be a criminal investigation. If it appears to be a knowingly false allegation, then sanctions should be imposed.

Training

In the past five years there has been a great deal of new research in objectively evaluating child sexual abuse reports. With on-going training for court-related professionals and more parent education, our society will better protect children from the serious harm of sexual abuse while avoiding the serious harm of making mistakes.   1/19/99

A Few of the Many Good Resources Available

Child Maltreatment: Journal of the American Professional Society on the Abuse of Children, SAGE Publications (Quarterly Journal since 1996)

Journal on Child Sexual Abuse, Haworth Press (Qtrly issues)

Jeopardy in the Courtroom, Ceci and Bruck, APA, 1995

True and False Allegations of Child Sexual Abuse, Ney, 1995

Inaccuracies in Children's Testimony, J. Meyer, 1997

Interviewing for Child Sexual Abuse: A Forensic Guide (Videotape), Kathleen C. Faller, Guilford Press, 1998.

New Ways Parent-Child Talk

When parents separate, having a talk with your children that includes some or all of the following may be helpful (presented in age-appropriate terms). You can say this separately or jointly to your children. It helps if you agree on when you are going to say this to them, and what details you have agreed upon to tell them. For example: parenting schedule, how you will communicate, and how decisions will be made.

1. **New ways in different houses:** We're going to be organizing our family in new ways from now on. Your mother/father and I are going to be living in different houses and bringing new people into our lives. While we are separating or getting a divorce, we are not separating from you. We will both do everything we can to keep our relationships with you loving and strong. You deserve the best from both of us.

2. **Positive ways with each other:** We're going to try to act in positive ways with each other. We're going to encourage you to have a strong relationship with both of us. We're going to avoid comparing ourselves to each other, by saying one of your parents is a better person than the

other. We both have made mistakes and I am working on myself to be a better person in my life. And we both have strengths that you can learn from, and I will remind you of your mother's/father's strengths in case you forget occasionally.

3. **Avoiding extreme behaviors:** As we organize your family in new ways, we are going to try to avoid extreme behaviors by using moderate behaviors, because families are hurt by extreme behaviors. If your mother/father does something extreme, I am still going to try to use moderate behaviors. Because one extreme behavior does not deserve another.

4. **Managing our emotions:** I am going to try to manage my own emotions as we go through this separation or divorce. You are not responsible for the separation or divorce, and you are not responsible for my feelings. I alone am responsible for how I manage my emotions and for protecting you from my most intense emotions. This will be a hard time and I will not be perfect.

5. **Emotions can be contagious:** I understand that emotions can be contagious, so I will try to reassure you that you do not have to have my emotions. You are a separate person and will have your own emotions about this separation or divorce. You should always feel free to talk about your feelings with me and I will respect your feelings, even when they are different from mine. The most important thing is that I will try to do my best to let you continue to be a child while I continue to be a parent.

6. **Flexible thinking:** I am going to use flexible thinking in handling our separation or divorce. This means that you can approach me with any ideas about what you and I can do together, and about the new ways our family will be operating. But remember that your mother/father and I will be doing the decision-making. This means I will try to solve problems without getting stuck in all-or-nothing thinking where I

only see one solution. There are many ways to make our lives work well together and I will be open-minded.

7. **Rules in both houses:** There will still be rules in each of our houses, even though some of the rules will be different. We both expect you to follow the other parent's rules when you are in the other's house.

Do you have any questions about these new ways of doing things?

References

Introduction

xv **issue in over 20%:** "Among custody-litigating families, the estimates are higher – 20% to 27%." Kelly, J. B. and Johnston, J. R. (2004). Rejoinder to Gardner's "Commentary on Kelly and Johnston's "The Alienated Child: A Reformulation of Parental Alienation Syndrome,'" Family Court Review, Vol. 42 (4), 622-628, 622.

xv **alleged in only about 2-5%:** Thoennes and Tjaden (1990) study of contested custody cases found only 2% had allegations of child sexual abuse, as cited in Sparta, S. N. and Koocher, G.P. (2006). Forensic Mental Health Assessment of Children and Adolescents. New York, NY: Oxford University Press, 130.   Also, in a survey of 131 family lawyers in 2006 in San Diego County, California, only 5% of contested custody cases were reported to include child sexual abuse allegations, whether believed true or false. Eddy, B. and Waldman, E. (as yet unpublished).

xxii **child abuse reduced:** Sedlak, A.J., Mettenburg, J., Basena, M., Petta, I., McPherson, K., Greene, A., and Li, S. (2010). Fourth National Incidence Study of Child Abuse and Neglect (NIS-4): Report to Congress. Washington, DC: U.S. Department of Health and Human Services, Administration for Children and Families.

xxii **personality disorders:** American Psychiatric Association. (2000). Diagnostic and Statistical Manual of Mental Disorders (4th ed.). Washington, DC. This is the manual mental health professionals use to identify types of disorders, so they can propose the best types of treatments. It includes 10 personality disorders. Five of them appear to be particularly associated with high-conflict behavior, which is described in Chapter 1.

xxiv **Splitting:** Eddy, W.A., (2004). Splitting: Protecting Yourself While Divorcing a Borderline or Narcissist. Milwaukee, WI: Eggshells Press. This book will be revised and released by New Harbinger Press in early 2011.

xxv **Oceans:** Eddy, C. R. (2003). Oceans of the Mind: Computer Science and Theory of Knowledge. San Diego, CA: William A. Eddy. The central feature of this book is the Principle of Multiple Models, which derives from comparing brains with computers.

Chapter 1: High-Conflict Divorce

3 **took the offer:** Borof, I. J. (2003). Honey, I Want the Kids: Part I-Temporary Custody Overview. Family Law News 25, 12-15, 12.

4 **Wall Street Journal:** Thernstrom, J. (2003). Untying the Knot. New York Times Magazine, August 24, 2003, 38-44.

4 **family court judges:** Brownstone, Mr. Justice Harvey. (2009). Tug of War: A Judge's Verdict on Separation, Custody Battles, and the Bitter Realities of Family Court. Toronto, Ontario, Canada: ECW Press. Justice Brownstone provides an excellent overview of family court, which applies equally to families in the United States and Canada. With more than 14 years as a family court judge, he states that some family courts today have "unprecedented and ever-increasing backlogs." The theme of his book is that "family court is not good for families, and litigation is not good for children."

4 **Johnston quote:** Johnston, J. R., Roseby, V., and Kuehnle, K. (2009). In the Name of the Child: A Developmental Approach to Understanding and Helping Children of Conflicted and Violent Divorce. New York, NY: Springer Publishing Company, LLC., 4. Used with permission.

7 **NIH study, regarding Borderline:** Grant, B. F., Chou, S. P., Goldstein, R. B., Huang, B., Stinson, F. S., Saha, T. D. (2008). Prevalence, correlates, disability and comorbidity of DSM-IV Borderline Personality disorder: Results from the Wave 2

national epidemiologic survey on alcohol and related conditions. Journal of Clinical Psychiatry, 69, 533-545.

7-8 **NIH study, regarding Narcissistic:** Stinson, R. S., Dawson, D. A., Goldstein, R. B. Chou, S. P., Huang, B., Smith, S. M. (2008). Prevalence, correlates, disability, and comorbidity of DSM-IV Narcissistic Personality Disorder: Results from the Wave 2 National Epidemiologic Survey on Alcohol and Related Conditions. Journal of Clinical Psychiatry, 69, 1033-1045.

8-9 **NIH study, regarding Paranoid, Antisocial and Histrionic:** Grant, B. F., Hasin, D. S., Stinson, R. S., Dawson, D. A., Chou, S. P., Ruan, W. J. (2004). Prevalence, correlates, and disability of personality disorders in the United States: Results from the National Epidemiologic Survey on Alcohol and Related Conditions. Journal of Clinical Psychiatry, 65, 948-958.

10-11 **Kreisman quote:** Kreisman, J.J. and Straus, H. (1989). I Hate You, Don't Leave Me: Understanding the Borderline Personality. New York, NY: Avon Books, Inc., 10-11.

11 **Beck quote:** Beck, A.T., Freeman, A., and Associates (1990). Cognitive Therapy of Personality Disorders. New York, NY: The Guildford Press, 187. Used with permission.

Chapter 2: Child Alienation

22 **Gardner quote:** Gardner, R.A. (2004). Commentary on Kelly and Johnston's "The Alienated Child: A Reformulation of Parental Alienation Syndrome" Family Court Review, 39(3), July 2001. Family Court Review, 42, (4), 611-621, 612.

23 **Bruch quote:** Bruch, C. (2001). Parental Alienation Syndrome and Parental Alienation: Getting It Wrong in Child Custody Cases. Family Law Quarterly, 35(3), 527-552, 533-534. Used with permission.

24 **sexual abuse and alienation percentages:** see references for xii above.

25-26 **agree on several points:** Fidler, B. J. and Bala, N. (Guest Eds.). (2010). Family Court Review: An Interdisciplinary Journal, 48, (1).

29 **love their parents, but hate the abuse:** Those who work primarily with domestic violence victims have also seen this dynamic. Jaffe, P. G., Lemon, N. K. D., and Poisson, S. E. (2003). Child Custody and Domestic Violence: A Call For Safety and Accountability. Thousand Oaks, CA: Sage Publications, 55: "In homes where there is domestic violence, children most often continue to love both parents." On the other hand, some researchers of child sexual abuse report: "Children who are victims of sexual abuse also have been observed to cling to their mothers (Finkelhor & Browne, cited in de Young, 1986)." Bancroft, L. and Silverman, J. G. (2002). The Batterer as Parent: Addressing the Impact of Domestic Violence on Family Dynamics. Thousand Oaks, CA: Sage Publications, 126.

39-40 **Justice Williams quote:** Williams, R. J. (2001). Should Judges Close the Gate on PAS and PA? Family Court Review, 39 (3), 267-281, 279. Used with permission.

40 **child murders increased 35%:** Malamud, M. (2010). Advocates: More Child Abuse Resources Needed. NASW News, January 2010, 9. "According to the report, between 2001 and 2007 there was a 35 percent increase in the number of children in the United States who died from abuse and neglect (1,300 in 2001 and 1,760 in 2007)."

42 **sexual abuse and alienation percentages:** see references for xii above.

43-44 **Kelly and Johnston quote:** Kelly, J. B. and Johnston, J. R. (2001). THE ALIENATED CHILD: A Reformulation of Parental Alienation Syndrome, Family Court Review, Vol. 39 (3), 249-266, 251. Used with permission.

44-45 **Johnston quote:** Johnston, J., Roseby, V., and Kuehnle, K. (2009). In the Name of the Child: A Developmental Approach to Understanding and Helping Children of Conflicted and Violent Divorce. New York, NY: Springer Publishing Company, LLC. 363-364. Used with permission.

Chapter 3: 1000 Little Bricks

49-51 **Tyler quote:** Tyler, Tracey (2009). Mom loses custody for "alienating" kids from their dad; Ruling a 'wake-up call' for parents who use kids to punish ex-partners. Toronto Star, January 25, 2009, A.1. Reprinted with permission – Torstar Syndication Services.

53 **Right and Left Brains:** Siegel, D. J. (2007). The Mindful Brain. New York, NY: W. W. Norton & Company, 44-47.

53-54 **children's right brains are dominant:** Schore, A. N. (2003). Affect Regulation and the Repair of the Self. New York, NY: W. W. Norton & Company, 61.

54 **at risk of becoming:** Johnston, J., Roseby, V., and Kuehnle, K. (2009). In the Name of the Child: A Developmental Approach to Understanding and Helping Children of Conflicted and Violent Divorce. New York, NY: Springer Publishing Company, LLC. 373. These authors point out that whether a child adapts to parent conflict by either: 1) adopting an "angry, rejecting, and alienated stance" against one parent or 2) adopting a "constricted, vigilant stance" toward both parents; they are at risk for developing personality disorders.

55-62 **attachment explanations:** Wallin, D. J. (2007). Attachment in Psychotherapy. New York, NY: Guilford Press. His entire book explains how children learn basic interpersonal skills by repeatedly interacting with their parents in a secure attachment relationship, and then interacting that way with others as well. Quotes used with permission.

65-66 **Kreisman quote:** Kreisman, J.J. and Straus, H. (1989). I Hate You, Don't Leave Me: Understanding the Borderline Personality. New York, NY: Avon Books, Inc., 48, 50.

73 **Auletta quote: Auletta, K. (2010). Non-Stop News:** With cable, the Web, and Tweets, Can the President—or the Press—Still Control the Story? The New Yorker, Jan. 25, 2010, 38. Used with permission.

Chapter 4: Emotions are Contagious

82-83 **The Amygdala:** Goleman, D. (2006). Social Intelligence: The New Science of Human Relationships. New York, NY: Bantam Dell, 39-40. See also: Schore, A. N. (2003). Affect Regulation and the Repair of the Self. New York, NY: W. W. Norton & Company, 82.

90-91 **Alday quote:** Alday, C. S. (2009). Anxiety-based school refusal: Helping parents cope. Brown University Child and Adolescent Behavior Letter, Jan. 2009 (1), 6-7. Used with permission.

96 **Marriage researchers:** Gottman, J. (1994). Why Marriages Succeed or Fail … And How You Can Make Yours Last. New York, NY: Simon & Schuster Paperbacks, 57.

96 **Parent-Child Interaction Therapy:** Timmer, S. G., Urquiza, A. J., Zebell, N. M. and McGrath, J. M. (2005). Parent-Child Interaction Therapy: Application to Maltreating Parent-Child Dyads. Child Abuse & Neglect, Vol. 29, 825-842.

96-97 **Ahrons quote:** Ahrons, C. (2004). We're Still Family: What Grown Children Have to Say About Their Parents' Divorce. New York, NY: HarperCollins Publishers, 229-230. Copyright © 2004 by Constance Ahrons. Reprinted by permission of the author and the Sandra Dijkstra Literary Agency. This is one of the easiest books to read about divorce outcomes, with many good tips on how to have a low-conflict rather than high-conflict divorce.

Chapter 5: All-or-Nothing Thinking

101 **Cognitive Distortions:** Burns, D. D. (1989). The Feeling Good Handbook. New York, NY: William Morrow and Company, 8-11.

107-108 **Sam Stone research:** Ceci, S. J. and Bruck, M. (1995). Jeopardy in the Courtroom: A Scientific Analysis of Children's Testimony. Washington, DC: American Psychological Association, 129-134.

109-110 **Carpenter quote:** Carpenter, S. (2008). Buried Prejudice. Scientific American Mind, Vol. 19 (2), 33-39, 35.

110-111 **"You've Got To Be Carefully Taught"** by Richard Rodgers and Oscar Hammerstein II Copyright © 1949 by Richard Rodgers and Oscar Hammerstein II

Copyright Renewed

WILLIAMSON MUSIC owner of publication and allied rights throughout the World International Copyright Secured   All Rights Reserved   Used by Permission

111 **Tribal Warfare:** Johnston, J., Roseby, V., and Kuehnle, K. (2009). In the Name of the Child: A Developmental Approach to Understanding and Helping Children of Conflicted and Violent Divorce. New York, NY: Springer Publishing Company, LLC. 21-24.

Chapter 6: Mirroring Bad Behavior

115 **Albert's example:** Gutierrez, K. K. (2008). Co-Parenting Counseling With High-Conflict Parents in the Presence of Domestic Violence. In J. Hamel (Ed.), Intimate Partner and Family Abuse: A Casebook of Gender-Inclusive Therapy (pp. 201-202). New York, NY: Springer Publishing Company.

116 **mirror neurons:** Iacoboni, M. (2008). Mirroring People: The New Science of How We Connect With Others. New York, NY: Farrar, Straus and Giroux.

117-118 **allegedly killed his brother:** Friedman, E. (December 4, 2009), "Andrew Conley Says He Was Inspired by 'Dexter' to Strangle Brother," abcNews/U.S., available at http://abcnews.go.com/US/teen-television-show-dexter-inspired-kill/story?id=9252620.

118 **girls equally engage in aggressive behavior:** Garbarino, J. (2006). See Jane Hit: Why Girls Are Growing More Violent and What We Can Do About It. New York, NY: Penguin Books, 13. Garbarino cites: Huesmann, L. R., Moise-Titus, J., Podolski, C., and Eron, L. D. (2003), Longitudinal Relations Between Children's Exposure to TV Violence and Their Aggressive and Violent Behavior in Young Adulthood: 1977-1992, Developmental Psychology, 39 (2), 201-221.

120 **"right-brain-to-right-brain" communication:** Schore, A. N. (2003). Affect Regulation and the Repair of the Self. New York, NY: W. W. Norton & Company, 58-66.

121 **cortisol – also known as the stress hormone:** Talbott, S. (2002). The Cortisol Connection: Why Stress Makes You Fat and Ruins Your Health – And What You Can Do About It. Alameda, CA: Hunter House, 68. "Prolonged exposure of brain cells (neurons) to cortisol reduces their ability to take up glucose (their only fuel source) and…causes them to shrink in size!"

122 **Teicher quote:** Teicher, M. H. (2002). Scars That Won't Heal: The Neurobiology of Child Abuse. Scientific American, 286 (3), 68-75, 72. Used with permission.

122 **Dialectical Behavior Therapy:** Linehan, M. M. (1993). Cognitive-Behavioral Treatment of Borderline Personality Disorder. New York, NY: Guilford Press. See also: Cloud, J. (2009). Minds on the Edge. Time, 173 (2), 42-46, 45: A Harvard

study of a group of those diagnosed with borderline personality disorder found that 88% no longer met the criteria for the diagnosis ten years later and that most had some improvement within just a year.

Chapter 7: Teaching Resilience

135 **Resilience is mostly learned:** Graziano, M. (2008). Tapping Into Strengths: A Systems Approach to Resilience. Psychotherapy Networker, May/June 2008, 21-22.

137-138 **Wallin quote:** Wallin, D. J. (2007). Attachment in Psychotherapy. Guildford Press: New York, 21, 48-49. Used with permission.

142-144 **Wallin quote from Fonagy:** See above, 49-51. Used with permission.

149-151 **different kinds of domestic violence:** Kelly, J. B. and Johnson, M. P. (2008). Differentiation Among Types of Intimate Partner Violence: Research Update and Implications For Interventions. Family Court Review, 46 (3), 476-499.

Chapter 8: Reasonable Parent's Dilemma

176 **interviewing children in child sexual abuse cases:** The American Professional Society on the Abuse of Children (APSAC) gives regular conferences and specialized training in interviewing children who may have been abused. "Interviewing alleged victims of child abuse has received intense scrutiny in recent years and increasingly requires specialized training and expertise." Website notice on January 27, 2010, available at http://webmail.aol.com/30462-111/aol-1/en-us/mail/PrintMessage.aspx.

177 **left brains will make up facts:** Damasio, A. (1999). The Feeling of What Happens: Body and Emotion in the Making of Consciousness. New York, NY: Harcourt Brace & Company, 187. Damasio is one of the top brain researchers and specializes in the treatment of brain injuries. He states: "Perhaps the most important revelation in human split-brain research is precisely this: that the left cerebral hemisphere of humans is prone to fabricating verbal narratives that do not necessarily accord with the truth."

Chapter 9: How Family and Friends Can Help

No references in this chapter.

Chapter 10: How Lawyers Can Help

197 **Baldwin quote:** Baldwin, A. (2008). A Promise to Ourselves: A Journey Through Fatherhood and Divorce. New York, NY: St. Martins Press, 185. Used with permission.

198 **75% without attorneys:** Elkins Family Law Task Force Draft Recommendations, Administrative Office of the Court, Judicial Council of California, December 2009, 2. "In many communities, more than 75 percent of family law cases have at least one self-represented party."

206-208 **Baker quote:** Baker, A.J.L. (2007). Adult Children of Parental Alienation Syndrome. New York, NY: W.W. Norton & Company, 204-205, 209, 212-214. Used with permission.

214 **McIntosh research:** McIntosh, J. (2009). Presentation at Opening Session: Back to the Future or Full Steam Ahead? What Research Really Shows About Children and Divorce. Association of Family and Conciliation Courts 46th Annual Conference. New Orleans, LA.

215 **parallel parenting plan:** Stahl, P. M. (1999). Complex Issues in Child Custody Evaluation. Thousand Oaks, CA: Sage Publications, 99-100. While many authors have described parallel parenting over the past two decades, Dr. Philip M. Stahl has been one of the most active in refining this concept and presenting it to family law professional organizations. He states: "Though the literature suggests that high-conflict parents cannot share parenting, Johnston (1994) states that parallel parenting may work. I agree and find that it is the goal to encourage."

215 **substantial time to the perpetrator:** Bancroft, L. and Silverman, J.G. (2002). The Batterer as Parent: Addressing the Impact of Domestic Violence on Family Dynamics. Thousand Oaks, CA: Sage Publications, 115-128.

Chapter 11: How Counselors Can Help

228 **Parent-Child Interaction Therapy:** Timmer, S. G., Urquiza, A. J., Zebell, N. M. and McGrath, J. M. (2005). Parent-Child Interaction Therapy: Application to Maltreating Parent-Child Dyads. Child Abuse & Neglect, Vol. 29, 825-842.

230 **Johnston quote:** Johnston, J. R., Roseby, V., and Kuehnle, K. (2009). In the Name of the Child: A Developmental Approach to Understanding and Helping Children of Conflicted and Violent Divorce. New York, NY: Springer Publishing Company, 373. Used with permission. Used with permission.

234 **New Ways for Families:** This is a method developed by Bill Eddy and High Conflict Institute. See resources by this author in front of this book. For information, contact www.HighConflictInstitute.com or www.NewWays4Families.com.

235 **Family Restructuring Therapy:** Private correspondence with Stephen Carter, March 1, 2010. See also www.chvb.ca. "Our website has a number of tip sheets that parents can access."

236-237 **Johnston quote:** Johnston, J. & Goldman, J.R. (2010). Outcomes of Family Counseling Interventions with Children Who Resist Visitation: An Addendum to Friedlander and Walters. Family Court Review, 48 (1), 112-114. Used with permission.

237-238 **Warshak quote:** Warshak, R. A. (2010). Family Bridges: Using Insights from Social Science to Reconnect Parents and Alienated Children. Family Court Review, 48 (1), 48-80. 61, 67-68, 77. Used with permission.

239-240 **Kelly quote:** Kelly, J. (2010). Commentary on "Family Bridges: Using Insights from Social Science to Reconnect Parents and Alienated Children." Family Court Review, 48 (1), 81-90, 83. Used with permission.

240-241 **Jaffe quote:** Jaffe, P., Ashbourne, D., and Mamo, A. A. (2010). Early Identification and Prevention of Parent-Child Alienation: A Framework for Balancing Risks and Benefits of Intervention. Family Court Review, 48 (1), 136-152. 138, 139. Used with permission.

241-242 **Sullivan quote:** Sullivan, M. J., Ward, P. A., and Deutsch, R. M. (2010). Overcoming Barriers Family Camp: A Program for High-Conflict Divorced Families Where a Child is Resisting Contact with a Parent. Family Court Review, 48 (1), 116-135, 124, 130. Used with permission.

Chapter 12: The Future of Family Courts

247-248 **Waldie quote:** Waldie, Paul. (2008). Judge Wants Divorced Couple to Legally Split–From the Courtroom. The Globe and Mail. May 8, 2008, A12. Used with permission.

251-252 **Martinson quote:** Martinson, D. J. (2010). One Case-One Specialized Judge: Why Courts Have an Obligation to Manage Alienation and Other High-Conflict Cases. Family Court Review, 48 (1), 180-189. Used with permission.

262 **Charlenni Ferreira:** Graham, T. (2010). Litany of Injuries Opens Child-Abuse Hearing. The Philadelphia Inquirer. January 13, 2010, A1, A4.

271 **Child-Inclusive Mediation:** McIntosh, J. E., Wells, Y. D., Smyth, B. M., & Long, C. M. (2008). Child-Focused and Child-Inclusive Divorce Mediation: Comparative Outcomes from a Prospective Study of Postseparation Adjustment. Family Court Review, 46, 105-124.

273 **Teicher quote:** Teicher, M. H. (2002). Scars That Won't Heal: The Neurobiology of Child Abuse. Scientific American, 286 (3), 68-75, 75. Used with permission.

Index

A

Ahrons, Constance, 96
alienation
  defined, xiii, 43,
  alienated child, 5, 25, 43, 288
  explicit and implicit, 108-110, 114
  reformulation by Kelly & Johnston, 43
  see child alienation
  see parental alienation
  see Parental Alienation Syndrome
all-or-nothing thinking, 1, 5, 9, 15, 18-19, 39, 48, 72, 73, 70, 99-114, 145, 185, 217
  court solutions to, 103
  stereotypes, 107-111
amygdala, 82-85, 86, 195
antisocial personality, 8, 62, 251, 257
assertive approach, 157-158, 162-163, 179, 204, 220
attachment
  behavior, 55-59, 65, 174
  dismissive, 60, 62, 141, 212
  fearful, 60-61, 62, 177, 212
  insecure, 55-68, 113, 141, 142, 225
  preoccupied, 60, 62, 139-140
  secure, 55-59, 70, 79, 120, 135-144, 151-152, 153, 216

B

Baker, Amy, 206-207, 317
Bancroft, Lundy, 230, 312, 317
borderline personality disorder, 7, 62, 66-67, 122
brain
  hemispheres, 53, 82, 119-122
  left brain, 53, 119-120, 177, 273-274
  right brain, 53, 70, 82, 111, 120, 177
  see amygdala
  see corpus callosum
  see dendrites
  see mirror neurons
bricks
  hot bricks, 137, 144, 146, 153
  cooling hot bricks, 137
  see 1000 Little Bricks theory
  "foundation" bricks, 152

About the Author

William A. ("Bill") Eddy is President of High Conflict Institute, LLC, based in Scottsdale, Arizona. He is a Certified Family Law Specialist in California with 17 years' experience representing clients in family court and providing divorce mediation out of court. Prior to becoming a lawyer, he worked as a Licensed Clinical Social Worker with 12 years' experience providing therapy to children, adults, couples and families in psychiatric hospitals and outpatient clinics.

As President and co-founder of High Conflict Institute, Bill has become an international speaker on the subject of high-conflict personalities to attorneys, judges, mediators, therapists and collaborative professionals, in over 25 states, Canada, France and Australia. High Conflict Institute is dedicated to providing training, resources and program development to professionals dealing with high-conflict personalities in legal disputes, workplace disputes, healthcare disputes, and education disputes. The New Ways for Families™ program was developed by Bill in 2009 for the High Conflict Institute as an intervention method for potentially high-conflict families in family courts.

He is part-time faculty of the National Judicial College providing training to state and federal judges in handling high-conflict people in court, and is also part-time faculty of the Strauss Institute for Dispute Resolution at the School of Law at Pepperdine University. He serves as the Senior Family Mediator at the National Conflict Resolution Center in San Diego, California and has taught Negotiation and Mediation for six years at the University of San Diego School of Law.

Bill obtained his law degree in 1992 from the University of San Diego, a Master of Social Work degree in 1981 from San Diego State University, and a Bachelors degree in Psychology in 1970 from Case Western Reserve University. He began his career as a youth social worker in a changing neighborhood in New York City. He considers conflict resolution the theme of his varied career. Contact Bill at:

www.HighConflictInstitute.com

or

www.NewWays4Families.com

High Conflict Institute, LLC
7701 E. Indian School Rd., Ste. F
Scottsdale, AZ 85251
(602) 606-7628
Toll-Free (888) 768-9874

If you would like to send me an email about your experiences, what you've learned from this book, or anything else, please read my blog at www.highconflictinstitute.com and click on "Blog" on the far right side. Or email me at info@highconflictinstitute.com.

Bill Eddy
High Conflict Institute

HIGH CONFLICT

INSTITUTE

About High Conflict Institute

High Conflict Institute, LLC, was co-founded by Bill Eddy, LCSW, Esq., and Megan L. Hunter, MBA, to provide education and resources to professionals handling high-conflict disputes, and to the general public. In 2009, they were joined by Michelle Jensen, JD, MSW, who serves as the New Ways Program Coordinator.

After years of working with High Conflict disputes in many settings, we came to the conclusion that these disputes are not driven by complex issues, but by High Conflict Personalities. Based on Bill Eddy's broad training in mental health, law and conflict resolution, he developed the High Conflict Personality Theory (the "HCP Theory") and has been teaching the necessary skills for handling HCPs to professionals in a wide variety of settings: legal, workplace, healthcare, education, government, business and others.

We provide seminars and consultation to organizations upon request, as well as providing our own seminars in different regions of the United States for any professional facing High Conflict cases or issues. Several helpful books can be found on our website.

new ways
FOR families

We are committed to changing the culture of conflict from one of all-or-nothing solutions, good and bad people, and shame and blame, to a culture of mutual empathy, attention and respect for all people while teaching new skills, assertively setting limits, and containing truly dangerous behavior.

www.HighConflictInstitute.com
(602) 606-7628
Toll-Free (888) 768-9874

About New Ways for Families™

New Ways for Families is a structured parenting skills method developed by Bill Eddy that includes short-term counseling to reduce the impact of conflict on children in potentially high-conflict cases. It can be used whenever a parent or the court believes one parent needs restricted parenting (supervised, no contact, limited time), at the start of a case or any time a parent requests restricted parenting – including post-judgment litigation.

This method emphasizes strengthening skills for positive future behavior (new ways), rather than focusing on past negative behavior – while still acknowledging it. It is designed to save courts time, to save parents money, and to protect children as their families re-organize in new ways after a separation or divorce, for married or never-married parents. This method's goals are:

1. To immunize families against becoming high-conflict families

2. To help parents teach their children resilience

3. To strengthen both parent's abilities to make parenting decisions

4. To assist professionals and the courts in assessing both parent's potential

5. To give parents a chance to change poor parenting behaviors

www.NewWays4Families.com

(602) 606-7628
Toll-Free (888) 768-9874

For questions about HCI Press, please call 602-606-7628
or visit us online at www.hcipress.com

Breinigsville, PA USA
10 June 2010
239543BV00003B/2/P